Charles G.D. Roberts

Selected Animal Stories

A Critical Edition

Edited by
Terry Whalen

The Tecumseh Press Ltd.
Ottawa, Canada
2005

Canadian Critical Editions

General Editors

John Moss and Gerald Lynch

Canadian Critical Editions offer, for academic study and the interested reader, authoritative texts of significant Canadian works within a comprehensive critical setting. Where appropriate, each edition provides extensive biographical and bibliographical background, reprints of documents, commentary to illuminate the context of its creation and the history of its reception, new essays written from a variety of critical perspectives, and a biography. These critical editions provide an excellent opportunity for appreciation of the works themselves, for understanding their place in the developing tradition, and for participating in the critical discourse surrounding each work. Making the best accessible, this is the key concept behind the Canadian Critical Editions.

Other titles in the Canadian Critical Editions available from Tecumseh Press

Stephen Leacock, *Sunshine Sketches of a Little Town*, editor Gerald Lynch, 1996.

Sara Jeannette Duncan, *The Imperialist*, editor Thomas E. Tausky, 1996.

Susanna Moodie, *Roughing It in the Bush; or, Life in Canada*, editor Elizabeth Thompson, 1997.

John Richardson, *Wacousta*, editor John Moss, 1998.

A Northern Romanticism: Poets of the Confederation, editor Tracy Ware, 2000.

Early Canadian Short Stories: Short Stories in English before World War I, editor Misao Dean, 2000.

Frances Brooke, *The History of Emily Montague*, editor Laura Moss, 2001.

Stephen Leacock, *Arcadian Adventures with the Idle Rich*, editor David Bentley, 2002.

J.G. Sime, *Sister Woman*, editor Sandra Campbell, 2004.

Titles in Preparation

A Northern Modernism: Poets Since Confederation, editor Tracy Ware.

James De Mille, *A Strange Manuscript Found in a Copper Cylinder*, editor Gwendolyn Davies.

Thomas Chandler Haliburton, *The Clockmaker*, editor Carrie MacMillan.

Ethel Wilson, *Swamp Angel*, editor Lei-Ping Geng.

Duncan Campbell Scott, *In the Village of Vigern*, editor Klay Dyer.

Charles G.D. Roberts
Selected Animal Stories

A Critical Edition

Edited by
Terry Whalen

The Tecumseh Press
Ottawa, Canada
2005

for
Maryann, Anna, David,
Jenna, and Jacob

Canada

The Publishers acknowledge the financial assistance of the Government of Canada through the Book Publishing Industry Development Program (BPIDP) for our publishing activities.

Library and Archives Canada Cataloguing in Publication

Roberts, Charles G. D., 1860-1943.
Selected animal stories / Charles G.D. Roberts; edited by Terry Whalen.

(Canadian critical editions; 10)
Includes bibliographical references.
ISBN 1-896133-50-9 (bound).–
ISBN 1-896133-48-7 (pbk.)

1. Animals—Fiction. 2. Roberts, Charles G.D., 1860-1943—Criticism and interpretation. I. Whalen, Terrence Anthony, 1944- II. Title. III. Series

PS8485.O24A6 2005 C813'.4 C2004-905646-8

Cover design by drt.2005, Ottawa

Printed and bound in Canada on acid-free paper.

Contents

Documentary

Reviews

Criticism

Editor's Preface

Charles G.D. Roberts (1860-1943) wrote over two hundred animal stories in his time. He often published these and other stories first as magazine offerings in such periodicals as *Appleton's Magazine*, *Atlantic*, *Canadian Magazine*, *Century Illustrated Magazine*, *Chamber's Journal*, *The Christian Herald*, *The Circle*, *The Criterion*, *Current Magazine*, *The Continent*, *The Delineator*, *Dominion Illustrated Monthly*, *Everybody's Magazine*, *Fortnightly Review*, *Frank Leslie's Popular Monthly*, *Good Housekeeping*, *Hampton's Magazine*, *Harper's Bazaar*, *Harper's Monthly*, *Harper's Young People*, *Illustrated American*, *The Independent*, *Ladies Home Journal*, *Living Age*, *John o' London's*, *Lippincott's Monthly Magazine*, *MacLean's Magazine*, *McClure's Magazine*, *The Metropolitan*, *New York Herald*, *Outing*, *Pall Mall Magazine*, *Pearson's Magazine*, *Scribner's Monthly*, *St. Nicholas Magazine*, *Red Book Magazine*, *Saturday Evening Post*, *Smart Set*, *The Strand*, *St. Nicholas Magazine*, *Sunday Magazine*, *Sunset*, *Toronto Star Weekly*, *Wide Awake*, *The Windsor Magazine*, and *Youth's Companion*. Roberts was a prolific writer of fiction and he wrote for a series of different audiences, sometimes for youth but mostly for adults. His animal stories were sold in collections—at least twenty of them—primarily in the United States, Canada and Britain. His works were translated into many languages and sold widely in Europe. His literary contribution was an international one.

The twenty animal stories retrieved in this edition are taken from across Roberts' career as an animal story writer, but there is more weighted emphasis on the early ones, as these seem to me of his best ones. We cannot read the selections made by earlier editors (see bibliography especially for the editions compiled by John Coldwell Adams, Ethel Hume Bennet, Joseph Gold, Alec Lucas, and Martin Ware) without becoming starkly aware of the extent to which Roberts' literary reputation shifts quite radically, dependent on which stories one chooses to hold up for attention. I have selected stories from across Roberts' career, well-written stories, ones in which the language is crisp and expressive. They are usually stories in which Roberts sought to come close-up to the lives of the animals themselves. As well, I have paid close attention to what he has said himself about the animal story genre, when making the selection.

The human being is present in a number (not a big number) of these stories, but usually as a second-string character. The most obvious exception to this second-string status is in the story "The Grip in Deep Hole," in which a man is trapped like an animal in a struggle for his life. Roberts saw many ways in which we and the animals are alike, and "The Grip in Deep Hole" captures the common existential fix of the human animal with other animals in a striking and dramatic way. It is an animal story insofar as it deals with the human being as an animal fighting for survival. Any way they are sorted, Roberts' animal stories are also stories about, or having consequences for, the human being in any event. This issue is dealt with in more detail in the Introduction and in the Reviews and the Criticism sections of the edition, and it is clear that Roberts was quite philosophical about the similarities between animal and human creatures. Knowledge of animals helped him to get his own existential bearings.

I am grateful to have permission to reprint here the well-written, informative, searching critical commentaries of Joseph Gold, W.J. Keith, T.D. MacLulich, and Misao Dean. All of these critics have read Roberts attentive to the details of his works. I have reprinted in this section an earlier critical essay of my own, and have used the space allotted for my Introduction as a location in which to talk about Roberts amidst the more general phenomenon of animal writing outside of literature, strictly speaking. In a way, the Introduction is as much an exercise in interesting the reader in many 'animal books' I have found particularly compelling as it is a general introduction to the stories and the cognate materials. It makes the reader aware of a number of books on animals which I have found especially engaging, readable and smart. That is why I have placed their full titles and dates of these books in the main text, hoping the suggestions of their titles will engage the reader further. I still hold to the views I expressed in my earlier critical essay, but wished to write an Introduction for this edition which is quite a bit different.

Readers will find that the Documentary and Reviews sections contain material which is strikingly in rhythm with discussion points dealt with by Roberts' more contemporary literary critics, and, indeed, some of the issues appear destined to be permanent ones in the consideration of his works. Roberts liked talking quite self-consciously about the animal story and about his craft, and all that he says on these points makes for illuminating prefatory material about what it is he thinks he is doing in his stories.

Roberts appears well-served by his publishers, at the production level, during his own time, and the many, relatively lavish editions of the stories are beautiful testament to this. His collections were often, even usually, illustrated by Charles Livingston Bull in the American first editions (and beyond). The cover visual to this critical edition is of a caribou done by Bull, one which appeared on the second inside page of L.C. Page's 1907 edition of *The Haunters of the Silences*. It is based on a caribou which appears in "A Stranger to the Wild," one seen returning a stallion's stare with a "glance of mild curiosity." Other Bull illustrations are placed throughout the edition, in the approximate locations where they originally appeared in the copy texts (the case of "Do Seek their Meat from God" is an exception to this rule). They are compelling examples of the inspired art Roberts' stories were capable of provoking.

I found one, a single typesetting error in all of the stories I have assembled here and I have corrected it without noise around the particulars. The texts of his stories are very 'clean' at their sources.

The twenty stories are arranged chronologically, as they first appeared in book collections. I have used first editions (American or British, but mostly American) as copy texts, and have indicated, when known, if any individual story had also appeared in a magazine form as well, prior to the date of the relevant book publication. John Coldwell Adams has compiled an extensive bibliography which includes a list of the locations in which many individual stories were published (see this in Glenn Clever's *The Sir Charles G.D. Roberts Symposium*). The spelling and most other conventions are as they appear in each of the editions, so no attempt has been made to standardize the spelling, even though indentation has been standardized throughout for comfort to the eye. Roberts loved to use hyphenated words, and he also favoured compound punctuation, so the reader should not be surprised to find some hyphenation and punctuation conventions at work in the texts which might seem at first a bit elaborate. I tried to choose stories which read well, and I think Roberts' style thrives, anyway, within his punctuation habits, and within his sometimes circumjacent sentence structure. Roberts is a very readable writer.

I can't begin to thank all of the people who have helped me with this edition—and they are often people who have encouraged me in ways which are extra-literary as much as literary. As for the research for the project, it feathers into much of the research I did when writing, years ago, a monograph on Roberts' fiction for ECW Press, though it includes more recent work as well. So I am especially grateful to George Henderson, archivist at the Queen's University Archives, who has always given me abundant help and encouragement with my work on Roberts and on Bliss Carman. I am indebted to the staff of the University of New Brunswick's Harriet Irving Library, and more recently the goodwill and assistance of Mary Flagg, University Archivist of the University of New Brunswick. For both Carman and Roberts materials assistance I am also grateful to Eric Swanick, who, as New Brunswick's Legislative Librarian, and as a person deeply committed to the dissemination of Canadian literary materials, supported my work intricately over the years. I am also grateful to Karen Black, Special Collections Librarian at the Killam Memorial Library, Dalhousie University, and to Patricia Gallant, Academic Librarian, Special Collections, at the Vaughan Memorial Library, Acadia University, for their assistance in helping me locate a number of first editions of Roberts' works. Douglas Vaisey, Head Reference Librarian at Saint Mary's University, has also kindly assisted me with this and with other projects. For technical support at a very crucial stage in the development of this edition, I am grateful to Jim Thompson, Director of Information Technology Systems and Support at Saint Mary's University.

A number of my colleagues at Saint Mary's University have been very supportive of this edition—they have encouraged me through to the completion of the project in ways that make me proud to be a member among them. A special thank you to Kenneth MacKinnon, who has encouraged my work on many occasions, and who has helped keep me positive about value of the labour involved. I have as well discussed the edition, and discussed animals, with a number of my other colleagues at Saint Mary's University, and they have variously offered their views on the project, on Roberts, on animals, and/or have checked on how I am 'doing' through it all. I thank them warmly—especially Janet Baker, Brian Bartlett, Cyril Byrne, Teresa Heffernan, Wendy Katz, Michael Larsen, David Pigot, Russell Perkin, Gillian Thomas, and Kathleen Tudor.

I am grateful to John Coldwell Adams, D.M.R. Bentley, Glenn Clever, Jack David, Stewart Donovan, W.J. Keith, Robert Lecker, Carrie MacMillan, Lorraine McMullen, Frank Tierney, Thomas B. Vincent, and Tracy Ware, for various kinds of support and goodwill they have shown to me for my work on Confederation writing, and in most cases, for support particularly in my work on Roberts.

I thank John E. Grantmyre, Andrew Humphrey, and Lori Wood for keeping me strong at various significant junctures in the progress of this edition.

I am grateful to the brink of a silence past words to Gerald Lynch, for his humanity and for the well-known blend of seriousness and ease he brings to his role as editor. He is one of the finest editors I have ever known.

Finally but foremost, I thank my wife, Maryann Antonia Whalen from the bottom of my heart, for her help with the project, and for that wise love of hers which makes my life so new each day.

Introduction

Terry Whalen
Charles G.D. Roberts' Animal Stories—We and the Animals Are Alike

In *After Theory* (2003), Terry Eagleton suggests that "The material body is what we share most significantly with the whole rest of our species, extended both in time and space" (155). Alasdair MacIntyre reminds us that "Human identity is primarily, even if not only, bodily and therefore animal identity" (qtd. in Eagleton 155), and in his *Meditations on Hunting* (1942), Jose Ortega y Gasset says that for us and for the other animals "life is brief and urgent" (23). We have much in common with other animals, but for all of this, our attitudes to the 'lesser' creatures is often one of superior ignorance. We use other animals for our food and clothing, as experimental objects in laboratories, as beasts of burden, and as sources of our amusement, in sports, and as pets, but our culture seldom notices their value as creatures in themselves. Roberts makes the case for viewing animals in their own *being*—in a way, from their own point of view. In many of the over two hundred animal stories he wrote, he dramatizes what it means to live in the world as a creature, and he does this by writing about animals in a newly observant fashion. In his commentary in the Criticism section of this edition, Joseph Gold says that Roberts liked to "brush out the line between animal and human." That is what makes his stories most fascinating for many of his readers—he is a writer of creature awareness who makes us think anew about ways in which we and the animals are alike.

The Biography section of this edition makes some connections between the life Roberts lived and the shape of his appreciation for the animal world. In a number of different ways, all of the contributions to the Criticism section of this edition relate Roberts' stories to the intellectual milieu of his own time, and that is essentially a post-Darwinist period of intellectual searching and spiritual doubt. As well, Roberts was born into a male culture in which he was encouraged to view hunting and fishing and trapping as laudable, even invigorating activities. He spent a great deal of time canoeing and hiking in the woods of New Brunswick, eventually becoming aware of animals in ways that appreciated their dignity and sympathized with their plight. He was smartly curious about his surroundings, and his appreciation of animals often took place at the level of his own observations. In addition, the fact that he wrote stories engaged with the lives of the animals themselves, accounts for a quality of 'realism' (not literalism) found in his stories and it differentiates his work from more projective types of animal stories written by earlier practitioners of the animal story genre. Many of his best stories are post-Darwinist melodramas and tragedies which are also efforts of literary observation.

Along with Ernest Thompson Seton, Roberts is a co-founder of the modern 'realistic' animal story. In that genre he tried to recreate an understanding sensation of animal life as it was lived in the Canadian wilds. Lorraine McMullen says in her "Ernest Thompson Seton" monograph that "most critics agree, or consider Roberts and Seton to have developed the ['realistic' animal] story simultaneously" (224), and Muriel Whittaker says in her Introduction to *The Best Canadian Animal Stories: Classic Tales by Master Storytellers* (1997), that "Charles G.D. Roberts and Ernest Thompson Seton developed almost simultaneously this ['realistic' animal story] genre which is Canada's original contribution to world literature" (2). For all of this, in his edition, *The Wild Animal Story* (1998), Ralph H. Lutts suggests that the genre also evolved out of the example of animal-centred classics from England like Anna Sewell's *Black Beauty* (1877) and Rudyard Kipling's *The Jungle Books* (1894, 1895), and he suggests that it had also an early manifestation in the work of American author, Charles Dudley Warner, whose "story 'A-Hunting of the Deer' (1878) depicted the hunt as the deer experienced it" (3). The modern realistic animal story was an evolving international genre, that is, and Roberts was lauded on both sides of the Atlantic as the best practitioner of its craft.

In *Survival: A Thematic Guide to Canadian Literature* (1972), Margaret Atwood highlights the fact that "the animal as victim is a persistent image in Canadian literature" (79), and this is an oft-repeated notion about the power politics of the

Canadian animal story, but it is not one necessarily applicable to Roberts in any significant way. Roberts was interested in American traditions of nature writing, and his works therefore participate in the American tradition of Literary Naturalism as a result, a tradition which is more scientific, philosophical and more existentialist, less purely nationalist in archetype than anything Atwood had in mind. My own piece in the Criticism section of this edition goes into Roberts' American connections in some detail, and I suggest that his literary legacy included a contribution to American literature as much as one to the literature of his own nation; he was a cosmopolitan writer whose writings show that he was in sync with much that was going on in the literary world beyond Canada.

Roberts thought out very carefully his aesthetic of animal fiction, and he was aware of the history of animal writing that preceded his own efforts. The documentary section of this edition contains reprints of a number of his clearest commentaries on animals and on the animal story and they show that he was aware of the history of animal literature, the form of his own aesthetic, and the pragmatic value of his new version of the genre. In one of those documents, his essay "The Animal Story," which is his Introduction to the selection, *The Kindred of the Wild: A Book of Animal Life* (1902), he recites the history of the genre as the record of a human withdrawal from the experiential world of creatures into the world of removed abstraction where authors employed fable, symbol, and other literary contrivances to typify animals merely:

> . . . as advancing civilization drew an ever widening line between man and animals, and men became more and more engrossed in the interests of their own kind, the personalities of the wild creatures which they had once known so well became obscured to them, and the creatures themselves came to be regarded, for the purposes of literature, as types or symbols merely, —except in those cases, equally obstructive to exact observation, where they were revered as temporary tenements of the spirits of departed kinsfolk (19).

Roberts knew that all art abstracted the animal inevitably, and thought there was something obvious about this, but he quarreled with the degree of that abstraction in some of its manifestations, and with the disfiguring that took place in that process. He saw that the disfigurations were often done rigidly in the name of the reigning mythology of the day. In his view Christianity, for example, too easily dismissed the animal as unworthy of human attention. Roberts thought that "the advent of Christianity, strange as it may seem at first glance, did not make for a closer understanding between man and the lower animals" (*Kindred* 20), because Christianity viewed nature as the enemy of the soul. Roberts felt that the dominant, received value system had evolved a self-serving view of animals, one that ignored the dignity of animals and their existential connection with humanity. More recent writers also speak of this cultural mistake as a central one. In their *Regarding Animals* (1996) Arnold Arluke and Clinton R. Sanders, for example, put the issue this way:

> A hierarchical model of animals has governed Western thought since Aristotle's notion that nature was ordered on a vertical scale that extended from lifeless things to man. For many centuries, new thinking in Western societies has continued to be influenced by ancient ideas about a "chain of being" . . . From the Middle Ages to the eighteenth century, it was thought that God fixed the place of all creatures in nature, with humans having dominion over animals. God was at the pinnacle in this rigid hierarchical chain of being, followed by his representatives and interpreters (church and state), then by the social tiers of feudalism, all of which sat above the kingdom of nonhuman animals, also having its respective ranking from primates to plants. Each living thing was seen as both similar yet different from those immediately above and below it on the scale.
>
> [Recent] Scholars have thoroughly criticized this way of classifying animals . . . arguing that the chain of being and the theological doctrine behind it wrongly allowed people to consider themselves

> inherently superior to animals and justified their exploitation of them (168).

In the same light, Paul Shepard, in his *The Others: How Animals Made Us Human* (1996), says that "Western religious ideas of animals, called 'theological zoology', by Florence Murdoch, comprise two thousand years of 'grotesque parodies of natural history'" (223). There are subversions of this 'theological zoology' in the past (Shepard 222-42), but the dominant view has set the attitudes that have kept animals marginalized right up to the present day. It is a view that Roberts wished to challenge, and his rebellion against it has often gone unnoticed. In a significantly-titled essay, "Renegotiating the Contacts," Barry Lopez has called our "determined degradation of the value of animal life" during the "agricultural, scientific and industrial revolutions" a kind of "deep and long-lived insult" (15) which he says accounts for why we "have lost our understanding of the place of awe and mystery in adult life, though it is still maintained by aboriginal peoples" (16). Roberts understood this prior to Lopez, and he saw the realistic animal story as having the potential for recovering a lost and vital awareness.

Immanuel Kant disagreed with Rene Descartes' view of the animal as little more than a machine. Kant said that "the lower animals, like man, act according to representations, and are not machines, as Descartes contends, and . . . despite their specific difference, they are living beings and as such generally kindred to man" (qtd. in Grenier 66). This is a difference that is huge and it is still with us today. It is often argued at the centre of animal rights debates and it goes to the commercial use of animals at many levels. Seton and Roberts come down on the side of Kant in the debate, Seton famously saying, in language very close to Kant's, that "we and the beasts are kin" (*Wild Animals* 11) and Roberts, in "The Animal Story," stressing the sentiment in tightly similar terms. Roberts thought that the realized presence of animals was a *spiritus loci* at which we might recoup a capacity for awe:

> looking deep into the eyes of certain of the four-footed kindred, we have been startled to see therein a

> something, before unrecognised, that answered to our inner and intellectual, if not spiritual selves. . . . It is as if one should step carelessly out of one's back door, and marvel to see unrolling before his new-awakened eyes the peaks and seas and misty valleys of an unknown world. (*The Kindred of the Wild* 23-24)

Roberts' urging here is a particularized variation on Aristotle's notion that "In all things in nature there is something of the marvelous" (qtd. in Shepard 127). By seeing the creature more in itself, we respect its otherness, and we also respect the animal as a stimulus to our own spiritual awareness. Any exploitation of the creature in this connection is a relatively benign one; we approach it for the wisdom it suggests to our imagination, for an appreciation of its mysterious *being*.

Roberts also thought we were kin to the beasts in our struggles for survival and in our deaths. This is especially clear in his many stories that include human survival like "Do Seek Their Meat from God" and "The Grip in Deep Hole," but it is also implicit in virtually all of his stories about animals separate from the human. He writes with a post-Darwinian sobriety about nature, so he sees the edifying mystery but also the pain in life and it is a pain that humans and animals both suffer in a kind of existential mutuality. There is a fickle quality in the outcome of events in many of Roberts' stories, and even though Chance is sometimes benevolent—see it at work this way in "Starnose of the Under Ways," "The Lord of the Air," or "A Stranger to the Wild," for example—it is often more malignant than good. See, for a central example, "The Sentry of the Sedge Flats" for a very usual working out of the indifferent formula. The lives of animals are governed as much by Chance, Irony, and Death, as by individual creature will and the simple wish to thrive.

The struggle and pain Roberts' animals suffer is sometimes an impersonal equivalent to the pain Roberts knew in his own life. So it is hard to read "The Panoply of Spears," for instance, without thinking of the death of Roberts' son Altheson in October of 1897. And it is easy to see the connection between Roberts' own sense of longing and restlessness and the similar emotions he depicts in a number of the animals in such stories as "The Homesickness of Kehonka," "A Stranger to the Wild," and "The Nest of The Mallard." Roberts often depicted a meaningful domesticity in animal life, and he perhaps wished he had such dynamic for his own family. He has many personal, biographical connections with his stories, and this in part accounts for a lyrical intensity in them which personalizes their philosophical concerns.

In terms of form, Roberts describes the animal story as "a psychological romance constructed on a framework of natural science" (*Kindred* 24), and he divides it into three categories of artistic enactment: the anecdote of observation; the animal adventure story; and the animal biography or psychological chronicle. In the Criticism section of this edition, W.J. Keith and Misao Dean both refer to constituents of the genre in some detail. In practice, Roberts employs ingredients from all three types of animal story within his own writing, but his brilliance as a writer lies in the way such forms facilitate his felt renderings of animal life, renderings that include a clear picture of the ferocity, energy, mystery, suspense, and beauty that go to make that life seem marvelous and urgent at once.

The 'realistic' animal story is the ideal type of story as Roberts states it, and it has in his view a spiritually therapeutic value, one he most sharply expresses in the final paragraph of "Animal Story":

> The animal story, as we now have it, is a potent emancipator. It frees us for a little from the world of shop-worn utilities, and from the mean tenement of self of which we do well to grow weary. It helps us to return to nature, without requiring that we at the same time return to barbarism. It leads us back to the old kinship of earth, without asking us to relinquish by way of toll any part of the wisdom of the ages, any "large result of time." The clear and candid life to which it reinitiates us, far behind though it lies in the long upward march of being, holds for us this quality. It has ever the more significance, it has ever the richer gift of refreshment and renewal, the more humane the heart and spiritual understanding which we bring to the intimacy (*Kindred* 29).

As Ortega similarly put it later, "Man cannot re-enter Nature except by temporarily rehabilitating that part of himself which is still animal" (121); Ortega sees the re-initiation as available in the act of intelligent hunting, while Roberts sees it as differently available in the magic of imaginative witness. We live both without and within nature, and the realistic animal story holds the promise that we might recover the latter half of this truth by reading. Thus, the animal story promises to enact a process of rehabilitation, of "re-initiation' (to recall Roberts' word) which is potentially rewarding to our spiritual needs.

The Documents section of this edition contains other comments by Roberts related to the animal story, items additional to the central "The Animal Story" essay I have quoted from at some length. It is clear from all of this material that Roberts went about his task of writing these stories in a highly conscious way. Most of the items in the Criticism section of this edition comment on Roberts' complicated interest in 'realism,' though they do so along with various other issues in mind as well. Roberts knew that the blend of observation and art was a difficult one in the 'realistic' animal story, but it was worth the challenge because of its potentially rehabilitating effect on its readers. As Keith suggests in the Criticism section of this edition, Roberts was aware of the limitations of subjectivism even as he sought an escape from it in his stories. The best of his animal stories contain the empiricist concerns of the naturalist and the creative vision of the writer all in one mix, and it was a blending that won him critical acclaim on both sides of the Atlantic as an animal writer who was different, one who ventured more close-up to the animal world than earlier practitioners of the genre.

Nevertheless, in the United States particularly, such a blending involved Roberts in a controversy over the accuracy of his observations and the validity of his knowledge about given individual species of animals. The accuracy of his observations about animals were questioned by figures as influential as John Burroughs and President Theodore Roosevelt. The details of the so-called "nature faker" controversy are concisely discussed in T.D. MacLulich's article in the Criticism section, and it is clear that Roberts was up to the debate on a number of grounds. For a lengthier treatment of the controversy see Ralph H. Lutts' full-length study, *The Nature Fakers: Wildlife, Science & Sentiment* (1990). As Lutts puts it, the controversy "was concerned with whether or not some of the most prominent nature writers of the time were really fraud naturalists" (x). Roberts got caught up in that debate and he defended himself in it very ably. It was a debate which sometimes took on a good-natured humorous dimension as well, and Roberts didn't mind that part of it at all.

The presence of subjectivism within 'realism' is always problematic in nature writing, and Roberts was conscious of this when theorizing about the animal story. Both the Criticism and the Review sections of this edition contain items that show it was a relevant literary-critical issue in Roberts' time and it remains a reference point for some debate in our time as well. When speaking primarily of Ernest Thompson Seton, Jack London and Roberts, Marian Scholtmeijer warns in *Animal Victims in Modern Fiction: From Sanctity to Sacrifice* (1993) that "Signs of ideological imposition, mistaken for realism, abound in their stories (119)," and Dean's article in the Criticism section works out some of the details of ideology in a significant number of Roberts' animal stories. Scholtmeijer and Dean remind us that Roberts' 'realism' cannot be taken at face value. Like all writing, it brings with it some of the cultural biases of its day. In the end, many of Roberts' animals were often what Burroughs names "human beings disguised as animals" (qtd. by MacLulich in the Criticism section), what MacLulich terms "miniature human beings" or what Dean memorably refers to as the many "(m)animals" in Roberts' world. There is a way in which the animals presented in Roberts' world contain a good deal of Roberts' own projective self, inevitably. It was Roberts' view, nonetheless, that the degree of projection was one the realistic animal story writer could hold in check with a familiarity with natural science and a willingness to observe the animal world anew. Many critics have defended this blend in Roberts' vision, but argument about the adequacy of the blend is likely to continue.

What we see as the details of Roberts' ideological biases depend very heavily upon the stories we choose to hold him to, so it is never an easy task to find certainty about Roberts' signature ideological claims. Accurate as it partly is, it is therefore only selectively accurate of Janice Kulyk Keefer, for example, to claim in *Under Eastern Eyes: A critical reading of Maritime fiction* (1987), that "Roberts maintains a social and moral hierarchy in his wilderness (85)" in which "lordly eagle and kingly moose are presented as nature's aristocrats and set over the middling beavers and porcupines, so the dutiful performance of familial responsibilities by porcupines and the unremitting industry of beavers are deemed superior to the gratuitous depredations of mole-shrew, or weasel (85)." Roberts varied those relationships immensely in his stories, not always in favour of the strong or the masculine, and his tone of expression was very different from Keefer's in that it contained within its emotion a characteristically compassionate note. Roberts thought that Chance, Irony, and Death were the real aristocrats in the wilderness, and his compassion for all creatures qualifies greatly all of his received ideological inclinations. The pathos of animal life is everywhere visible in Roberts' stories, and it takes particularly violent and poignant turns in stories like "Do Seek their Meat from God," "The Young Ravens," and "The Winged Scourge of the Dark." Sensitivity to suffering lies at the centre of Roberts' animal stories as a whole, and it assures a moral capaciousness in their temper, notwithstanding their inclusion of some traces of Roberts' ideological environment.

It is likely that Roberts would have agreed with the insights in Jeffrey Moussaieff Masson's *The Emperor's Embrace: Reflections on Animal Families and Fatherhood* (1999), where Masson outlines tenderness and altruism as positive qualities often found in male animals in the wilds, qualities chartable as evidence against a stock claim that male animals are capable of only selfish, dominating and fierce behaviour. "The Winged Scourge of the Dark," among others, is a story where positive male qualities are dramatized, and it is a story which celebrates maternal values as well. There are stories in which Roberts admires the morality of both female and male creatures, and of each gender separately. And Roberts sometimes makes female creatures superior to male ones, so there is no easy cornering of creature virtue in his works. Such stories as "The Panoply of Spears," The Nest of the Mallard," "The Black Fisherman," "When Twilight Falls on the Stump Lots," and "The Citadel in the Grass," to mention only a few, demonstrate a broad range of praise for both male and female animals, and they are all stories united by a basic respect Roberts has for qualities of kindness and courage. The gender biases of individual stories are not easily nudged into representation of his work as a whole. His sense of the role of Chance, Irony, and Death in nature was so strong that he often demonstrated how swiftly all hierarchies might be turned to dust in an instant, rendered beside the point in a hurry. "The Iron Edge of Winter," and particularly "The Sentry of the Sedge Flats," among many others, make this point with a starkness all their own. Hierarchical glitter for any creature in Roberts' fiction is a fleeting glory at best.

Roberts claimed that animals had thinking powers analogous to but not identical to human reason, and, even though the details of his claims on this subject were quite precise, it was a claim that further added to the controversial nature of his efforts as an animal story writer. In 1871 Charles Darwin had said that "Only a few persons now dispute that animals possess some power of reason," adding that "Animals may constantly be seen to pause, deliberate and resolve" (qtd. in Derr 159). As Eagleton has recently quipped, "Some dolphins can distinguish the sentence 'Take the surfboard to the frisbee' from 'Take the frisbee on the surfboard', an operation which even some world leaders might find difficulty with" (61). Roberts viewed the intelligence of animals in a similarly praising light, but a number of his "nature faker" critics thought that he gave animals too much credit for an intelligence which he merely projected or willed into their brains from the outside. Roberts is far from alone in his respect for animal intelligence, clearly, and a contemporary novelist such as Barbara Gowdy, on the evidence of her novel about elephants, *The White Bone* (1998), might agree with Roberts that animals do indeed think in highly complex, deliberate and often very sensitive ways. There is a distinguished tradition of animal writing that respects animal intelligence, and Roberts writes in rhythm with that tradition in his stories.

In some instances, and as imagined in Roberts' novel *Red Fox* (1905), given animals are much more sophisticated thinkers than given human beings. Roberts was not a conservative evolutionist. Some of his stories suggest that some human beings are far less sensitive, less instinctively intelligent, and even less moral than highly developed individual animals who think in their own ways in a manner that includes deliberation, quick decision, and a good heart. A number of contemporary naturalists and biologists would sanction happily Roberts' insistence on the complications of animal thought. In a recent work on animal thinking, *Winter World: The Ingenuity of Animal Survival* (2003), biologist Bernd Heinrich suggests that even weasels, for instance, are "fairly intelligent" and that according "to at least one anecdote that I trust, weasels can count (or at least have a sophisticated concept of quantity) up to six" (49). Significantly, though, the issue of animal intelligence is often an issue of learned instinct more than anything else. Heinrich argues that the ability of many animals to survive the winter in the northern climates is due to an instinctive wisdom accumulated at a basic level over thousands of years. In a sense, their thinking is in their bones.

Ortega claims that "*something like* reason operates in the domestic animal" (81) because the species divide is narrower in that particular relationship with humans. A number of biologists would agree further with Roberts that wild animals as well are capable of very complicated levels of thought. Marc D. Hauser's recent *Wild Minds: What Animals Really Think* (2000) is a study which implicitly supports Darwin and Roberts' claims about animal intelligence. Intelligence in Roberts' animals varies from the low-key kind instanced in his "By the Winter Tide" to the highly sophisticated and almost incredible mental activity he enacts in "The Citadel in the Grass." There is also a sort of whimsicality or play of mind in some of Roberts' animals, and he enacts this nicely in "The Iron Edge of Winter." He would have recognized exactly what Hauser is talking about, here, in a rendition about certain birds:

> . . . canaries and warblers, create new song variants each season in much the same way that Wagner created thematic variations or leitmotivs during such operatic masterpieces as *The Ring*. In both single-and multiple-dialect species, different populations main-

> tain long-lasting song traditions, themes passed down from generation to generation. The final class of song learners consists of the great mimics, species such as the mockingbirds, lyrebirds, and starlings. These species build an impressive repertoire of sounds, including songs from local fauna as well as sounds from some of the inanimate objects in the vicinity. In the London area, a chaffinch learned to reproduce the ring of the British telephone company, and then appeared to use it as a prank to cause the master of the house to rush outside. (119)

Hauser's study of animal intelligence is punctuated with many telling examples like this and he ends his study with the serious conclusion that:

> We share the planet with thinking animals. Each species, with its uniquely sculpted mind, endowed by nature and shaped by evolution, is capable of meeting the most fundamental challenges that the physical and psychological world presents. Although the human mind leaves a characteristically different imprint on the planet, we are certainly not alone in this process. (257)

Hauser is a contemporary professor in the Mind, Brain, and Behavior Program at Harvard University, but we might also take some comfort from the authority of Heinrich (whom I have already quoted earlier), who tells us that kinglets can survive in the winter because they "defy the odds and laws of physics, and prove that the fabulous is possible" (316), not because they read books on physics, but because as a subspecies they have learned by a sort of deliberative adaptation to survive.

Animals are also implicit teachers to humans, since they relay various bits of wisdom to us in the ways in which they live their lives. Shepard details how we are very close to animals in our daily lives: "Domestic animals have gradually become surrogate companions, siblings, lovers, victims, workers, parents, competitors, deities, oracles, enemies, kinfolk, caretaker-watchmen, and so on." (142) More importantly, though, we have learned much from animals that we take into our behaviour as humans. We have, for example, learned music from the birds, hunting from innumerable animals, and much of our linguistic expression emerged, in his view, from observation of animal activity:

> The emphasis on what the animal does has influenced language. Speech itself may have emerged in concert with sounds for actions borrowed from the names of animals. We verb the animals not only in games but in ordinary speech. We duck our heads, crane our necks, clam up, crab at one another, carp, rat, crow, or grouse vocally. We cow, quail, toady, lionize, and fawn in servility, admiration and fear. We fish for compliments, hog what should be shared, wolf it down, skunk others in total defeat, and hawk our wares. We outfox and buffalo those whom we dupe; we bug and badger in harassment. We hound or dog in pursuit, bear our burdens, lark and horse around in frolic. We bull, ram, or worm our way, monkey with things, weasel, and chicken out. We know loan sharks, possum players, and bullshitters. (*The Others* 86-87)

Animals help us express ourselves, and our culture is rife with the signification of animals in moral stories and in commercial symbols. We are attracted to their potential for meaning, even if many of us are unsure of, or hardly care about, what they might suggest to us in themselves. We habitually exploit animals for all sorts of reasons, and the range of usage is a wide one. In *Animal Geographies: Place, Politics, and Identity in the Nature-Culture Borderlands* (1998) Jody Emel and Jennifer Wolch note a few of the symbolic usages:

> The Berenstain Bears, Winnie the Pooh, Barney, Paddington Bear, Brer Fox and Brer Rabbit teach children morality, kindness, good manners, and self-respect. That animals are deeply ensconced in children's folk culture is a reality not lost upon toy-makers, particularly those who manufacture soft,

> cuddly animal companions and children's books. Products for adults are equally susceptible to animal-based marketing campaigns, however. Black rhinos and vervet monkeys sell Nissan Pathfinders. Wolves and black panthers sell Jeeps, and an alligator with frogs on its tail walks off a pier with a case of Budweiser. A quick look at the movie industry's production of animal movies for family consumption illustrates a growing trend. Disney's *101 Dalmations* is the seventh-highest-grossing film of all time. (17)

Alexander Wilson suggests that in many nature and wilderness movies we are far away from animals in any true sense of the word. Such movies, he says, are "one expression of a long human tradition of investing the natural world with meaning. Those meanings are as often as not laden with sexism, colonialism, and species hierarchy—witness the number of cars, tractors, and military machines named after animals" (qtd. in Wolch and Emel 140). In many films and movies, animals are little more than four-legged social archetypes, exploited for their abstract use as human tools of meaning—in many instances, tools of established, conventional social powers. Animals are seldom seen in themselves; they are part of the nature we have lost contact with, the nature Roberts beckons us to see afresh. We cannot learn from them if we are content to use them as merely emblems of our own human concerns.

Even zoos are morally bizarre, distancing mediums that manipulate animal identity in a pedagogically artificial manner. In his *About Looking* (1980) John Berger says that "Everywhere animals disappear," and, "In zoos they constitute the living monument to their own disappearance." (24) The zoo is little more than a site of confusion about animals, a place where the "captive wild animal is regarded as a human in animal skin. Perhaps one of the best examples of this transformation is the giant panda. Many of the panda's physical features—the round head, large eyes, and vertical posture—facilitate its anthropomorphization." (Arluke and Sanders 17) In zoos, animals are presented as merely ourselves with fur on. As Shepard would have it, "For centuries animals have been seen as demented persons" (231), and that is one of the more prominent presentations of the animal in the zoo context. In some zoos, animals are little more than prisoners who have not committed crimes. Animals are in zoos so that we can come to know them, but what is most centrally shown, intentionally or not, is that they are subservient to us and little more than toys for our entertainment.

Otherwise, animals are abused for the knowledge that comes out of technoscientific experimentation, and this is in keeping with the conviction that they are lesser beings, machines without feelings or thoughts. By a sinister shift of logic, this can also have an effect on the way groups of human beings are sometimes discriminated against without conscience. Once a person or a group of people are viewed as animal-like in their identity, their mistreatment is, by extension, all the more readily tolerated. In her *The Dreaded Comparison: Human and Animal Slavery* (1988), for example, Marjorie Spiegel relates how in the "eyes of the white slaveholders, black people were 'just animals'"(43); and Arluke and Sanders see how, "At times, certain minorities and powerless groups of people—retarded children, prisoners, the poor, enlisted soldiers—have been defined as different enough from most humans to be used as lab animals. Like lab animals, they are seen as lower on the social ladder, lesser humans, and therefore eligible for use in experiments that involve greater risk and suffering than those thought appropriate for other humans." (174) How we view animals relates to how we treat human beings.

Today, in some cancer research projects, transgenetic mice are bred with cancer in their bodies and thereby made ready for research. This so-called "OncoMouse" is the first animal in the world that has been patented for profit reasons—with all of the implications of animal-as-machine that suggests—and it shows that biotechnology has evolved a new level of animal suffering in the name of medical research. Animal rights advocates like Donna J. Haraway are outraged by such practices, and many agree with Jeffrey Moussaieff Masson and Susan McCarthy that violence against animals in the laboratory is tolerated only because we have lost an awareness of the creature identity of animals themselves. Descartes strikes again, and we can see Roberts' contrary, positive importance in this connection. For Masson and McCarthy we have lost the awareness that we, too, are creatures and we have a moral responsibility to view animals in an intelligent moral perspective. As Roger Grenier has said (after Jeremy Bentham), in his *The Difficulty of Being a Dog* (1998), "animals experience suffering just as much as we do (66)." In their *When Elephants Weep: The Emotional Lives of Animals* (1995), Masson and McCarthy ask us to realize that:

> Animals are not there for us to drill holes into, clamp down, dissect, pull apart, render helpless, and subject to agonizing experiments. John Lilly, one of the first to work scientifically with dolphins, was recently quoted as saying that he no longer works with dolphins because he "didn't want to run a concentration camp for highly developed beings." Animals are, like us, endangered species on an endangered planet, and we are the ones who are endangering them, it, and ourselves. They are the innocent sufferers in a hell of our making. We owe them, in the very least, to refrain from harming them further. If no more, we could leave them be. (236)

These are strong and coherent words. James Polk a long time ago (see Bibliography for his work on Roberts) cast Roberts as a writer aware of animal rights as an important issue, and it is clear that Roberts' sensitivity to animal pain and suffering suggests such an inclination in his stories. He eventually gave up hunting as he matured (see Documents for his comments on this), and he would likely agree with Mahatma Ghandi, as quoted in Raymond Merritt and Miles Barth's *1000 Dogs* (2000), that the "greatness of a nation and its moral progress can be measured by the way its animals are treated." (468) Roberts' fiction records many instances of human contempt for animal welfare, and initiation plots in Roberts' fiction often involve education into a gentler view. The more mature view appreciates the moral innocence of animals and also a moral dignity that is sometimes visible in the way they conduct their lives. Acting like an animal is not always, in Roberts' view, a lesser way to behave.

H.L. Mencken once wittily remarked that "Living with a dog is easy—like living with an idealist" (qtd. in Meritt and Barth 330) and Cynthia Heimel has quipped that "Dogs are us, only innocent" (qtd. in Merritt and Barth 374). Both comments remind us of a quality of innocence in animals, and Roberts typically records such a value in his stories. His more 'realistic' animal stories are not usually moral fables of the kind he dislikes in his "The Animal Story" essay, but they do offer moral commentary on life. Eagleton says that "Non-human animals behave as though they have beliefs" (61), in the sense that they live in accordance with certain codes of behaviour which are tacit to their lives. Roberts views animals similarly, I think, and he sees a moral *exemplum* in the loyalty of animals, in their capacity for love, and in their courage next to the overwhelming odds Nature stacks against them. He does not include all animals in his roster of the morally correct, and he will sometimes express a contempt in his stories for the weasel, among others, and for sinister figures like the white owl in "The Winged Scourge of the Dark," animals that remind him of bullies who prey on the weak. Nevertheless, what commonly comes through as the aggregate of his moral vision of the animal world is a vision of exemplary activity. He commonly views animals as heroic and as tragic, courageous and pathetic at the same time.

In *Animal Others: On Ethics, Ontology, and Animal Life* (1999), H. Peter Steeves remarks that "Perhaps it is the case that our finest ethical traits are not human traits which we need to polish up when we meet animal Others, but rather animal traits which we need to call forth and display proudly when dealing with Otherness of all kinds." (10) And Masson says that when we look at given animals we have to agree with Darwin that, for all of the ferocity in the animal world, the behaviour of many animals must make us feel that "the mystery of kindness lies before our eyes, unfathomable, yet real." (1999, 210) Like Roberts, Steeves respects the ready courage of animals next to adversity. As Steeves suggests, "courage arises from our animal nature; courage is on its finest display in penguins, wrens and bees—we are destined to be called great if we are capable of living up to half their standard" (10). This feeling for the moral wisdom of the animal world is one Roberts understood and emphasized in his fiction.

In his understanding of animals as marginalized, unacknowledged creatures with potentially enabling connections to the human, Roberts has forward-looking affinities with a series of contemporary animal writers, fiction writers and non-fiction writers alike. He shares with many of the animal commentators I have quoted throughout this Introduction a desire to bring his audience close-up to the mystery, beauty, innocence, wisdom and courage of the animal kindred. Other animals are an important part of our existence. Ignorance of them, in Roberts' view, is a very expensive proposition.

Works Cited

Atwood, Margaret. *Survival: A Thematic Guide to Canadian Literature.* Anansi, 1972.

Arluke, Arnold, and Clinton R. Sanders. *Regarding Animals.* Philadelphia: Temple U P, 1996.

Berger, John. *About Looking*, New York: Pantheon, 1980.

Derr, Mark. *Dog's Best Friend: Annals of the Dog-Human Relationship.* 1997. Chicago: U Chicago P, 2004.

Eagleton, Terry. *After Theory*, London: Allan Lane, 2003.

Gasset, Jose Ortega y. *Meditations on Hunting.* 1942. Trans. Howard B. Wescott, introd. Paul Shepard. New York: Scribner's, 1972.

Grenier, Roger. *The Difficulty of Being a Dog.* 1998. Trans. Alice Kaplan. Chicago: U Chicago P, 2000.

Hauser, Mark D. *Wild Minds: What Animals Really Think. 2000.* New York: Henry Holt, 2001.

Heinrich, Bernd. *Winter World: The Ingenuity of Animal Survival.* 2003. New York: HarperCollins, 2004.

Kulyk Keefer, Janice. *Under Eastern Eyes: a critical reading of Maritime fiction.* Toronto: U Toronto P, 1987.

Merritt, Raymond, and Miles Barth. *1000 Dogs.* New York: Taschen, 2000.

Lopez, Barry. "Renegotiating the Contacts." *Parabola: Myth and Quest for Meaning*, (Special Issue on Animals) 7.2 (1983): 14-19.

Lutts, Ralph. *The Nature Fakers: Wildlife, Science & Sentiment.* Golden, Colorado: Fulcrum, 1990.

———. ed. *The Wild Animal Story.* Philadelphia: Temple U P, 1998.

Masson, Jeffrey Moussaieff. *The Emperor's Embrace: Reflections on Animal Families and Fatherhhod.* New York: Simon & Schuster, 1999.

Masson, Jeffrey Moussaieff, and Susan McCarthy. *When Elephants Weep: The Emotional Lives of Animals*. New York: Delacorte, 1995.

McMullen, Lorraine. "Ernest Thompson Seton," *Canadian Writers and Their Works* (Fiction Series). eds. Robert Lecker, Jack David and Ellen Quigley. Toronto: ECW Press, 1989. 217-70.

Roberts, Charles G.D. "The Animal Story," Intro. to *The Kindred of the Wild: A Book of Animal Life*. 1902. Boston: L.C. Page, 1940.

Scholtmeijer, Marian. *Animal Victims in Modern Fiction: From Sanctity to Sacrifice*. Toronto: U Toronto P, 1993.

Seton, Ernest Thompson. Introduction to *Wild Animals I Have Known*. 1898. Introd. Alec Lucas. New Canadian Library, No. 141. Toronto: McClelland and Stewart, 1983.

Shepard, Paul. *The Others: How Animals Made Us Human*. 1996. Washington: Island / Shearwater, 1997.

Spiegel, Marjorie. *The Dreaded Comparison: Human and Animal Slavery*. Philadelphia: Heritage Books and New Society, 1988.

Steeves, H. Peter. *Animal Others: On Ethics, Ontology, and Animal Life*. Albany: State U of New York, 1999.

Whitaker, Muriel. ed. *The Best Canadian Animal Stories: Classic Tales by Master Storytellers*. Toronto: McClelland and Stewart, 1997.

Wolch, Jennifer, and Jody Emel. *Animal Geographies: Place, Politics, and Identity in the Nature-Culture Borderlands*. London: Verso, 1998.

"OUT OF A SHADOWY HOLLOW BEHIND A LONG, WHITE ROCK . . . CAME SOFTLY A GREAT PANTHER."

Do Seek their Meat from God*

One side of the ravine was in darkness. The darkness was soft and rich, suggesting thick foliage. Along the crest of the slope tree-tops came into view—great pines and hemlocks of the ancient unviolated forest—revealed against the orange disk of a full moon just rising. The low rays slanting through the moveless tops lit strangely the upper portion of the opposite steep,—the western wall of the ravine, barren, unlike its fellow, bossed with great rocky projections, and harsh with stunted junipers. Out of the sluggish dark that lay along the ravine as in a trough, rose the brawl of a swollen, obstructed stream.

Out of a shadowy hollow behind a long white rock, on the lower edge of that part of the steep which lay in the moonlight, came softly a great panther. In common daylight his coat would have shown a warm fulvous hue, but in the elvish decolorizing rays of that half hidden moon he seemed to wear a sort of spectral gray. He lifted his smooth round head to gaze on the increasing flame, which presently he greeted with a shrill cry. That terrible cry, at once plaintive and menacing, with an undertone like the fierce protestations of a saw beneath the file, was a summons to his mate, telling her that the hour had come when they should seek their prey. From the lair behind the rock, where the cubs were being suckled by their dam, came no immediate answer. Only a pair of crows, that had their nest in a giant fir-tree across the gulf, woke up and croaked harshly their indignation. These three summers past they had built in the same spot, and had been nightly awakened to vent the same rasping complaints.

The panther walked restlessly up and down, half a score of paces each way, along the edge of the shadow, keeping his wide-open green eyes upon the rising light. His short, muscular tail twitched impatiently, but he made no sound. Soon the breadth of confused brightness had spread itself further down the steep, disclosing the foot of the white rock, and the bones and antlers of a deer which had been dragged thither and devoured.

---

* From *Earth's Enigmas* (Boston: L.C. Page, 1896), 1-17. "Do Seek their Meat from God" also appeared in *Harper's Monthly* (Dec. 1892). The Charles Livingston Bull illustration reprinted with this story appeared in a 1903 edition of *Earth's Enigmas,* also published by L.C. Page.

By this time the cubs had made their meal, and their dam was ready for such enterprise as must be accomplished ere her own hunger, now grown savage, could hope to be assuaged. She glided supplely forth into the glimmer, raised her head, and screamed at the moon in a voice as terrible as her mate's. Again the crows stirred, croaking harshly; and the two beasts, noiselessly mounting the steep, stole into the shadows of the forest that clothed the high plateau.

The panthers were fierce with hunger. These two days past their hunting had been wellnigh fruitless. What scant prey they had slain had for the most part been devoured by the female; for had she not those small blind cubs at home to nourish, who soon must suffer at any lack of hers? The settlements of late had been making great inroads on the world of ancient forest, driving before them the deer and smaller game. Hence the sharp hunger of the panther parents, and hence it came that on this night they hunted together. They purposed to steal upon the settlements in their sleep, and take tribute of the enemies' flocks.

Through the dark of the thick woods, here and there pierced by the moonlight, they moved swiftly and silently. Now and again a dry twig would snap beneath the discreet and padded footfalls. Now and again, as they rustled some low tree, a pewee or a nuthatch would give a startled chirp. For an hour the noiseless journeying continued, and ever and anon the two gray, sinuous shapes would come for a moment into the view of the now well-risen moon. Suddenly there fell upon their ears, far off and faint, but clearly defined against the vast stillness of the Northern forest, a sound which made those stealthy hunters pause and lift their heads. It was the voice of a child crying,—crying long and loud, hopelessly, as if there were no one by to comfort it. The panthers turned aside from their former course and glided toward the sound. They were not yet come to the outskirts of the settlement, but they knew of a solitary cabin lying in the thick of the woods a mile and more from the nearest neighbor. Thither they bent their way, fired with fierce hope. Soon would they break their bitter fast.

Up to noon of the previous day the lonely cabin had been occupied. Then its owner, a shiftless fellow, who spent his days for the most part at the corner tavern three miles distant, had suddenly grown disgusted with a land wherein one must work to live, and had betaken himself with his seven-year-old boy to seek some more indolent clime. During the long lonely days when his father was away at the tavern the little boy had been wont to visit the house of the next neighbor, to play with a child of some five summers, who had no other playmate. The next neighbor was a prosperous pioneer, being master of a substantial frame house in the midst of a large and well-tilled clearing. At times, though rarely, because it was forbidden, the younger child would make his way by a rough wood road to visit his poor little disreputable playmate. At length it had appeared that the five-year-old was learning unsavory language from the elder boy, who rarely had an opportunity of hearing speech more desirable. To the bitter grief of both children, the companionship had at length been stopped by unalterable decree of the master of the frame house.

Hence it had come to pass that the little boy was unaware of his comrade's departure. Yielding at last to an eager longing for that comrade, he had stolen away late in the afternoon, traversed with endless misgivings the lonely stretch of wood road, and reached the cabin only to find it empty. The door, on its leathern hinges, swung idly open. The one room had been stripped of its few poor furnishings. After looking in the rickety shed, whence darted two wild and hawklike chickens, the child had seated himself on the hacked threshold, and sobbed passionately with a grief that he did not fully comprehend. Then seeing the shadows lengthen across the tiny clearing, he had grown afraid to start for home. As the dusk gathered, he had crept trembling into the cabin, whose door would not stay shut. When it grew quite dark, he crouched in the inmost corner of the room, desperate with fear and loneliness, and lifted up his voice piteously. From time to time his lamentations would be choked by sobs, or he would grow breathless, and in the terrifying silence would listen hard to hear if any one or anything were coming. Then again would the shrill childish wailings arise, startling the unexpectant night, and piercing the forest depths, even to the ears of those great beasts which had set forth to seek their meat from God.

The lonely cabin stood some distance, perhaps a quarter of a mile, back from the highway connecting the settlements.

Along this main road a man was plodding wearily. All day he had been walking, and now as he neared home his steps began to quicken with anticipation of rest. Over his shoulder projected a doubled-barrelled fowling-piece, from which was slung a bundle of such necessities as he had purchased in town that morning. It was the prosperous settler, the master of the frame house. His mare being with foal, he had chosen to make the tedious journey on foot.

The settler passed the mouth of the wood road leading to the cabin. He had gone perhaps a furlong beyond, when his ears were startled by the sound of a child crying in the woods. He stopped, lowered his burden to the road, and stood straining ears and eyes in the direction of the sound. It was just at this time that the two panthers also stopped, and lifted their heads to listen. Their ears were keener than those of the man, and the sound had reached them at a greater distance.

Presently the settler realized whence the cries were coming. He called to mind the cabin; but he did not know the cabin's owner had departed. He cherished a hearty contempt for the drunker squatter; and on the drunken squatter's child he looked with small favor, especially as a playmate for his own boy. Nevertheless he hesitated before resuming his journey.

"Poor little devil!" he muttered, half in wrath. "I reckon his precious father's drunk down at 'the Corners,' and him crying for loneliness!" Then he reshouldered his burden and strode on doggedly.

But louder, shriller, more hopeless and more appealing, arose the childish voice, and the settler paused again, irresolute, and with deepening indignation. In his fancy he saw the steaming supper his wife would have awaiting him. He loathed the thought of retracing his steps, and then stumbling a quarter of a mile through the stumps and bog of the wood road. He was foot-sore as well as hungry, and he cursed the vagabond squatter with serious emphasis; but in that wailing was a terror which would not let him go on. He thought of his own little one left in such a position, and straightway his heart melted. He turned, dropped his bundle behind some bushes, grasped his gun, and made speed back for the cabin.

"Who knows," he said to himself, "but that drunken idiot has left his youngster without a bite to eat in the whole miserable shanty? Or maybe he's locked out, and the poor little beggar's half scared to death. *Sounds* as if he was scared;" and at this thought the settler quickened his pace.

As the hungry panthers drew near the cabin, and the cries of the lonely child grew clearer, they hastened their steps, and their eyes opened to a wider circle, flaming with a greener fire. It would be thoughtless superstition to say the beasts were cruel. They were simply keen with hunger, and alive with the eager passion of the chase. They were not ferocious with any anticipation of battle, for they knew the voice was the voice of a child, and something in the voice told them the child was solitary. Theirs was no hideous or unnatural rage, as it is the custom to describe it. They were but seeking with the strength, the cunning, the deadly swiftness given them to that end, the food convenient for them. On their success in accomplishing that for which nature had so exquisitely designed them depended not only their own, but the lives of their blind and helpless young, now whimpering in the cave on the slope of the moon-lit ravine. They crept through a wet alder thicket, bounded lightly over the ragged brush fence, and paused to reconnoitre on the edge of the clearing, in the full glare of the moon. At the same moment the settler emerged from the darkness of the wood-road on the opposite side of the clearing. He saw the two great beasts, heads down and snouts thrust forward, gliding toward the open cabin door.

For a few moments the child had been silent. Now his voice rose again in pitiful appeal, a very ecstasy of loneliness and terror. There was a note in the cry that shook the settler's soul. He had a vision of his own boy, at home with his mother, safe-guarded from even the thought of peril. And here was this little one left to the wild beasts! "Thank God! Thank God I came!" murmured the settler, as he dropped on one knee to take a surer aim. There was a loud report (not like the sharp crack of a rifle), and the female panther, shot through the loins, fell in a heap, snarling furiously and striking with her forepaws.

The male walked around her in fierce and anxious amazement. Presently, as the smoke lifted, he discerned the settler kneeling for a second shot. With a high screech of fury, the lithe brute sprang upon his enemy, taking a bullet full in his chest without seeming to know he was hit. Ere the man could slip in another cartridge the beast was upon him, bearing him to the ground and fixing keen fangs in his shoulder. Without a word, the man set his strong fingers desperately into the brute's throat, wrenched himself partly free, and was struggling to rise, when the panther's body collapsed upon him all at once, a dead weight which he easily flung aside. The bullet had done its work just in time.

Quivering from the swift and dreadful contest, bleeding profusely from his mangled shoulder, the settler stepped up to the cabin door and peered in. He heard sobs in the darkness.

"Don't be scared, sonny," he said, in a reassuring voice. "I'm going to take you home along with me. Poor little lad, *I'll* look after you if folks that ought to don't."

Out of the dark corner came a shout of delight, in a voice which made the settler's heart stand still. "*Daddy*, daddy," it said, "I *knew* you'd come. I was so frightened when it got dark!" And a little figure launched itself into the settler's arms, and clung to him trembling. The man sat down on the threshold and strained the child to his breast. He remembered how near he had been to disregarding the far-off cries, and great beads of sweat broke out upon his forehead.

Not many weeks afterwards the settler was following the fresh trail of a bear which had killed his sheep. The trail led him at last along the slope of a deep ravine, from whose bottom came the brawl of a swollen and obstructed stream. In the ravine he found a shallow cave, behind a great white rock. The cave was plainly a wild beast's lair, and he entered circumspectly. There were bones scattered about, and on some dry herbage in the deepest corner of the den, he found the dead bodies, now rapidly decaying, of two small panther cubs.

"The Young Ravens that Call upon Him"*

It was just before dawn, and a grayness was beginning to trouble the dark about the top of the mountain.

Even at that cold height there was no wind. The veil of cloud that hid the stars hung but a hand-breadth above the naked summit. To eastward the peak broke away sheer, beetling in a perpetual menace to the valleys and the lower hills. Just under the brow, on a splintered and creviced ledge, was the nest of the eagles.

As the thick dark shrank down the steep like a receding tide, and the grayness reached the ragged heap of branches forming the nest, the young eagles stirred uneasily under the loose droop of the mother's wings. She raised her head and peered about her, slightly lifting her wings as she did so; and the nestlings, complaining at the chill air that came in upon their unfledged bodies, thrust themselves up amid the warm feathers of her thighs. The male bird, perched on a jutting fragment beside the nest, did not move. But he was awake. His white, narrow, flat-crowned head was turned to one side, and his yellow eye, under its straight, fierce lid, watched the pale streak that was growing along the distant eastern sea-line.

The great birds were racked with hunger. Even the nestlings, to meet the petitions of whose gaping beaks they stinted themselves without mercy, felt meagre and uncomforted. Day after day the parent birds had fished almost in vain; day after day their wide and tireless hunting had brought them scant reward. The schools of alewives, mackerel, and herring seemed to shun their shores that spring. The rabbits seemed to have fled from all the coverts about their mountain.

The mother eagle, larger and of mightier wing than her mate, looked as if she had met with misadventure. Her plumage was disordered. Her eyes, fiercely and restlessly anxious, at moments grew dull as if with exhaustion. On the day before, while circling at her viewless height above a lake far

---

* From *Earth's Enigmas* (Boston: L.C. Page, 1896), 52-61. "The Young Ravens that Call upon Him" also appeared in *Lippincott's Monthly Magazine* (May 1894) and *Current Literature* (July 1903).

inland, she had marked a huge lake-trout, basking near the surface of the water. Dropping upon it with half-closed, hissing wings, she had fixed her talons in its back. But the fish had proved too powerful for her. Again and again it had dragged her under water, and she had been almost drowned before she could unloose the terrible grip of her claws. Hardly, and late, had she beaten her way back to the mountain-top.

And now the pale streak in the east grew ruddy. Rust-red stains and purple, crawling fissures began to show on the rocky face of the peak. A piece of scarlet cloth, woven among the fagots of the nest, glowed like new blood in the increasing light. And presently a wave of rose appeared to break and wash down over the summit, as the rim of the sun came above the horizon.

The male eagle stretched his head far out over the depth, lifted his wings and screamed harshly, as if in greeting of the day. He paused a moment in that position, rolling his eye upon the nest. Then his head went lower, his wings spread wider, and he launched himself smoothly and swiftly into the abyss of air as a swimmer glides into the sea. The female watched him, a faint wraith of a bird darting through the gloom, till presently, completing his mighty arc, he rose again into the full light of the morning. Then on level, all but moveless wing, he sailed away toward the horizon.

As the sun rose higher and higher, the darkness began to melt on the tops of the lower hills and to diminish on the slopes of the upland pastures, lingering in the valleys as the snow delays there in the spring. As point by point the landscape uncovered itself to his view, the eagle shaped his flight into a vast circle, or rather into a series of stupendous loops. His neck was stretched toward the earth, in the intensity of his search for something to ease the bitter hunger of his nestlings and his mate.

Not far from the sea, and still in darkness, stood a low, round hill, or swelling upland. Bleak and shelterless, whipped by every wind that the heavens could let loose, it bore no bush but an occasional juniper scrub. It was covered with mossy hillocks, and with a short grass, meagre but sweet. There in the chilly gloom, straining her ears to catch the lightest footfall of approaching peril, but hearing only the hushed thunder of the surf, stood a lonely ewe over the lamb to which she had given birth in the night.

Having lost the flock when the pangs of travail came upon her, the unwonted solitude filled her with apprehension. But as soon as the first feeble bleating of the lamb fell upon her ear, everything was changed. Her terrors all at once increased tenfold,—but they were for her young, not for herself; and with them came a strange boldness such as her heart had never know before. As the little weakling shivered against her side, she uttered low, short bleats and murmurs of tenderness. When an owl hooted in the woods across the valley, she raised her head angrily and faced the sound, suspecting a menace to her young. When a mouse scurried past her, with a small, rustling noise amid the withered mosses of the hillock, she stamped fiercely, and would have charged had the intruder been a lion.

When the first gray of dawn descended over the pasture, the ewe feasted her eyes with the sight of the trembling little creature, as it lay on the wet grass. With gentle nose she coaxed it and caressed it, till presently it struggled to its feet, and, with its pathetically awkward legs spread wide apart to preserve its balance, it began to nurse. Turning her head as far around as she could, the ewe watched its every motion with soft murmurings of delight.

And now that wave of rose, which had long ago washed the mountain and waked the eagles, spread tenderly across the open pasture. The lamb stopped nursing; and the ewe, moving forward two or three steps, tried to persuade it to follow her. She was anxious that it should as soon as possible learn to walk freely, so they might together rejoin the flock. She felt that the open pasture was full of dangers.

The lamb seemed afraid to take so many steps. It shook its ears and bleated piteously. The mother returned to its side, caressed it anew, pushed it with her nose, and again moved away a few feet, urging it to go with her. Again the feeble little creature refused, bleating loudly. At this moment there came a terrible hissing rush out of the sky, and a great form fell upon the lamb. The ewe wheeled and charged madly; but at the same instant the eagle, with two mighty buffetings of his wings, rose beyond her reach and soared away toward the mountain. The lamb hung limp from his talons; and with piteous cries the ewe ran beneath, gazing upward, and stumbling over the hillocks and juniper bushes.

In the nest of the eagles there was content. The pain of their hunger appeased, the nestlings lay dozing in the sun, the neck of one resting across the back of the other. The triumphant male sat erect upon his perch, staring out over the splendid world that displayed itself beneath him. Now and again he half lifted his wings and screamed joyously at the sun. The mother bird, perched upon a limb on the edge of the nest, busily rearranged her plumage. At times she stooped her head into the nest to utter over her sleeping eaglets a soft chuckling noise, which seemed to come from the bottom of her throat.

But hither and thither over the round bleak hill wandered the ewe, calling for her lamb, unmindful of the flock, which had been moved to other pastures.

Strayed *

In the Cabineau Camp, of unlucky reputation, there was a young ox of splendid build, but of a wild and restless nature.

He was one of a yoke, of part Devon blood, large, dark-red, all muscle and nerve, and with wide magnificent horns. His yoke-fellow was a docile steady worker, the pride of his owner's heart; but he himself seemed never to have been more than half broken in. The woods appeared to draw him by some spell. He wanted to get back to the pastures where he had roamed untrammelled of old with his fellow-steers. The remembrance was in his heart of the dewy mornings when the herd used to feed together on the sweet grassy hillocks, and of the clover-smelling heats of June when they would gather hock-deep in the pools under the green willow-shadows. He hated the yoke, he hated the winter; and he imagined that in the wild pastures he remembered it would be for ever summer. If only he could get back to those pastures!

One day there came the longed-for opportunity; and he seized it. He was standing unyoked beside his mate, and none of the teamsters were near. His head went up in the air, and with a snort of triumph he dashed away through the forest.

For a little while there was a vain pursuit. At last the lumbermen gave it up. "Let him be!" said his owner, "an' I rayther guess he'll turn up agin when he gits peckish. He kaint browse on spruce buds an' lung-wort."

Plunging on with long gallop through the snow he was soon miles from camp. Growing weary he slackened his pace. He came down to a walk. As the lonely red of the winter sunset began to stream through the openings of the forest, flushing the snows of the tiny glades and swales, he grew hungry, and began to swallow unsatisfying mouthfuls of the long moss which roughened the tree-trunks. Ere the moon got up he had filled himself with this fodder, and then he lay down in a little thicket for the night.

---

* From *Earth's Enigmas* (Boston: L.C. Page, 1896), 238-47. "Strayed" also appeared in *Harper's Young People* (July 2, 1889).

But some miles back from his retreat a bear had chanced upon his foot-prints. A strayed steer! That would be an easy prey. The bear started straightway in pursuit. The moon was high in heaven when the crouched ox heard his pursuer's approach. He had no idea what was coming, but he rose to his feet and waited.

The bear plunged boldly into the thicket, never dreaming of resistance. With a muffled roar the ox charged upon him and bore him to the ground. Then he wheeled, and charged again, and the astonished bear was beaten at once. Gored by those keen horns he had no stomach for further encounter, and would fain have made his escape; but as he retreated the ox charged him again, dashing him against a huge trunk. The bear dragged himself up with difficulty, beyond his opponent's reach; and the ox turned scornfully back to his lair.

At the first yellow of dawn the restless creature was again upon the march. He pulled more mosses by the way, but he disliked them the more intensely now because he thought he must be nearing his ancient pastures with their tender grass and their streams. The snow was deeper about him, and his hatred of the winter grew apace. He came out upon a hill-side, partly open, whence the pine had years before been stripped, and where now grew young birches thick together. Here he browsed on the aromatic twigs, but for him it was harsh fare.

As his hunger increased he thought a little longingly of the camp he had deserted, but he dreamed not of turning back. He would keep on till he reached his pastures, and the glad herd of his comrades licking salt out of the trough beside the accustomed pool. He had some blind instinct as to his direction, and kept his course to the south very strictly, the desire in his heart continually leading him aright.

That afternoon he was attacked by a panther, which dropped out of a tree and tore his throat. He dashed under a low branch and scraped his assailant off, then, wheeling about savagely, put the brute to flight with his first mad charge. The panther sprang back into his tree, and the ox continued his quest.

Soon his steps grew weaker, for the panther's cruel claws had gone deep into his neck, and his path was marked with blood. Yet the dream in his great wild eyes was not dimmed as his strength ebbed away. His weakness he never noticed or heeded. The desire that was urging him absorbed all other thoughts,—even, almost, his sense of hunger. This, however, it was easy for him to assuage, after a fashion, for the long, gray, unnourishing mosses were abundant.

By and by his path led him into the bed of a stream, whose waters could be heard faintly tinkling on thin pebbles beneath their coverlet of ice and snow. His slow steps conducted him far along this open course. Soon after he had disappeared, around a curve in the distance there came the panther, following stealthily upon his crimsoned trail. The crafty beast was waiting till the bleeding and the hunger should do its work, and the object of its inexorable pursuit should have no more heart left for resistance.

This was late in the afternoon. The ox was now possessed with his desire, and would not lie down for any rest. All night long, through the gleaming silver of the open spaces, through the weird and checkered gloom of the deep forest, heedless even of his hunger, or perhaps driven the more by it as he thought of the wild clover bunches and tender timothy awaiting him, the solitary ox strove on. And all night, lagging far behind in his unabating caution, the panther followed him.

At sunrise the worn and stumbling animal came out upon the borders of the great lake, stretching its leagues of unshadowed snow away to the south before him. There was his path, and without hesitation he followed it. The wide and frost-bound water here and there had been swept clear of its snows by the wind, but for the most part its covering lay unruffled; and the pale dove-colors, and saffrons, and rose-lilacs of the dawn were sweetly reflected on its surface.

The doomed ox was now journeying very slowly, and with the greatest labor. He staggered at every step, and his beautiful head drooped almost to the snow. When he had got a great way out upon the lake, at the forest's edge appeared the pursuing panther, emerging cautiously from the coverts. The round tawny face and malignant green eyes were raised to peer out across the expanse. The laboring progress of the ox was promptly marked. Dropping its nose again to the ensanguined snow, the beast resumed his pursuit, first at a slow trot, and then at a long, elastic gallop. By this time the ox's quest was nearly done. He plunged forward upon his knees, rose again with difficulty, stood still, and looked around him. His eyes were clouding over, but he saw, dimly, the tawny brute that was now hard upon his steps. Back came a flash of the old courage, and he turned, horns lowered, to face the attack. With the last of his strength he charged, and the panther paused irresolutely; but the wanderer's knees gave way beneath his own impetus, and his horns ploughed the snow. With a deep bellowing groan he rolled over on his side, and the longing, and the dream of the pleasant pastures, faded from his eyes. With a great spring the panther was upon him, and the eager teeth were at his throat,—but he knew nought of it. No wild beast, but his own desire, had conquered him.

When the panther had slaked his thirst for blood, he raised his head, and stood with his fore-paws resting on the dead ox's side, and gazed all about him.

To one watching from the lake shore, had there been any one to watch in that solitude, the wild beast and his prey would have seemed but a speck of black on the gleaming waste. At the same hour, league upon league back in the depth of the ancient forest, a lonely ox was lowing in his stanchions, restless, refusing to eat, grieving for the absence of his yoke-fellow.

The Moonlight Trails*

There was no wind. The young fir-trees stood up straight and tall and stiffly pointed from the noiseless white levels of the snow. The blue-white moon of midwinter, sharply glittering like an icicle, hung high in a heaven clear as tempered steel.

The young fir-trees were a second growth, on lands once well cleared, but afterward reclaimed by the forest. They rose in serried phalanxes, with here and there a solitary sentinel of spruce, and here and there a little huddling group of yellow birches. The snow-spaces between formed sparkling alleys, and long, mysterious vistas, expanding frequently into amphitheatres of breathless stillness and flooding radiance. There was no trace of that most ghostly and elusive winter haze which represents the fine breathing of the forest. Rather the air seemed like diamonds held in solution, fluent as by miracle, and not without strange peril to be jarred by sound or motion.

Yet presently the exaggerated tension of the stillness was broken, and no disaster followed. Two small, white, furry shapes came leaping, one behind the other, down a corridor of radiance, as lightly as if a wind were lifting and drifting them. It was as if some of the gentler spirits of the winter and the wild had seized the magic hour for an incarnation. Leaping at gay leisure, their little bodies would lengthen out to a span of nearly three feet, then round themselves together so that the soft pads of their hinder paws would touch the snow within a couple of inches of the prints from which their fore paws were even then starting to rise. The trail thus drawn down the white aisle consisted of an orderly succession of close triplicate bunches of footprints, like no other trail of the wild folk. From time to time the two harmonious shapes would halt, sit up on their hindquarters, erect their long, attentive ears, glance about warily with their bulging eyes which, in this position, could see behind as well as in front of their narrow heads, wrinkle those cleft nostrils which were cunning to differentiate every

* From *The Kindred of the Wild* (Boston: L.C. Page, 1902), 33-52. "The Moonlight Trails" also appeared in *Outing* (Jan. 1901).

"ALL THE PLAYERS WERE MOTIONLESS, WITH EARS ONE WAY."

scent upon the sharp air, and then browse hastily but with a cheerful relish at the spicy shoots of the young yellow birch. Feeding, however, was plainly not their chief purpose. Always within a few moments they would resume their leaping progress through the white glitter and the hard, black shadows.

Very soon their path led them out into a wide glade, fenced all about with the serried and formal ranks of the young firs. It seemed as if the blue-white moon stared down into this space with a glassiness of brilliance even more deluding and magical than elsewhere. The snow here was crossed by a tangle of the fine triplicate tracks. Doubling upon themselves in all directions and with obvious irresponsibility, they were evidently the trails of play rather than of business or of flight. Their pattern was the pattern of mirth; and some half dozen wild white rabbits were gaily weaving at it when the two newcomers joined them. Long ears twinkling, round eyes softly shining, they leaped lightly hither and thither, pausing every now and then to touch each other with their sensitive noses, or to pound on the snow with their strong hind legs in mock challenge. It seemed to be the play of care-free children, almost a kind of confused dance, a spontaneous expression of the joy of life. Nevertheless, for all the mirth of it, there was never a moment when two or more of the company were not to be seen sitting erect, with watchful ears and eyes, close in the shadow of the young fir-trees. For the night that was so favourable to the wild rabbits was favourable also to the fox, the wildcat, and the weasel. And death stalks joy forever among the kindred of the wild.

From time to time one or another of the leaping players would take himself off through the fir-trees, while others continued to arrive along the moonlight trails. This went on till the moon had swung perhaps an hour's distance on her shining course; then, suddenly it stopped; and just for a fleeting fraction of a breath all the players were motionless, with ears one way. From one or another of the watchers there had come some signal, swift, but to the rabbits instantly clear. No onlooker not of the cleft-nose, long-ear clan could have told in what the signal consisted, or what was its full significance. But whatever it was, in a moment the players were gone, vanishing to the east and west and south, all at once, as if blown off by a mighty breath. Only toward the north side of the open there went not one.

Nevertheless, the moon, peering down with sharp scrutiny into the unshadowed northern fringes of the open, failed to spy out any lurking shape of fox, wildcat, or weasel. Whatever the form in which fate had approached, it chose not to unmask its menace. Thereafter, for an hour or more, the sparkling glade with its woven devices was empty. Then, throughout the rest of the night, an occasional rabbit would go bounding across it hastily, on affairs intent, and paying no heed to its significant hieroglyphs. And once, just before moon-set, came a large red fox and sniffed about the tangled trails with an interest not untinged with scorn.

II.

The young fir wood covered a tract of poor land some miles in width, between the outskirts of the ancient forest and a small settlement known as Far Bazziley. In the best house of Far Bazziley—that of the parish clergyman—there lived a boy whom chance, and the capricious destiny of the wild folk, led to take a sudden lively interest in the moonlight trails. Belonging to a different class from the other children of the settlement, he was kept from the district school and tutored at home, with more or less regularity, by his father. His lesson hours, as a rule, fell when the other boys were busy at their chores—and it was the tradition of Far Bazziley that boys were born to work, not play. Thus it happened that the boy had little of the companionship of his fellows.

Being of too eager and adventurous a spirit to spend much of his leisure in reading, he was thrown upon his own resources, and often found himself hungry for new interests. Animals he loved, and of all cruelty toward them he was fiercely intolerant. Great or small, it hurt him to see them hurt; and he was not slow to resent and resist that kind of discomfort.

On more than one occasion he had thrashed other boys of the settlement for torturing, with boyish playfulness and ingenuity, superfluous kittens which thrifty housewives had confided to them to drown. These rough interferences with custom did him no harm, for the boys were forced to respect his prowess, and they knew well enough that kittens had some kind of claim upon civilisation. But when it came to his overbearing championship of snakes, that was another matter, and he made himself unpopular. It was rank tyranny, and disgustingly unnatural, if they could not crush a snake's back with stones and then lay it out in the sun to die gradually, without the risk of getting a black eye and bloodied nose for it.

It was in vain the boy explained, on the incontrovertible authority of his father, that the brilliant garter-snake, the dainty little green snake, and indeed all the snakes of the neighbourhood without exception, were as harmless as lady-bugs. A snake was a snake; and in the eyes of Far Bazziley to kill one, with such additions of painfulness in the process as could be devised on the moment, was to obey Biblical injunction. The boy, not unnaturally, was thrust more and more into the lonely eminence of his isolation.

But one unfailing resource he had always with him, and that was the hired man. His mother might be, as she usually was, too absorbed in household cares to give adequate heed to his searching interrogations. His father might spend huge blanks of his time in interminable drives to outlying parts of his parish. But the hired man was always at hand. It was not always the same hired man. But whether his name were Bill or Tom, Henry or Mart or Chris, the boy found that he could safely look for some uniformity of characteristics, and that he could depend upon each in turn for some teaching that seemed to him more practical and timely than equations or the conjugation of *nolo, nolle, nolui*.

At this particular time of the frequenting of the moonlight trails, the boy was unusually fortunate in his hired man. The latter was a boyish, enthusiastic fellow, by the name of Andy, who had an interest in the kind of things which the boy held important. One morning as he was helping Andy with the barn work, the man said:

"It's about full moon now, and right handy weather for rabbit-snarin'. What say if we git off to the woods this afternoon, if your father'll let us, an' set some snares fer to-night, afore a new snow comes and spiles the tracks?"

The silent and mysterious winter woods, the shining spaces of the snow marked here and there with strange footprints leading to unknown lairs, the clear glooms, the awe and the sense of unseen presences—these were what came thronging into the boy's mind at Andy's suggestion. All the wonderful possibilities of it! The wild spirit of adventure, the hunting zest of elemental man, stirred in his veins at the idea. Had he seen a rabbit being hurt he would have rushed with indignant pity to the rescue. But the idea of rabbit-snaring, as presented by Andy's exciting words, fired a side of his imagination so remote from pity as to have no communication with it whatever along the nerves of sympathy or association. He was a vigorous and normal boy, and the jewel of consistency (which is usually paste) was therefore of as little consequence to him as to the most enlightened of his elders. He threw himself with fervour into Andy's scheme, plied him with exhaustive questions as to the methods of making and setting snares, and spent the rest of the morning, under direction, in whittling with his pocket-knife the required uprights and crosspieces, and twisting the deadly nooses of fine copper wire. In the prime of the afternoon the two, on their snowshoes, set off gaily for the wood of the young fir-trees.

Up the long slope of the snowy pasture lots, where the drifted hillocks sparkled crisply, and the black stumps here and there broke through in suggestive, fantastic shapes, and the gray rampikes towered bleakly to the upper air, the two climbed with brisk steps, the dry cold a tonic to nerve and vein. As they entered the fir woods a fine, balsamy tang breathed up to greet them, and the boy's nostrils took eager note of it.

The first tracks to meet their eyes were the delicate footprints of the red squirrel, ending abruptly at the foot of a tree somewhat larger than its fellows. Then the boy's sharp eyes marked a trail very slender and precise—small, clear dots one after the other; and he had a feeling of protective tenderness to the maker of that innocent little trail, till Andy told him that he of the dainty footprints was the bloodthirsty and indomitable weasel, the scourge of all the lesser forest kin.

The weasel's trail led them presently to another track, consisting of those triplicate clusters of prints, dropped lightly and far apart; and Andy said, "Rabbits! and the weasel's after them!" The words made a swift picture in the boy's imagination; and he never forgot the trail of the wild rabbit or the trail of the weasel.

Crossing these tracks, they soon came to one more beaten, along which it was plain that many rabbits had fared. This they followed, one going on either side of it that it might not be obliterated by the broad trail of their snowshoes; and in a little time it led them out upon the sheltered glade whereon the merrymakers of the night before had held their revels.

In the unclouded downpour of the sunlight the tracks stood forth with emphasised distinctness, a melting, vapourous violet against the gold-white of the snowy surface; and to the boy's eyes, though not to the man's, was revealed a formal and intricate pattern in the tangled markings. To Andy it was incomprehensible; but he saw at once that in the ways leading to the open it would be well to plant the snares. The boy, on the other hand, had a keener insight, and exclaimed at once, "What fun they must have been having!" But his sympathy was asleep. Nothing, at that moment, could wake it up so far as to make him realise the part he was about to play toward those childlike revellers of the moonlight trails.

Skirting the glade, and stepping carefully over the trails, they proceeded to set their snares at the openings of three of the main alleys; and for a little while the strokes of their hatchets rang out frostily on the still air as they chopped down fragrant armfuls of the young fir branches.

Each of the three snares was set in this fashion: First they stuck the fir branches into the snow to form a thick green fence on both sides of the trail, with a passage only wide enough for one rabbit at a time to pass through. On each side of this passageway they drove securely a slender stake, notched on the inner face. Over the opening they bent down a springy sapling, securing its top, by a strong cord, to a small wooden cross-piece which was caught and held in the notches of the two uprights. From the under side of this cross-piece was suspended the easy-running noose of copper wire, just ample enough for a rabbit's head, with the ears lying back, to enter readily.

By the time the snares were set it was near sundown, and the young fir-trees were casting long, pointed, purple shadows. With the drawing on of evening the boy felt stirrings of a wild, predatory instinct. His skin tingled with a still excitement which he did not understand, and he went with a fierce yet furtive wariness, peering into the shadows as if for prey. As he and Andy emerged from the woods, and strode silently down the desolate slopes of the pasture lots, he could think of nothing but his return on the morrow to see what prizes had fallen to his snares. His tenderness of heart, his enlightened sympathy with the four-footed kindred, much of his civilisation, in fact, had vanished for the moment, burnt out in the flame of an instinct handed down to him from his primeval ancestors.

III.

That night the moon rose over the young fir woods, blue-white and glittering as on the night before. The air was of the same biting stillness and vitreous transparency. The magic of it stirred up the same merry madness in the veins of the wild rabbits, and set them to aimless gambolling instead of their usual cautious browsing in the thickets of yellow birch. One by one and two by two the white shapes came drifting down the shadowed alleys and moonlight trails of the fir wood toward the bright glade which they seemed to have adopted, for the time, as their playground. The lanes and ways were many that gave entrance to the glade; and presently some half dozen rabbits came bounding, from different directions, across the radiant open. But on the instant they stopped and sat straight up on their haunches, ears erect, struck with consternation.

There at the mouth of one of the alleys a white form jerked high into the air. It hung, silently struggling, whirling round and round, and at the same time swaying up and down with the bending of the sapling-top from which it swung. The startled spectators had no comprehension of the sight, no signal-code to express the kind of peril it portended, and how to flee from it. They sat gazing in terror. Then, at the next entrance, there shot up into the brilliant air another like horror; and at the next, in the same breath, another. The three hung kicking in a hideous silence.

The spell was broken. The spectators, trembling under the imminence of a doom which they could not understand, vanished with long bounds by the opposite side of the glade. All was still again under the blue-white, wizard scrutiny of the moon but those three kicking shapes. And these, too, in a few minutes hung motionless as the fir-trees and the snow. As the glassy cold took hold upon them they slowly stiffened.

About an hour later a big red fox came trotting into the glade. The hanging shapes caught his eye at once. He knew all about snares, being an old fox, for years at odds with the settlement of Far Bazziley. Casting a sharp glance about, he trotted over to the nearest snare and sniffed up desirously toward the white rabbit dangling above him. It was beyond his reach, and one unavailing spring convinced him of the fact. The second hung equally remote. But with the third he was more fortunate. The sapling was slender, and drooped its burden closer to the snow. With an easy leap the fox seized the dangling body, dragged it down, gnawed off its head to release the noose, and bore away the spoils in triumph, conscious of having scored against his human rivals in the hunt.

Late in the morning, when the sun was pale in a sky that threatened snowfall, the boy and Andy came, thrilling with anticipation, to see what the snares had captured. At the sight of the first victim, the stiff, furry body hanging in the air from the bowed top of the sapling, the boy's nerves tingled with a novel and fierce sense of triumph. His heart leapt, his eyes flamed, and he sprang forward, with a little cry, as a young beast might in sighting its first quarry. His companion, long used to the hunter's enthusiasm, was less excited. He went to the next snare, removed the victim, reset the catch and noose; while the boy, slinging his trophy over his shoulder with the air of a veteran (as he had seen it done in pictures), hastened on to the third to see why it had failed him. To his untrained eye the trampled snow, the torn head, and the blood spots told the story in part; and as he looked a sense of the tragedy of it began to stir achingly at the roots of his heart. "A fox," remarked Andy, in a matter-of-fact voice, coming up at the moment, with his prize hanging rigidly, by the pathetically babyish hind legs, from the grasp of his mittened fist.

The boy felt a spasm of indignation against the fox. Then, turning his gaze upon Andy's capture, he was struck by the cruel marks of the noose under its jaws and behind its ears. He saw, for the first time, the half-open mouth, the small, jutting tongue, the expression of the dead eyes; and his face changed. He removed his own trophy from his shoulder and stared at it for some moments. Then two big tears rolled over his ruddy cheeks. With an angry exclamation he flung the dead rabbit down on the snow and ran to break up the snares.

"We won't snare any more rabbits, Andy," he cried, averting his face, and starting homeward with a dogged set to his shoulder. Andy, picking up the rejected spoils with a grin that was half bewilderment, half indulgent comprehension, philosophically followed the penitent.

The Lord of the Air *

"HE SAW HIS WIDE-WINGED MATE, TOO, LEAVE THE NEST."

The chill glitter of the northern summer sunrise was washing down over the rounded top of old Sugar Loaf. The sombre and solitary peak, bald save for a ragged veil of blueberry and juniper scrub, seemed to topple over the deep enshadowed valley at its foot. The valley was brimmed with crawling vapours, and around its rim emerged spectrally the jagged crests of the fir wood. On either side of the shrouded valley, to east and west, stretched a chain of similar basins, but more ample, and less deeply wrapped in mist. From these, where the vapours had begun to lift, came radiances of unruffled water.

* From *The Kindred of the Wild* (Boston: L.C. Page, 1902), 55-90. "The Lord of the Air" also appeared in *Frank Leslie's Popular Monthly* (May 1902) and *Pearson's Magazine* (Jan. 1903).

Where the peak leaned to the valley, the trunk of a giant pine jutted forth slantingly from a roothold a little below the summit. Its top had long ago been shattered by lightning and hurled away into the depths; but from a point some ten or twelve feet below the fracture, one gaunt limb still waved green with persistent, indomitable life. This bleached stub, thrust out over the vast basin, hummed about by the untrammelled winds, was the watch-tower of the great bald eagle who ruled supreme over all the aerial vicinage of the Squatooks.

When the earliest of the morning light fell palely on the crest of Sugar Loaf, the great eagle came to his watch-tower, leaving the nest on the other side of the peak, where the two nestlings had begun to stir hungrily at the first premonition of dawn. Launching majestically from the edge of the nest, he had swooped down into the cold shadow, then, rising into the light by a splendid spiral, with muffled resonance of wing-stroke, he had taken a survey of the empty, glimmering world. It was still quite too dark for hunting, down there on earth, hungry though the nestlings were. He soared, and soared, till presently he saw his wide-winged mate, too, leave the nest, and beat swiftly off toward the Tuladi Lakes, her own special hunting-grounds. Then he dropped quietly to his blanched pine-top on the leaning side of the summit.

Erect and moveless he sat in the growing light, his snowy, flat-crowned head thrust a little forward, consciously lord of the air. His powerful beak, long and scythe-edged, curved over sharply at the end in a rending hook. His eyes, clear, direct, unacquainted with fear, had a certain hardness in their vitreous brilliancy, perhaps by reason of the sharp contrast between the bright gold iris and the unfathomable pupil, and the straight line of the low overhanging brow gave them a savage intensity of penetration. His neck and tail were of the same snowy whiteness as his snake-like head, while the rest of his body was a deep, shadowy brown, close kin to black.

Suddenly, far, far down, winging swiftly in a straight line through the topmost fold of the mist drift, he saw a duck flying from one lake to another. The errand of the duck was probably an unwonted one, of some special urgency, or he would not have flown so high and taken the straight route over the forest; for at this season the duck of inland waters is apt to fly low and follow the watercourse. However that may be, he had forgotten the piercing eyes that kept watch from the peak of old Sugar Loaf.

The eagle lifted and spread the sombre amplitude of his wings, and glided from his perch in a long curve, till he balanced above the unconscious voyager. Then down went his head; his wings shut close, his feathers hardened till he was like a wedge of steel, and down he shot with breathless, appalling speed. But the duck was travelling fast, and the great eagle saw that the mere speed of dropping like a thunderbolt was insufficient for his purpose. Two or three quick, short, fierce thrusts of his pinions, and the speed of his descent was more than doubled. The duck heard an awful hissing in the air above him. But before he could swerve to look up he was struck, whirled away, blotted out of life.

Carried downward with his quarry by the rush of his descent, the eagle spread his pinions and rose sharply just before he reached the nearest tree-tops. High he mounted on still wings with that tremendous impulse. Then, as the impulse failed, his wings began to flap strongly, and he flew off with business-like directness toward the eyrie on the other slope of Sugar Loaf. The head and legs of the duck hung limply from the clutch of his talons.

The nest was a seemingly haphazard collection of sticks, like a hay-cart load of rubbish, deposited on a ledge of the mountainside. In reality, every stick in the structure had been selected with care, and so adeptly fitted that the nest stood unshaken beneath the wildest storms that swept old Sugar Loaf. The ground below the ledge was strewn with the faggots and branches which the careful builders had rejected. The nest had the appearance of being merely laid upon the ledge, but in reality its foundations were firmly locked into a ragged crevice which cleft the ledge at that point.

As the eagle drew near with his prey, he saw his mate winging heavily from the Tuladis, a large fish hanging from her talons. They met at the nest's edge, and two heavy-bodied, soot-coloured, half-fledged nestlings, with wings half spread in eagerness, thrust up hungry, gaping beaks to greet them. The fish, as being the choicer morsel, was first torn to fragments and fed to these greedy beaks; and the duck followed in a few moments, the young ones gulping their meal with grotesque contortions and ecstatic liftings of their wings. Being already much more than half the size of their parents, and growing almost visibly, and expending vast vitality in the production of their first feathers, their appetites were prodigious. Not until these appetites seemed to be, for the moment, stayed, and the eaglets sank back contentedly upon the nest, did the old birds fly off to forage for themselves, leaving a bloody garniture of bones and feathers upon the threshold of their home.

The king—who, though smaller than his mate, was her lord by virtue of superior initiative and more assured, equable daring—returned at once to his watch-tower on the lake side of the summit. It had become his habit to initiate every enterprise from that starting-point. Perching motionless for a few minutes, he surveyed the whole wide landscape of the Squatook Lakes, with the great waters of Lake Temiscouata gleaming to the northwest, and the peak of Bald Mountain, old Sugar Loaf's rival, lifting a defiant front from the shores of Nictau Lake, far to the south.

The last wisp of vapour had vanished, drunk up by the rising sun, and the eagle's eye had clear command of every district of his realm. It was upon the little lake far below him that his interest presently centred itself. There, at no great height above the unruffled waters, he saw a fish-hawk sailing, now tilted to one side or the other on moveless wing, now flapping hurriedly to another course, as if he were scrupulously quartering the whole lake surface.

The king recognised with satisfaction the diligence of this, the most serviceable, though most unwilling, of his subjects. In leisurely fashion he swung off from his perch, and presently was whirling in slow spirals directly over the centre of the lake. Up, up he mounted, till he was a mere speck in the blue, and seemingly oblivious of all that went on below; but, as he wheeled, there in his supreme altitude, his grim white head was stretched ever earthward, and his eyes lost no detail of the fish-hawk's diligence.

All at once, the fish-hawk was seen to poise on steady wing. Then his wings closed, and he shot downward like a javelin. The still waters of the lake were broken with a violent splash and the fish-hawk's body for a moment almost disappeared. Then, with a struggle and a heavy flapping of wings, the daring fisher arose, grasping in his victorious claws a large "togue" or gray lake trout. He rose till he was well above the tree-tops of the near-by shore, and then headed for his nest in the cedar swamp.

This was the moment for which the eagle had been waiting, up in the blue. Again his vast wings folded themselves. Again his plumage hardened to a wedge of steel. Again he dropped like a plummet. But this time he had no slaughterous intent. He was merely descending out of the heavens to take tribute. Before he reached the hurrying fish-hawk he swerved upward, steadied himself, and flapped a menacing wing in the fish-hawk's face, heading it out again toward the centre of the lake.

Frightened, angry, and obstinate, the big hawk clutched his prize the closer, and made futile efforts to reach the tree-tops. But, fleet though he was, he was no match for the fleetness of his master. The great eagle was over him, under him, around him, all at once, yet never striking him. The king was simply indicating, quite unmistakably, his pleasure, which was that the fish should be delivered up.

Suddenly, however, seeing that the fish-hawk was obstinate, the eagle lost patience. It was time, he concluded, to end the folly. He had no wish to harm the fish-hawk,—a most useful creature, and none too abundant for his kingly needs. In fact, he was always careful not to exact too heavy a tribute from the industrious fisherman, lest the latter should grow discouraged and remove to freer waters. Of the spoils of his fishing the big hawk was always allowed to keep enough to satisfy the requirements of himself and his nestlings. But it was necessary that there should be no foolish misunderstanding on the subject.

The eagle swung away, wheeled sharply with an ominous, harsh rustling of stiffened feathers, and then came at the hawk with a yelp and a sudden tremendous rush. His beak was half open. His great talons were drawn forward and extended for a deadly stroke. His wings darkened broadly over the fugitive. His sound, his shadow,—they were doom itself, annihilation to the frightened hawk.

But that deadly stroke was not delivered. The threat was enough. Shrinking aside with a scream the fish-hawk opened his claws, and the trout fell, a gleaming bar of silver in the morning light. On the instant the eagle half closed his wings, tilted sideways, and swooped. He did not drop, as he had descended upon the voyaging duck, but with a peculiar shortened wing-stroke, he flew straight downward for perhaps a hundred feet. Then, with this tremendous impulse driving him, he shot down like lightning, caught the fish some twenty feet above the water, turned, and rose in a long, magnificent slant, with the tribute borne in his talons. He sailed away majestically to his watch-tower on old Sugar Loaf, to make his meal at leisure, while the ruffled hawk beat away rapidly down the river to try his luck in the lower lake.

Holding the fish firmly in the clutch of one great talon, the eagle tore it to pieces and swallowed it with savage haste. Then he straightened himself, twisted and stretched his neck once or twice, settled back into erect and tranquil dignity, and swept a kingly glance over all his domain, from the far head of Big Squatook, to the alder-crowded outlet of Fourth Lake. He saw unmoved the fish-hawk capture another prize, and fly off with it in triumph to his hidden nest in the swamp. He saw two more ducks winging their way from a sheltered cove to a wide, green reed-bed at the head of the thoroughfare. Being a right kingly monarch, he had no desire to trouble them. Untainted by the lust of killing, he killed only when the need was upon him.

Having preened himself with some care, polished his great beak on the dry wood of the stub, and stretched each wing, deliberately and slowly, the one after the other, with crisp rustling noises, till each strong-shanked plume tingled pleasantly in its socket and fitted with the utmost nicety to its overlapping fellows, he bethought him once more of the appetites of his nestlings. There were no more industrious fish-hawks in sight. Neither hare nor grouse was stirring in the brushy opens. No living creatures were visible save a pair of loons chasing each other off the point of Sugar Loaf Island, and an Indian in his canoe just paddling down to the outlet to spear suckers.

The eagle knew that the loons were no concern of his. They were never to be caught napping. They could dive quicker than he could swoop and strike. The Indian also he knew, and from long experience had learned to regard him as inoffensive. He had often watched, with feelings as near akin to jealousy as his arrogant heart could entertain, the spearing of suckers and whitefish. And now the sight determined him to go fishing on his own account. He remembered a point of shoals on Big Squatook where large fish were wont to lie basking in the sun, and where sick or disabled fish were frequently washed ashore. Here he might gather some spoil of the shallows, pending the time when he could again take tribute of the fish-hawk. Once more he launched himself from his watch-tower under the peak of Sugar Loaf, and sailed away over the serried green tops of the forest.

II.

Now it chanced that the old Indian, who was the most cunning trapper in all the wilderness of Northern New Brunswick, though he seemed so intent upon his fishing, was in reality watching the great eagle. He had anticipated, and indeed prepared for the regal bird's expedition to those shoals of the Big Squatook; and now, as he marked the direction of his flight, hc clucked grimly to himself with satisfaction, and deftly landed a large sucker in the canoe.

That very morning, before the first pallor of dawn had spread over Squatook, the Indian had scattered some fish, trout and suckers, on the shore adjoining the shoal water. The point he chose was where a dense growth of huckleberry and withewood ran out to within a few feet of the water's edge, and where the sand of the beach was dotted thickly with tufts of grass. The fish, partly hidden among these tufts of grass, were all distributed over a circular area of a diameter not greater than six or seven feet; and just at the centre of the baited circle the Indian had placed a stone about a foot high, such as any reasonable eagle would like to perch upon when making a hasty meal. He was crafty with all the cunning of the woods, was this old trapper, and he knew that a wise and experienced bird like the king of Sugar Loaf was not to be snared by any ordinary methods. But to snare him he was resolved, though it should take all the rest of the summer to accomplish it; for a rich American, visiting Edmundston on the Madawaska in the spring, had promised him fifty dollars for a fine specimen of the great white headed and white tailed eagle of the New Brunswick lakes, if delivered at Edmundston alive and unhurt.

When the eagle came to the point of shoals he noticed a slight change. That big stone was something new, and therefore to be suspected. He flew over it without stopping, and alighted on the top of a dead birch-tree near by. A piercing scrutiny convinced him that the presence of the stone at a point where he was accustomed to hop awkwardly on the level sand, was in no way portentous, but rather a provision of destiny for his convenience. He sailed down and alighted upon the stone.

When he saw a dead sucker lying under a grass tuft he considered again. Had the fish lain at the water's edge he would have understood; but up among the grasses, that was a singular situation for a dead fish to get itself into. He now peered suspiciously into the neighbouring bushes, scanned every tuft of grass, and cast a sweeping survey up and down the shores. Everything was as it should be. He hopped down, captured the fish, and was about to fly away with it to his nestlings, when he caught sight of another, and yet another. Further search revealed two more. Plainly the wilderness, in one of those caprices which even his old wisdom had not yet learned to comprehend, was caring very lavishly for the king. He hastily tore and swallowed two of the fish, and then flew away with the biggest of the lot to the nest behind the top of old Sugar Loaf. That same day he came twice again to the point of shoals, till there was not another fish left among the grass tufts. But on the following day, when he came again, with hope rather than expectation in his heart, he found that the supply had been miraculously renewed. His labours thus were greatly lightened. He had more time to sit upon his wind-swept watch-tower under the peak, viewing widely his domain, and leaving the diligent fish-hawks to toil in peace. He fell at once into the custom of perching on the stone at every visit, and then devouring at least one fish before carrying a meal to the nest. His surprise and curiosity as to the source of the supply had died out on the second day. The wild creatures quickly learn to accept a simple obvious good, however extraordinary, as one of those beneficences which the unseen powers bestow without explanation.

By the time the eagle had come to this frame of mind, the old Indian was ready for the next move in his crafty game. He made a strong hoop of plaited withe-wood, about seven feet in diameter. To this he fastened an ample bag of strong salmon-netting, which he had brought with him from Edmundston for this purpose. To the hoop he fixed securely a stiff birch sapling for a handle, so that the affair when completed was a monster scoop-net, stout and durable in every part. On a moonlight night when he knew that the eagle was safely out of sight, on his eyrie around at the back of Sugar Loaf, the Indian stuck this gigantic scoop into the bow of his canoe, and paddled over to the point of shoals. He had never heard of any one trying to catch an eagle in a net; but, on the other hand, he had never heard of any one wanting an eagle alive, and being willing to emphasise his wants with fifty dollars. The case was plainly one that called for new ideas, and the Indian, who had freed himself from the conservatism of his race, was keenly interested in the plan which he had devised.

The handle of the great scoop-net was about eight feet in length. Its butt the trapper drove slantingly into the sand where the water was an inch or two deep, bracing it securely with stones. He fixed it at an angle so acute that the rim of the net lay almost flat at a height of about four feet above the stone whereon the eagle was wont to perch. Under the uppermost edge of the hoop the trapper fixed a firm prop, making the structure steady and secure. The drooping slack of the net he then caught up and held lightly in place on three or four willow twigs, so that it all lay flat within the rim. This accomplished to his satisfaction, he scattered fish upon the ground as usual, most of them close about the stone and within the area overshadowed by the net, but two or three well outside. Then he paddled noiselessly away across the moon-silvered mirror of the lake, and disappeared into the blackness about the outlet.

On the following morning, the king sat upon his watch-tower while the first light gilded the leaning summit of Sugar Loaf. His gaze swept the vast and shadowy basin of the landscape with its pointed tree-tops dimly emerging above the vapour-drift, and its blank, pallid spaces whereunder the lakes lay veiled in dream. His golden eye flamed fiercely under the straight and fierce white brow; nevertheless, when he saw, far down, two ducks winging their way across the lake, now for a second visible, now vanishing in the mist, he suffered them to go unstricken. The clear light gilded the white feathers of his head and tail, but sank and was absorbed in the cloudy gloom of his wings. For fully half an hour he sat in regal immobility. But when at last the waters of Big Squatook were revealed, stripped and gleaming, he dropped from his perch in a tremendous, leisurely curve, and flew over to the point of shoals.

As he drew near, he was puzzled and annoyed to see the queer structure that had been erected during the night above his rock. It was inexplicable. He at once checked his flight and began whirling in great circles, higher and higher, over the spot, trying in vain to make out what it was. He could see that the dead fish were there as usual. And at length he satisfied himself that no hidden peril lurked in the near-by huckleberry thicket. Then he descended to the nearest tree-top and spent a good half-hour in moveless watching of the net. He little guessed that a dusky figure, equally moveless and far more patient, was watching him in turn from a thicket across the lake.

At the end of this long scrutiny, the eagle decided that a closer investigation was desirable. He flew down and alighted on the level sand well away from the net. There he found a fish which he devoured. Then he found another; and this he carried away to the eyrie. He had not solved the mystery of the strange structure overhanging the rock, but he had proved that it was not actively inimical. It had not interfered with his morning meal, or attempted to hinder him from carrying off his customary spoils. When he returned an hour later to the point of shoals the net looked less strange to him. He even perched on the sloping handle, balancing himself with outspread wings till the swaying ceased. The thing was manifestly harmless. He hopped down, looked with keen interested eyes at the fish beside the rock, hopped in and clutched one out with beak and claw, hopped back again in a great hurry, and flew away with the prize to his watch-tower on Sugar Loaf. This caution he repeated at every visit throughout that day. But when he came again on the morrow, he had grown once more utterly confident. He went under the net without haste or apprehension, and perched unconcernedly on the stone in the midst of his banquet. And the stony face of the old Indian, in his thicket across the lake, flashed for one instant with a furtive grin. He grunted, melted back into the woods, and slipped away to resume his fishing at the outlet.

The next morning, about an hour before dawn, a ghostly birch canoe slipped up to the point of shoals, and came to land about a hundred yards from the net. The Indian stepped out, lifted it from the water, and hid it in the bushes. Then he proceeded to make some important changes in the arrangement of the net.

To the topmost rim of the hoop he tied a strong cord, brought the free end to the ground, led it under a willow root, and carried it some ten paces back into the thicket. Next he removed the supporting prop. Going back into the thicket, he pulled the cord. It ran freely under the willow root, and the net swayed down till it covered the rock, to rebound to its former position the moment he released the cord. Then he restored the prop to its place; but this time, instead of planting its butt firmly in the sand, he balanced it on a small flat stone, so that the least pull would instantaneously dislodge it. To the base of the prop he fixed another cord; and this also he ran under the willow root and carried back into the thicket. To the free end of this second cord he tied a scrap of red flannel, that there might be no mistake at a critical moment. The butt of the handle he loosened, so that if the prop were removed the net would almost fall of its own weight; and on the upper side of the butt, to give steadiness and speed of action, he leaned two heavy stones. Finally, he baited his trap with the usual dead fish, bunching them now under the centre of the net. Then, satisfying himself that all was in working order, he wormed his way into the heart of the thicket. A few leafy branches, cunningly disposed around and above his hiding-place, made his concealment perfect, while his keen black beads of eyes commanded a clear view of the stone beneath the net. The ends of the two cords were between his lean fingers. No waiting fox or hiding grouse could have lain more immovable, could have held his muscles in more patient perfect stillness, than did the wary old trapper through the chill hour of growing dawn.

At last there came a sound that thrilled even such stoic nerves as his. Mighty wings hissed in the air above his head. The next moment he saw the eagle alight upon the level sand beside the net. This time there was no hesitation. The great bird, for all his wisdom, had been lured into accepting the structure as a part of the established order of things. He hopped with undignified alacrity right under the net, clutched a large whitefish, and perched himself on the stone to enjoy his meal.

At that instant he felt, rather than saw, the shadow of a movement in the thicket. Or rather, perhaps, some inward, unaccredited guardian signalled to him of danger. His muscles gathered themselves for that instantaneous spring wherewith he was wont to hurl himself into the air. But even that electric speed of his was too slow for this demand. Ere he could spring, the great net came down about him with a vicious swish; and in a moment beating wings, tearing beak, and clutching talons were helplessly intertangled in the meshes. Before he could rip himself free, a blanket was thrown over him. He was ignominiously rolled into a bundle, picked up, and carried off under the old Indian's arm.

III.

When the king was gone, it seemed as if a hush had fallen over the country of the Squatooks. When the old pine beneath the toppling peak of Sugar Loaf had stood vacant all the long golden hours of the morning, two crows flew upon from the fir-woods to investigate. They hopped up and down on the sacred seat, cawing impertinently and excitedly. Then in a sudden flurry of apprehension they darted away. News of the great eagle's mysterious absence spread quickly among the woodfolk,—not by direct communication, indeed, except in the case of the crows, but subtly and silently, as if by some telepathic code intelligible alike to mink and wood-mouse, kingfisher and lucifee.

When the noon had gone by, and the shadow of Sugar Loaf began to creep over the edge of the nest, the old mother eagle grew uneasy at the prolonged absence of her mate. Never before since the nestlings broke the shell had he been so long away. Never before had she been compelled to realise how insatiable were the appetites of her young. She flew around to the pine-tree on the other side of the peak,—and finding it vacant, something told her it had been long unoccupied. Then she flew hither and thither over all the lakes, a fierce loneliness growing in her heart. From the long grasses around the mouth of the thoroughfare between third and fourth lakes a heron arose, flapping wide bluish wings, and she dropped upon it savagely. However her wild heart ached, the nestlings must be fed. With the long limp neck and slender legs of the heron trailing from her talons, she flew away to the eyrie; and she came no more to the Squatooks.

The knowledge of all the woodfolk around the lakes had been flashed in upon her, and she knew some mysterious doom had fallen upon her mate. Thereafter, though the country of the Squatooks was closer at hand and equally well stocked with game, and though the responsibilities of her hunting had been doubled, she kept strictly to her old hunting-ground of the Tuladis. Everything on the north side of old Sugar Loaf had grown hateful to her; and unmolested within half a mile of the eyrie, the diligent fish-hawks plied their craft, screaming triumphantly over every capture. The male, indeed, growing audacious after the king had been a whole week absent, presumed so far as to adopt the old pine-tree under the peak for his perch, to the loud and disconcerting derision of the crows. They flocked blackly about with vituperative malice, driving him to forsake his seat of usurpation and soar indignantly to heights where they could not follow. But at last the game palled upon their whimsical fancies, and they left him in peace to his aping of the king.

Meanwhile, in the village of Edmundston, in the yard of a house that stood ever enfolded in the sleepless roar of the Falls of Madawaska, the king was eating out his sorrowful and tameless heart. Around one steely-scaled leg, just above the spread of the mighty claws, he wore the ragged ignominy of a bandage of soiled red flannel. This was to prevent the chafing of the clumsy and rusty dog-chain which secured him to his perch in an open shed that looked out upon the river. Across the river, across the cultivated valley with its roofs, and farther across the forest hills than any human eye could see, his eye could see a dim summit, as it were a faint blue cloud on the horizon, his own lost realm of Sugar Loaf. Hour after hour he would sit upon his rude perch, unstirring, unwinking, and gaze upon this faint blue cloud of his desire.

From his jailers he accepted scornfully his daily rations of fish, ignoring the food while any one was by, but tearing it and gorging it savagely when left alone. As week after week dragged on, his hatred of his captors gathered force, but he showed no sign. Fear he was hardly conscious of; or, at least, he had never felt that panic fear which unnerves even kings, except during the one appalling moment when he felt the falling net encumber his wings, and the trapper's smothering blanket shut out the sun from his eyes. Now, when any one of his jailers approached and sought to win his confidence, he would shrink within himself and harden his feathers with wild inward aversion, but his eye of piercing gold would neither dim nor waver, and a clear perception of the limits of his chain would prevent any futile and ignoble struggle to escape. Had he shown more fear, more wildness, his jailers would have more hope of subduing him in some measure; but as it was, being back country men with some knowledge of the wilderness folk, they presently gave him up as tameless and left off troubling him with their attentions. They took good care of him, however, for they were to be well paid for their trouble when the rich American came for his prize.

At last he came; and when he saw the king he was glad. Trophies he had at home in abundance,—the skins of lions which he had shot on the Zambesi, of tigers from Himalayan foot-hills, of grizzlies from Alaskan cañons, and noble heads of moose and caribou from these very highlands of Squatook, whereon the king had been wont to look from his dizzy gyres of flight above old Sugar Loaf. But the great white-headed eagle, who year after year had baffled his woodcraft and eluded his rifle, he had come to love so that he coveted him alive. Now, having been apprised of the capture of so fine and well-known a bird as the king of old Sugar Loaf, he had brought with him an anklet of thick, soft leather for the illustrious captive's leg, and a chain of wrought steel links, slender, delicate, and strong. On the morning after his arrival the new chain was to be fitted.

The great eagle was sitting erect upon his perch, gazing at the faint blue cloud which he alone could see, when two men came to the shed beside the river. One he knew. It was his chief jailer, the man who usually brought fish. The other was a stranger, who carried in his hand a long, glittering thing that jangled and stirred a vague apprehension in his heart. The jailer approached, and with a quick movement wrapped him in a coat, till beak and wings and talons alike were helpless. There was one instinctive, convulsive spasm within the wrapping, and the bundle was still, the great bird being too proud as well as too wise to waste force in a vain struggle.

"Seems pretty tame already," remarked the stranger, in a tone of satisfaction.

"Tame!" exclaimed the countryman. "Them's the kind as don't tame. I've give up trying to tame him. Ef you keep him, an' feed him, an' coax him for ten year, he'll be as wild as the day Gabe snared him up on Big Squatook."

"We'll see," said the stranger, who had confidence in his knowledge of the wild folk.

Seating himself on a broken-backed chair just outside the shadow of the shed, where the light was good, the countryman held the motionless bundle firmly across his knees, and proceeded cautiously to free the fettered leg. He held it in an inflexible grip, respecting those knife-edged claws. Having removed the rusty dog-chain and the ignominious red flannel bandage, he fitted dexterously the soft leather anklet, with its three tiny silver buckles, and its daintily engraved plate, bearing the king's name with the place and date of his capture. Then he reached out his hand for the new steel chain.

The eagle, meanwhile, had been slowly and imperceptibly working his head free; and now, behind the countryman's arm, he looked out from the imprisoning folds of the coat. Fierce, wild, but unaffrighted, his eye caught the glitter of the chain as the stranger held it out. That glitter moved him strangely. On a sudden impulse he opened his mighty beak, and tore savagely at the countryman's leg.

With a yell of pain and surprise the man attempted to jump away from this assault. But as the assailant was on his lap this was obviously impossible. The muscles of his leg stiffened out instinctively,—and the broken-backed chair gave way under the strain. Arms and legs flew wildly in the air as he sprawled backward,—and the coat fell apart,—and the eagle found himself free. The stranger sprang forward to clutch his treasured captive, but received a blinding buffet from the great wings undestined to captivity. The next moment the king bounded upward. The air whistled under his tremendous wing-strokes.

Up, up he mounted, leaving the men to gape after him, flushed and foolish. Then he headed his flight for that faint blue cloud beyond the hills.

That afternoon there was a difference in the country of the Squatooks. The nestlings in the eyrie—bigger and blacker and more clamorous they were now than when he went away—found more abundant satisfaction to their growing appetites. Their wide-winged mother, hunting away on Tuladi, hunted with more joyous heart. The fish-hawks on the Squatook waters came no more near the blasted pine; but they fished more diligently, and their hearts were big with indignation over the spoils which they had been forced to deliver up.

The crows far down in the fir-tops were garrulous about the king's return, and the news spread swiftly among the mallards, the muskrats, the hares, and the careful beavers. And the solitude about the toppling peak of old Sugar Loaf seemed to resume some lost sublimity, as the king resumed his throne among the winds.

The Homesickness of Kehonka*

The April night, softly chill and full of the sense of thaw, was closing down over the wide salt marshes. Near at hand the waters of the Tantramar, resting at full tide, glimmered through the dusk and lapped faintly among the winter-ruined remnants of the sedge. Far off—infinitely far it seemed in that illusive atmosphere, which was clear, yet full of the ghosts of rain—the last of daylight lay in a thin streak, pale and sharp, along a vast arc of the horizon. Overhead it was quite dark; for there was no moon, and the tenuous spring clouds were sufficient to shut out the stars. They clung in mid-heaven, but kept to their shadowy ranks without descending to obscure the lower air. Space and mystery, mystery and space, lay abroad upon the vague levels of marsh and tide.

Presently, from far along the dark heights of the sky, came voices, hollow, musical, confused. Swiftly they journeyed nearer; they grew louder. The sound—not vibrant, yet strangely far-carrying—was a clamorous monotony of honk-a-honk, honk-a-honk, honka, honka, honk, honk. It hinted of wide distance voyaged over on tireless wings, of a tropic winter passed in feeding amid remote, high-watered meadows of Mexico and Texas, of long flights yet to go, toward the rocky tarns of Labrador and the reed beds of Ungava. As the sound passed straight overhead the listener on the marsh below imagined, though he could not see, the strongly beating wings, the outstretched necks and heads, the round, unswerving eyes of the wild goose flock in its V-shaped array, winnowing steadily northward through the night. But this particular flock was not set, as it chanced, upon an all-night journey. The wise old gander winging at the head of the V knew of good feeding-grounds near by, which he was ready to revisit. He led the flock straight on, above the many windings of the Tantramar, till its full-flooded sheen far below him narrowed and narrowed to a mere brook. Here, in the neighbourhood of the uplands, were a number of shallow, weedy, fresh-water lakes,

* From *The Kindred of the Wild* (Boston: L.C. Page, 1902), 117-40. "The Homesickness of Kehonka" also appeared in *Outing* (May 1901).

with shores so choked with thickets and fenced apart with bogs as to afford a security which his years and broad experience had taught him to value. Into one of these lakes, a pale blur amid the thick shadows of the shores, the flock dropped with heavy splashings. A scream or two of the full-throated content, a few flappings of wings and rufflings of plumage in the cool, and the voyagers settled into quiet.

All night there was silence around the flock, save for the whispering seepage of the snow patches that still lingered among the thickets. With the first creeping pallor of dawn the geese began to feed, plunging their long black necks deep into the water and feeling with the sensitive inner edges of their bills for the swelling root-buds of weed and sedge. When the sun was about the edge of the horizon, and the first rays came sparkling, of a chilly pink most luminous and pure, through the lean traceries of the brushwood, the leader raised his head high and screamed a signal. With answering cries and a tempestuous splashing the flock flapped for a few yards along the surface of the water. Then they rose clear, formed quickly into rank, and in their spacious V went honking northward over the half-lighted, mysterious landscape. But, as it chanced, not all of the flock set out with that morning departure. There was one pair, last year's birds, upon whom had fallen a weariness of travel. Perhaps in the coils of their brains lurked some inherited memory of these safe resting-places and secluded feeding-grounds of the Midgic lakes. However that may have been, they chose to stay where they were, feeling in their blood no call from the cold north solitudes. Dipping and bowing, black neck by neck, they gave no heed to the leader's signal, nor to the noisy going of the flock. Pushing briskly with the black webs of their feet against the discoloured water, they swam to the shore and cast about for a place to build their nest.

There was no urgent hurry, so they chose not on that day nor the next. When they chose, it was a little bushy islet off a point of land, well tangled with alder and osier and a light flotsam of driftwood. The nest, in the heart of the tangle, was an apparently haphazard collection of sticks and twigs, well raised above the damp, well lined with moss and feathers. Here, in course of days, there accumulated a shining cluster of six large white eggs. But by this time the spring freshet had gone down. The islet was an islet no longer, but a mere adjunct of the point, which any inquisitive foot might reach dry shod. Now just at this time it happened that a young farmer, who had a curious taste for all the wild kindred of wood, and flood, and air, came up from the Lower Tantramar with a wagon-load of grist for the Midgic mill. While his buckwheat and barley were a-grinding, he thought of a current opinion to the effect that the wild geese were given to nesting in the Midgic lakes. "If so," said he to himself, "this is the time they would be about it." Full of interest, a half-hour's tramp through difficult woods brought him to the nearest of the waters. An instinct, an intuition born of his sympathy with the furtive folk, led him to the point, and out along the point to that once islet, with its secret in the heart of the tangle. Vain were the furious hissings, the opposing wings, the wide black bills that threatened and oppugned him. With the eager delight of a boy he pounced upon those six great eggs, and carried them all away. "They will soon turn out another clutch," said he to himself, as he left the bereaved pair, and tramped elatedly back to the mill. As for the bereaved pair, being of a philosophic spirit, they set themselves to fulfil as soon as possible his prophecy.

On the farm by the Lower Tantramar, in a hogshead half filled with straw and laid on its side in a dark corner of the tool-shed, those six eggs were diligently brooded for four weeks and two days by a comfortable gray and white goose of the common stock. When they hatched, the good gray and white mother may have been surprised to find her goslings of an olive green hue, instead of the bright golden yellow which her past experience and that of her fellows had taught her to expect. She may have marveled, too, at their unwonted slenderness and activity. These trivial details, however, in no way dampened the zeal with which she led them to the goose pond, or the fidelity with which she pastured and protected them. But rats, skunks, sundry obscure aliments, and the heavy wheels of the farm wagon, are among the perils which, the summer through, lie in wait for all the children of the feathered kin upon the farm; and so it came about that of the six young ones so successfully hatched from the wild goose eggs, only two lived till the coming of autumn brought them full plumage and the power of flight. Before the time of the southward migration

"HE WOULD STAND MOTIONLESS, HIS COMPACT, GLOSSY HEAD HIGH IN AIR."

came near, the young farmer took these two and clipped from each the strong primaries of their right wings. "They seem contented enough, and tame as any," he said to himself, "but you never can tell what'll happen when the instinct strikes 'em."

Both the young wild geese were fine males. Their heads and long, slim necks were black, as were also their tails, great wing feathers, bills, and feet. Under the tail their feathers were of snowiest white, and all the other portions of their bodies a rich grayish brown. Each bore on the side of its face a sharply defined triangular patch of white, mottled with faint brown markings that would disappear after his first moult. In one the white cheek patches met under the throat. This was a large, strongly built bird, of a placid and domestic temper. He was satisfied with the undistinguished gray companions of the flock. He was content, like them, to gutter noisily with his discriminating bill along the shallow edges of the pond, to float and dive and flap in the deeper centre, to pasture at random over the wet meadow, biting off the short grasses with quick, sharp, yet gracefully curving dabs. Goose pond and wet meadow and cattle-trodden barnyard bounded his aspirations. When his adult voice came to him, all he would say was honk, honk, contemplatively, and sometimes honk-a-honk when he flapped his wings in the exhilarating coolness of the sunrise. The other captive was of a more restless temperament, slenderer in build, more eager and alert of eye, less companionable of mood. He was, somehow, never seen in the centre of the flock—he never seemed a part of it. He fed, swam, rested, preened himself, always a little apart. Often, when the others were happily occupied with their familiar needs and satisfactions, he would stand motionless, his compact, glossy head high in air, looking to the north as if in expectation, listening as if he awaited longed-for tidings. The triangular white patch on each side of his head was very narrow, and gave him an expression of wildness; yet in reality he was no more wild, or rather no more shy, than any others of the flock. None, indeed, had so confident a fearlessness as he. He would take oats out of the farmer's hand, which none of the rest quite dared to do.

Until late in the autumn, the lonely, uncomraded bird was always silent. But when the migrating flocks began to pass overhead, on the long southward trail, and their hollow clamour was heard over the farmstead night and morning, he grew more restless. He would take a short run with outspread wings, and then, feeling their crippled inefficiency, would stretch himself to his full height and call, a sonorous, far-reaching cry—ke-honk-a, ke-honk-a. From this call, so often repeated throughout October and November, the farmer named him Kehonka. The farmer's wife favoured the more domesticated and manageable brother, who could be trusted never to stray. But the farmer, who mused deeply over his furrows, and half wistfully loved the wild kindred, loved Kehonka, and used to say he would not lose the bird for the price of a steer. "That there bird," he would say, "has got dreams away down in his heart. Like as not, he remembers things his father and mother have seen, up amongst the ice cakes and the northern lights, or down amongst the bayous and the big southern lilies." But all his sympathy failed to make him repent of having clipped Kehonka's wing.

During the long winter, when the winds swept fiercely the open marshes of the Tantramar, and the snow piled in high drifts around the barns and wood piles, and the sheds were darkened, and in the sun at noonday the strawy dungheaps steamed, the rest of the geese remained listlessly content. But not so Kehonka. Somewhere back of his brain he cherished pre-natal memories of warm pools in the South, where leafy screens grew rank, and the sweet-rooted water-plants pulled easily from the deep black mud, and his true kindred were screaming to each other at the oncoming of the tropic dark. While the flock was out in the barnyard, pulling lazily at the trampled litter, and snatching scraps of the cattle's chopped turnips, Kehonka would stand aloof by the water-trough, his head erect, listening, longing. As the winter sun sank early over the fir woods back of the farm, his wings would open, and his desirous cry would go echoing three or four times across the still countryside—ke-honk-a—ke-honk-a—ke-honk-a! Wherat the farmer's wife, turning her buckwheat pancakes over the hot kitchen stove, would mutter impatiently; but the farmer, slipping to the door of the cow-stable with the bucket of feed in his hand, would look with deep eyes of sympathy at the unsatisfied bird. "He wants something that we don't grow round here," he would say to himself; and little by little the bird's restlessness came to seem to him the concrete embodiment of certain dim outreachings of his own. He, too, caught himself straining his gaze beyond the marsh horizons of Tantramar.

When the winter broke, and the seeping drifts shrank together, and the brown of the ploughed fields came through the snow in patches, and the slopes leading down to the marshland were suddenly loud with running water, Kehonka's restlessness grew so eager that he almost forgot to feed. It was time, he thought, for the northward flight to begin. He would stand for hours, turning first one dark eye, then the other, toward the soft sky overhead, expectant of the V-shaped journeying flock, and the far-off clamour of voices from the South crying to him in his own tongue. At last, when the snow was about gone from the open fields, one evening at the shutting-in of dark, the voices came. He was lingering at the edge of the goose pond, the rest having settled themselves for the night, when he heard the expected sounds. Honk-a-honk, honk-a-honk, honka, honka, honk, honk, they came up against the light April wind, nearer, nearer, nearer. Even his keen eye could not detect them against the blackness; but up went his wings, and again and again he screamed to them sonorously. In response to his call, their flight swung lower, and the confusion of their honking seemed as if it were going to descend about him. But the wary old gander, their leader, discerned the roofs, man's handiwork, and suspected treachery. At his sharp signal the flock, rising again, streamed off swiftly toward safer feeding-grounds, and left Kehonka to call and call unanswered. Up to this moment all his restlessness had not led him to think of actually deserting the farmstead and the alien flock. Though not of them he had felt it necessary to be with them. His instinct for other scenes and another fellowship had been too little tangible to move him to the snapping of established ties. But now, all his desires at once took concrete form. It was his, it belonged to himself—that strong, free flight, that calling through the sky, that voyaging northward to secret nesting-places. In that wild flock which had for a moment swerved downward to his summons, or in some other flock, was his mate. It was mating season, and not until now had he known it.

Nature does sometimes, under the pressure of great and concentrated desires, make unexpected effort to meet unforeseen demands. All winter long, though it was not the season for such growth, Kehonka's clipped wing-primaries had been striving to develop. They had now, contrary to all custom, attained to an inch or so of effective flying web. Kehonka's heart was near bursting with his desire as the voices of the unseen flock died away. He spread his wings to their full extent, ran some ten paces along the ground, and then, with all his energies concentrated to the effort, he rose into the air, and flew with swift-beating wings out into the dark upon the northward trail. His trouble was not the lack of wing surface, but the lack of balance. One wing being so much less in spread than the other, he felt a fierce force striving to turn him over at every stroke. It was the struggle to counteract this tendency that wore him out. His first desperate effort carried him half a mile. Then he dropped to earth, in a bed of withered salt-grass all awash with the full tide of Tantramar. Resting amid the salt-grass, he tasted such an exultation of freedom that his heart forgot its soreness over the flock which had vanished. Presently, however, he heard again the sound that so thrilled his every vein. Weird, hollow, echoing with memories and tidings, it came throbbing up the wind. His own strong cry went out at once to meet it—ke-honk-a, ke-honk-a, ke-honk-a. The voyagers this time were flying very low. They came near, nearer, and at last, in a sudden silence of voices, but a great flapping of wings, they settled down in the salt-grass all about him.

The place was well enough for a night's halt—a shallow, marshy pool which caught the overflow of the highest spring tides, and so was not emptied by the ebb. After its first splashing descent into the water, which glimmered in pale patches among the grass stems, every member of the flock sat for some moments motionless as statues, watchful for unknown menace; and Kehonka, his very soul trembling with desire achieved, sat motionless among them. Then, there being no sign of peril at hand, there was a time of quiet paddling to and fro, a scuttling of practised bills among the grass-roots, and Kehonka found himself easily accepted as a member of the flock. Happiness kept him restless and on the move long after the others had their bills tucked under their wings. In the earliest gray of dawn, when the flock awoke to feed, Kehonka fed among them as if he had been with them all the way on their flight from the Mexican plains. But his feeding was always by the side of a young female who had not yet paired. It was interrupted by many little courtesies of touching bill and bowing head, which were received with plain favour; for Kehonka was a handsome and well marked bird. By the time the sky was red along the east and strewn with pale, blown feathers of amber pink toward the zenith, his swift wooing was next door to winning. He had forgotten his captivity and clipped wing. He was thinking of a nest in the wide emptiness of the North.

When the signal-cry came, and the flock took flight, Kehonka rose with them. But his preliminary rush along the water was longer than that of the others, and when the flock formed into flying order he fell in at the end of the longer leg of the V, behind the weakest of the young geese. This would have been a humiliation to him, had he taken thought of it at all; but his attention was all absorbed in keeping his balance. When the flock found its pace, and the cold sunrise air began to whistle past the straight, bullet-like rush of their flight, a terror grew upon him. He flew much better than he had flown the night before; but he soon saw that this speed of theirs was beyond him. He would not yield, however. He would not lag behind. Every force of his body and his brain went into that flight, till his eyes blurred and his heart seemed on the point of bursting. Then, suddenly, with a faint, despairing note, he lurched aside, shot downward, and fell with a great splash into the channel of the Tantramar. With strong wings, and level, unpausing flight, the flock went on to its North without him.

Dazed by the fall, and exhausted by the intensity of his effort, Kehonka floated, moveless, for many minutes. The flood-tide, however, racing inland, was carrying him still northward; and presently he began to swim in the same direction. In his sick heart glowed still the vision of the nest in the far-off solitudes, and he felt that he would find there, waiting for him, the strong-winged mate who had left him behind. Half an hour later another flock passed honking overhead, and he called to them; but they were high up, and feeding time was past. They gave no sign in answer. He made no attempt to fly after them. Hour after hour he swam on with the current, working ever north. When the tide turned he went ashore, still following the river, till its course changed toward the east; whereupon he ascended the channel of a small tributary which flowed in on the north bank. Here and there he snatched quick mouthfuls of sprouting grasses, but he was too driven by his desire to pause for food. Sometimes he tried his wings again, covering now some miles at each flight, till by and by, losing the stream because its direction failed him, he found himself in a broken upland country, where progress was slow and toilsome. Soon after sunset, troubled because there was no water near, he again took wing, and over dark woods which filled him with apprehension he made his longest flight. When about spent he caught a small gleaming of water far below him, and alighted in a little woodland glade wherein a brook had overflowed low banks.

The noise of his abrupt descent loudly startled the wet and dreaming woods. It was a matter of interest to all the furry, furtive ears of the forest for a half-mile round. But it was in no way repeated. For perhaps fifteen minutes Kehonka floated, neck erect, head high and watchful, in the middle of the pool, with no movement except the slight, unseen oaring of his black-webbed feet, necessary to keep the current from bearing him into the gloom of the woods. This gloom, hedging him on every side, troubled him with a vague fear. But in the open of the mid-pool, with two or three stars peering faintly through the misted sky above him, he felt comparatively safe. At last, very far above, he heard again that wild calling of his fellow,—honk-a-honk, honk-a-honk, honka, honka, honk, honk,—high and dim and ghostly, for these rough woodlands had no appeal for the journeying flocks. Remote as the voices were, however, Kehonka answered at once. His keen, sonorous, passionate cry rang strangely on the night, three times. The flock paid no heed to it whatever, but sped on northward with unvarying flight and clamour; and as the wizard noise passed beyond, Kehonka, too weary to take wing, followed eagerly to the northerly shore of the pool, ran up the wet bank, and stood straining after it.

His wings were half spread as he stood there, quivering with his passion. In his heart was the hunger of the quest. In his eyes was the vision of nest and mate, where the serviceberry thicket grew by the wide sub-arctic waters. The night wind blew steadily away from him to the under-brush close by, or even in his absorption he would have noticed the approach of a menacing, musky smell. But every sense was now numb in the presence of his great desire. There was no warning for him.

The underbrush rustled, ever so softly. Then a small, delicately moving, fine-furred shape, the discourager of quests, darted stealthily forth, and with a bound that was feathery in its blown lightness, seeming to be uplifted by the wide-plumed tail that balanced it, descended on Kehonka's body. There was a thin honk, cut short by keen teeth meeting with a crunch and a twist in the glossy slim blackness of Kehonka's neck. The struggle lasted scarcely more than two heart-beats. The wide wings pounded twice or thrice upon the ground, in fierce convulsion. Then the red fox, with a side-wise jerk of his head, flung the heavy, trailing carcass into a position for its easy carrying, and trotted off with it into the darkness of the woods.

The Haunter of the Pine Gloom*

For a moment the Boy felt afraid—afraid in his own woods. He felt that he was being followed, that there were hostile eyes burning into the back of his jacket. The sensation was novel to him, as well as unpleasant, and he resented it. He knew it was all nonsense. There was nothing in these woods bigger than a weasel, he was sure of that. Angry at himself, he would not look round, but swung along carelessly through the thicket, being in haste because it was already late and the cows should have been home and milked before sundown. Suddenly, however, he remembered that it was going flat against all woodcraft to disregard a warning. And was he not, indeed, deliberately seeking to cultivate and sharpen his instincts, in the effort to get closer to the wild woods folk and know them in their furtive lives? Moreover, he was certainly getting more and more afraid! He stopped, and peered into the pine glooms which surrounded him.

Standing motionless as a stump, and breathing with perfect soundlessness, he strained his ears to help his eyes in their questioning of this obscure menace. He could see nothing. He could hear nothing. Yet he knew his eyes and ears were cunning to pierce all the wilderness disguises. But stay—was that a deeper shadow, merely, far among the pine trunks? And—did it move? He stole forward; but even as he did so, whatever of unusual he saw or fancied in the object upon which his eyes were fixed, melted away. It became but a shadow among other shadows, and motionless as they—all motionless in the calm of the tranquil sunset. He ran forward now, impatient to satisfy himself beyond suspicion. Yes—of course—it was just this gray spruce stump! He turned away, a little puzzled and annoyed in spite of himself. Thrashing noisily hither and thither through the underbrush,—quite contrary to his wonted quietude while in the domains of the wood folk,—and calling loudly in his clear young voice, "Co-petty! Co-petty! Co-petty! Co-o-o-petty" over and over, he at length found the wilful

---

* From *The Kindred of the Wild* (Boston: L.C. Page, 1902), 199-237. 'The Haunter of the Pine Gloom" also appeared in *Outing* (Feb. 1902).

young cow which had been eluding him. Then he drove the herd slowly homeward, with mellow *tink-a-tonk, tank-tonk* of the cow-bells, to the farmyard and the milking.

Several evenings later, when his search for the wilful young cow chanced to lead him again through the corner of this second growth pine wood, the Boy had a repetition of the disturbing experience. This time his response was instant and aggressive. As soon as he felt that sensation of unfriendly eyes pursuing him, he turned, swept the shadows with his piercing scrutiny, plunged into the thickets with a rush, then stopped short as if frozen, almost holding his breath in the tensity of his stillness. By this procedure he hoped to catch the unknown haunter of the glooms under the disadvantage of motion. But again he was baffled. Neither eye nor ear revealed him anything. He went home troubled and wondering.

Some evenings afterward the same thing happened at another corner of the pasture; and again one morning when he was fishing in the brook a mile back into the woods, where it ran through a tangled growth of birch and fir. He began to feel that he was either the object of a malicious scrutiny, or that he was going back to those baby days when he used to be afraid of the dark. Being just at the age of ripe boyhood when childishness in himself would seem least endurable, the latter supposition was not to be considered. He therefore set himself to investigate the mystery, and to pit his woodcraft against the evasiveness of this troubler of his peace.

The Boy's confidence in his woodcraft was well founded. His natural aptitude for the study of the wild kindred had been cultivated to the utmost of his opportunity, in all the time that could be stolen from his lesson-hours and from his unexacting duties about his father's place. Impatient and boyish in other matters, he had trained himself to the patience of an Indian in regard to all matters appertaining to the wood folk. He had a pet theory that the human animal was more competent, as a mere animal, than it gets the credit of being; and it was his particular pride to outdo the wild creatures at their own games. He could hide, unstirring as a hidden grouse. He could run down a deer by sheer endurance—only to spare it at the last and let it go, observed and mastered, but unhurt. And he could see, as few indeed among the wild things could. This was his peculiar triumph. His eyes could discriminate where theirs could not. Perfect movelessness was apt to deceive the keenest of them; but his sight was not to be so foiled. He could differentiate gradually the shape of the brown hare crouching motionless on its brown form; and separate the yellow weasel from the tuft of yellow weeds; and distinguish the slumbering night-hawk from the knot on the hemlock limb. He could hear, too, as well as most of the wild kindred, and better, indeed, than some; but in this he had to acknowledge himself hopelessly outclassed by not a few. He knew that the wood-mouse and the hare, for instance, would simply make a mock of him in any test of ears; and as for the owl—well, that gifted hearer of infinitesimal sounds would be justified in calling him stone-deaf.

The Boy was a good shot, but very seldom was it that he cared to display his skill in that direction. It was his ambition to "name all the birds without a gun." He would know the wild folk living, not dead. From the feebler of the wild folk he wanted trust, not fear; and he himself had no fear, on the other hand, of the undisputed Master of the Woods, the big black bear. His faith, justified by experience, was that the bear had sense, knew how to mind his own business, and was ready to let other people mind theirs. He knew the bear well, from patient, secret observation when the big beast little imagined himself observed. From the neighbourhood of a bull-moose in rutting season he would have taken pains to absent himself; and if he had ever come across any trace of a panther in those regions, he would have studied that uncertain beast with his rifle always at hand in case of need. For the rest, he felt safe in the woods, as an initiate of their secrets, and it was unusual for him to carry in his wanderings any weapon but a stout stick and the sheath-knife in his belt.

Now, however, when he set himself to discover what it was that haunted his footsteps in the gloom, he took his little rifle—and in this act betrayed to himself more uneasiness than he had been willing to acknowledge.

This especial afternoon he got the hired man to look after the cows for him, and betook himself early, about two hours before sundown, to the young pine wood where the mystery had begun. In the heart of a little thicket, where he was partly concealed and where the gray-brown of his clothes blended with the stems and dead branches, he seated himself comfortably with his back against a stump. Experience had taught him that, in order to hold himself long in one position, the position chosen must be an easy one. Soon his muscles relaxed, and all his senses rested, watchful but unstrained. He had learned that tensity was a thing to be held in reserve until occasion should call for it.

In a little while his presence was ignored or forgotten by the chipmunks, the chickadees, the white-throats, and other unafraid creatures. Once a chipmunk, on weighty business bent, ran over his legs rather than go around so unoffending an obstacle. The chickadees played antics on the branches, and the air was beaded sweetly everywhere with their familiar *sic-a-dee, dee-ee*. A white-throat in the tree right over his head whistled his mellow *dear, dear eedlede—eedledee—eedledee*, over and over. But there was nothing new in all this: and at length he began to grow conscious of his position, and desirous of changing it slightly.

Before he had quite made up his mind to this momentous step there came upon his ear a beating of wings, and a fine cock grouse alighted on a log some forty paces distant. He stretched himself, strutted, spread his ruff and wings and tail, and was about to begin drumming. But before the first sonorous note rolled out there was a rustle and a pounce. The beautiful bird bounded into the air as if hurled from a spring; and a great lynx landed on the log, digging his claws fiercely into the spot where the grouse had stood. As the bird rocketed off through the trees the lynx glared after him, and emitted a loud, screeching snarl of rage. His disappointment was so obvious and childish that the Boy almost laughed out.

"Lucifee," said he to himself, giving it the name it went by in all the back settlements. "That's the fellow that has been haunting me. I didn't think there were any lynxes this side of the mountain. He hasn't seen me, that's sure. So now it's my turn to haunt him a bit."

The lucifee, indeed, had for the moment thrown off all concealment, in his fury at the grouse's escape. His stub of a tail twitched and his pale bright eyes looked around for something on which to vent his feelings. Suddenly, however, a wandering puff of air blew the scent of the Boy to his nostrils.

On the instant, like the soundless melting of a shadow, he was down behind the log, taking observations through the veil of a leafy branch.

Though the animal was looking straight toward him, the Boy felt sure he was not seen. The eyes, indeed, were but following the nose. The lynx's nose is not so keen and accurate in its information as are the noses of most of the other wild folk, and the animal was puzzled. The scent was very familiar to him, for had he not been investigating the owner of it for over a week, following him at every opportunity with mingled curiosity and hatred? Now, judging by the scent, the object of his curiosity was close at hand—yet incomprehensibly invisible. After sniffing and peering for some minutes he came out from behind the log and crept forward, moving like a shadow, and following up the scent. From bush to tree-trunk, from thicket to stump, he glided with incredible smoothness and rapidity, elusive to the eye, utterly inaudible; and behind each shelter he crouched to again take observations. The Boy thought of him, now, as a sort of malevolent ghost in fur, and no longer wondered that he had failed to catch a glimpse of him before.

The lynx (this was the first of its tribe the Boy had ever seen, but he knew the kind by reputation) was a somewhat doggish-looking cat, perhaps four or five times the weight of an ordinary Tom, and with a very uncatlike length of leg in proportion to its length of body. Its hindquarters were disproportionately high, its tail ridiculously short. Spiky tufts to its ears and a peculiar brushing back of the fur beneath its chin gave its round and fierce-eyed countenance an expression at once savage and grotesque. Most grotesque of all were the huge, noiseless pads of its feet, muffled in fur. Its colour was a tawny, weather-beaten gray-brown; its eyes pale, round, brilliant, and coldly cruel.

At length the animal, on a stronger puff of air, located the scent more closely. This was obvious from a sudden stiffening of his muscles. His eyes began to discern a peculiarity in the pine trunk some twenty paces ahead. Surely that was no ordinary pine trunk, that! No, indeed, that was where the scent of the Boy came from—and the hair on his back bristled fiercely. In fact, it *was* the Boy! The lucifee's first impulse, on the discovery, was to shrink off like a mist, and leave further investigation to a more favourable opportunity. But he thought better of it because the Boy was so still. Could he be asleep? Or, perhaps, dead? At any rate, it would seem, he was for the moment harmless. Curiosity overcoming discretion, and possibly hatred suggesting a chance of advantageous attack, the animal lay down, his paws folded under him, contemplatively, and studied with round, fierce eyes the passive figure beneath the tree.

The Boy, meanwhile, returned the stare with like interest, but through narrowed lids, lest his eyes should betray him; and his heart beat fast with the excitement of the situation. There was a most thrilling uncertainty, indeed, as to what the animal would do next. He was glad he had brought his rifle.

Presently the lucifee arose and began creeping stealthily closer, at the same time swerving off to the right as if to get behind the tree. Whether his purpose in this was to escape unseen or to attack from the rear, the Boy could not decide; but what he did decide was that the game was becoming hazardous and should be brought to immediate close. He did not want to be compelled to shoot the beast in self-defence, for, this being the first lynx he had ever seen, he wanted to study him. So, sudddenly, with the least possible movement of his features, he squeaked like a wood-mouse, then *quit-quit*-ed like a grouse, then gave to a nicety the sonorous call of the great horned owl.

The astonished lynx seemed to shrink into himself, as he flattened against the ground, grown moveless as a stone. It was incredible, appalling indeed, that these familiar and well-understood voices should all come from that same impassive figure. He crouched unstirring for so long that at last the shadows began to deepen perceptibly. The Boy remembered that he had heard, some time ago, the bells of the returning cows; and he realised that it might not be well to give his adversary the advantage of the dark. Nevertheless, the experience was one of absorbing interest and he hated to close it.

At length the lucifee came to the conclusion that the mystery should be probed more fully. Once more he rose upon his padded, soundless paws, and edged around stealthily to get behind the tree. This was not to be permitted. The Boy burst into a peal of laughter and rose slowly to his feet. On the instant the lucifee gave a bound, like a great rubber ball, backward into a thicket. It seemed as if his big feet were all feathers, and as if every tree trunk bent to intervene and screen his going. The Boy rubbed his eyes, bewildered at so complete and instantaneous an exit. Grasping his rifle in readiness, he hurried forward, searching every thicket, looking behind every stump and trunk. The haunter of the gloom had disappeared.

After this, however, the Boy was no more troubled by the mysterious pursuit. The lynx had evidently found out all he required to know about him. On the other hand the Boy was balked in his purpose of finding out all he wanted to know about the lynx. That wary animal eluded all his most patient and ingenious lyings-in-wait, until the Boy began to feel that his woodcraft was being turned to a derision. Only once more that autumn did he catch a glimpse of his shy opponent, and then by chance, when he was on another trail. Hidden at the top of a thick-wooded bank he was watching a mink at its fishing in the brook below. But as it turned out, the dark little fisherman had another watcher as well. The pool in the brook was full of large suckers. The mink had just brought one to land in his triangular jaws and was proceeding to devour it, when a silent gray thunderbolt fell upon him. There was a squeak and a snarl; and the long, snaky body of the mink lay as still as that of the fish which had been its prey. Crouching over his double booty, a paw on each, the lynx glared about him in exultant pride. The scent of the Boy, high on the bank above, did not come to him. The fish, as the more highly prized tidbit, he devoured at once. Then, after licking his lips and polishing his whiskers, he went loping off through the woods with the limp body of the mink hanging from his jaws, to eat it at leisure in his lair. The Boy made up his mind to find out where that lair was hidden. But his searchings were all vain, and he tried to console himself with the theory that the animal was wont to travel great distances in his hunting—a theory which he knew in his heart to be contrary to the customs of the cat-kindred.

During the winter he was continually tantalised by coming across the lucifee's tracks—great footprints, big enough to do for the trail-signature of the panther himself. If he followed these tracks far he was sure to find interesting records of wilderness adventure—here a spot where the lynx had sprung

"A SILENT GRAY THUNDERBOLT FELL UPON HIM."

upon a grouse, and missed it, or upon a hare, and caught it; and once he found the place where the big furry paws had dug down to the secret white retreat where a grouse lay sleeping under the snow. But by and by the tracks would cross each other, and make wide circles, or end in a tree where there was no lucifee to be found. And the Boy was too busy at home to give the time which he saw it would require to unravel the maze to its end. But he refused to consider himself defeated. He merely regarded his triumph as postponed.

Early in the spring the triumph came—though not just the triumph he had expected. Before the snow was quite gone, and when the sap was beginning to flow from the sugar maples, he went with the hired man to tap a grove of extra fine trees some five miles east from the settlement. Among the trees they had a sugar camp; and when not at the sugar-making, the Boy explored a near-by burnt-land ridge, very rocky and rich in coverts, where he had often thought the old lynx, his adversary, might have made his lair. Here, the second day after his arrival, he came upon a lucifee track. But it was not the track with which he was familiar. It was smaller, and the print of the right forefoot lacked a toe.

The Boy grinned happily and rubbed his mittened hands. "Aha!" said he to himself, "better and better! There is a Mrs. Lucifee. Now we'll see where she hides her kittens."

The trail was an easy one this time, for no enemies had been looked for in that desert neighbourhood. He followed it for about half a mile, and then caught sight of a hollow under an overhanging rock, to which the tracks seemed to lead. Working around to get the wind in his face, he stole cautiously nearer, till he saw that the hollow was indeed the entrance to a cave, and that the tracks led directly into it. He had no desire to investigate further, with the risk of finding the lucifee at home; and it was getting too late for him to undertake his usual watching tactics. He withdrew stealthily and returned to the camp in exultation.

In the night a thaw set in, so the Boy was spared the necessity of waiting for the noon sun to soften the snow and make the walking noiseless. He set out on the very edge of sunrise, and reached his hiding-place while the mouth of the cave was still in shadow. On the usual crisp mornings of sugar season the snow at such an hour would have borne a crust, to crackle sharply under every footstep and proclaim an intruding presence to all the wood folk for a quarter of a mile about.

After waiting for a good half-hour, his eyes glued to a small black opening under the rock, his heart gave a leap of strong, joyous excitement. He saw the lucifee's head appear in the doorway. She peered about her cautiously, little dreaming, however, that there was any cause for caution. Then she came forth into the blue morning light, yawned hugely, and stretched herself like a cat. She was smaller than the Boy's old adversary, somewhat browner in hue, leaner, and of a peculiarly malignant expression. The Boy had an instant intuition that she would be the more dangerous antagonist of the two; and a feeling of sharp hostility toward her, such as he had never felt toward her mate, arose in his heart.

When she had stretched to her satisfaction, and washed her face perfunctorily with two or three sweeps of her big paw, she went back into the cave. In two or three minutes she reappeared, and this time with a brisk air of purpose. She turned to the right, along a well-worn trail, ran up a tree to take a survey of the country, descended hastily, and glided away among the thickets.

"It's breakfast she's after," said the Boy to himself, "and she'll take some time to find it."

When she had been some ten minutes gone, the Boy went boldly down to the cave. He had no fear of encountering the male, because he knew from an old hunter who had taught him his first wood-lore that the male lucifee is not popular with his mate at whelping time, having a truly Saturnian fashion of devouring his own offspring. But there was the possibility, remote, indeed, but disquieting, of the mother turning back to see to some neglected duty; and with this chance in view he held his rifle ready.

Inside the cave he stood still and waited for his eyes to get used to the gloom. Then he discovered, in one corner, on a nest of fur and dry grass, a litter of five lucifee whelps. They were evidently very young, little larger than ordinary kittens, and too young to know fear, but their eyes were wide open, and they stood up on strong legs when he touched them softly with his palm. Disappointed in their expectation of being nursed, they mewed, and there was something in their cries that sounded strangely wild and fierce. To the Boy's great surprise, they were quite different in colour from their gray-brown, unmarked parents, being striped vividly and profusely, like a tabby or tiger. The Boy was delighted with them, and made up his mind that when they were a few days older he would take two of them home with him to be brought up in the ways of civilisation.

Three days later he again visited the den, this time with a basket in which to carry away his prizes. After waiting an hour to see if the mother were anywhere about, he grew impatient. Stealing as close to the cave's mouth as the covert would permit, he squeaked like a wood-mouse several times. This seductive sound bringing no response, he concluded that the old lucifee must be absent. He went up to the mouth of the cave and peered in, holding his rifle in front of his face in readiness for an instant shot. When his eyes got command of the dusk, he saw to his surprise that the den was empty. He entered and felt the vacant nest. It was quite cold, and had a deserted air. Then he realised what had happened, and cursed his clumsiness. The old lucifee, when she came back to her den, had learned by means of her nose that her enemy had discovered her hiding-place and touched her young with his defiling human hands, thereupon in wrath she had carried them away to some remote and unviolated lair. Till they were grown to nearly the full stature of lucifee destructiveness, the Boy saw no more of his wonderful lucifee kittens.

Toward the latter part of the summer, however, he began to think that perhaps he had made a mistake in leaving these fierce beasts to multiply. He no longer succeeded in catching sight of them as they went about their furtive business, for they had somehow become aware of his woodcraft and distrustful of their own shifts. But on all sides he found trace of their depredations among the weaker creatures. He observed that the rabbits were growing scarce about the settlement; and even the grouse were less numerous in the upland thickets of young birch. As all the harmless wood folk were his friends, he began to feel that he had been false to them in sparing their enemies. Thereupon, he took to carrying his rifle whenever he went exploring. He had not really declared war upon the haunters of the glooms, but his relations with them were becoming distinctly strained.

At length the rupture came; and it was violent. In one of the upland pastures, far back from the settlement, he came upon the torn carcass of a half-grown lamb. He knew that this was no work of a bear, for the berries were abundant that autumn, and the bear prefers berries to mutton. Moreover, when a bear kills a sheep he skins it deftly and has the politeness to leave the pelt rolled up in a neat bundle, just to indicate to the farmer that he has been robbed by a gentleman. But this carcass was torn and mangled most untidily; and the Boy divined the culprits.

It was early in the afternoon when he made his find, and he concluded that the lucifees were likely to return to their prey before evening. He hid himself, therefore, behind a log thickly fringed with juniper, not twenty-five paces from the carcass; and waited, rifle in hand.

A little before sunset appeared the five young lucifees, now nearly full grown. They fell at once to tearing at the carcass, with much jealous snarling and fighting. Soon afterwards came the mother, with a well-fed, leisurely air; and at her heels, the big male of the Boy's first acquaintance. It was evident that, now that the rabbits were getting scarce, the lucifees were hunting in packs, a custom very unusual with these unsocial beasts under ordinary circumstances, and only adopted when seeking big game. The big male cuffed the cubs aside without ceremony, mounted the carcass with an air of lordship, glared about him, and suddenly, with a snarl of wrath, fixed his eyes upon the green branches wherein the Boy lay concealed. At the same time the female, who had stopped short, sniffing and peering suspiciously, crouched to her belly, and began to crawl very softly and stealthily, as a cat crawls upon an unsuspecting bird, toward the innocent-looking juniper thicket.

The Boy realised that he had presumed too far upon the efficacy of stillness, and that the lynxes, at this close range, had detected him. He realised, too, that now, jealous in the possession of their prey, they had somehow laid aside their wonted fear of him; and he congratulated himself heartily that his little rifle was a repeater. Softly he raised it to take aim at the nearest, and to him the most dangerous of his foes, the cruel-eyed female; but in doing so he stirred, ever so little, the veiling fringe of juniper. At the motion the big male sprang forward, with two great bounds, and crouched within ten yards of the log. His stub of a tail twitched savagely. He was plainly nerving himself to the attack.

There was no time to lose. Taking quick but careful aim, the Boy fired. The bullet found its mark between the brute's eyes, and he straightened out where he lay, without a kick. At the sound and the flash the female doubled upon herself as quick as light; and before the Boy could get a shot at her she was behind a stump some rods away, shrinking small, and fleeing like a gray shred of vapour. The whelps, too, had vanished with almost equal skill—all but one. He, less alert and intelligent than his fellows, tried concealment behind a clump of pink fireweed. But the Boy's eyes pierced the screen; and the next bullet, cutting the fireweed stalks, took vengeance for many slaughtered hares and grouse.

After this the Boy saw no more of his enemies for some months, but though they had grown still more wary their experience had not made them less audacious. Before the snow fell they had killed another sheep; and the Boy was sure that they, rather than any skunks or foxes, were to blame for the disappearance of several geese from his flock. His primeval hunting instincts were now aroused, and he was no longer merely the tender-hearted and sympathetic observer. It was only toward the marauding lucifees, however, that his feelings had changed. The rest of the wild folk he loved as well as before, but for the time he was too busy to think of them.

When the snow came, and footsteps left their telltale records, the Boy found to his surprise that he had but one lucifee to deal with. Every lynx track in the neighbourhood had a toe missing on the right forefoot. It was clear that the whelps of last spring had shirked the contest and betaken themselves to other and safer hunting-grounds; but he felt that between himself and the vindictive old female it was war to the knife. Her tracks fairly quartered the outlying fields all about his father's farm, and were even to be found now and again around the sheep-pen and the fowl-house. Yet never, devise he ever so cunningly, did he get a glimpse of so much as her gray stub tail.

At last, through an open window, she invaded the sheep-pen by night and killed two young ewes. To the Boy this seemed mere wantonness of cruelty, and he set his mind to a vengeance which he had hitherto been unwilling to consider. He resolved to trap his enemy, since he could not shoot her.

Now, as a mere matter of woodcraft, he knew all about trapping and snaring; but ever since the day, now five years gone, when he had been heart-stricken by his first success in rabbit-snaring, he had hated everything like a snare or trap. Now, however, in the interests of all the helpless creatures of the neighbourhood, wild or tame, he made up his mind to snare the lucifee. He went about it with his utmost skill, in a fashion taught him by an old Indian trapper.

Close beside one of his foe's remoter runways, in an upland field where the hares were still abundant, the Boy set his snare. It was just a greatly exaggerated rabbit snare, of extra heavy wire and a cord of triple strength. But instead of being attached to the top of a bent-down sapling, it was fastened to a billet of wood about four feet long and nearly two inches in diameter. This substantial stick was supported on two forked uprights driven into the snow beside the runway. Then young fir-bushes were stuck about it carefully in a way to conceal evidence of his handiwork; and an artful arrangement of twigs disguised the ambushed loop of wire.

Just behind the loop of wire, and some inches below it, the Boy arranged his bait. This consisted of the head and skin of a hare, stuffed carefully with straw, and posed in a lifelike attitude. It seemed, indeed, to be comfortably sleeping on the snow, under the branches of a young fir-tree; and the Boy felt confident that the tempting sight would prevent the wily old lucifee from taking any thought to the surroundings before securing the prize.

Late that afternoon, when rose and gold were in the sky, and the snowy open spaces were of a fainter rose, and the shadows took on an ashy purple under the edges of the pines and firs, the old lucifee came drifting along like a phantom. She peered hungrily under every bush, hoping to catch some careless hare asleep. On a sudden a greenish fire flamed into her wide eyes. She crouched, and moved even more stealthily than was her wont. The snow, the trees, the still, sweet evening light, seemed to invest her with silence. Very soundly it slept, that doomed hare, crouching under the fir-bush! And now, she was within reach of her spring. She shot forward, straight and strong and true.

Her great paws covered the prey, indeed; but at the same instant a sharp, firm grip clutched her throat with a jerk, and then something hit her a sharp rap over the shoulders. With a wild leap backward and aside she sought to evade the mysterious attack. But the noose settled firmly behind her ears, and the billet of wood, with a nasty tug at her throat, leapt after her.

So this paltry thing was her assailant! She flew into a wild rage at the stick, tearing at it with her teeth and claws. But this made no difference with the grip about her throat, so she backed off again. The stick followed—and the grip tightened. Bracing her forepaws upon the wood she pulled fiercely to free herself; and the wire drew taut till her throat was almost closed. Her rage had hastened her doom, fixing the noose where there was no such thing as clawing it off. Then fear took the place of rage in her savage heart. Her lungs seemed bursting. She began to realise that it was not the stick, but some more potent enemy whom she must circumvent or overcome. She picked up the billet between her jaws, climbed a big birch-tree which grew close by, ran out upon a limb some twenty feet from the ground, and dropped the stick, thinking thus to rid herself of the throttling burden.

The shock, as the billet reached the end of its drop, jerked her from her perch; but clutching frantically she gained a foothold on another limb eight or ten feet lower down. There she clung, her tongue out, her eyes filming, her breath stopped, strange colours of flame and darkness rioting in her brain. Bracing herself with all her remaining strength against the pull of the dangling stick, she got one paw firmly fixed against a small jutting branch. Thus it happened that when, a minute later, her life went out and she fell, she fell on the other side of the limb. The billet of wood flew up, caught in a fork, and held fast; and the limp, tawny body, twitching for a minute convulsively, hung some six or seven feet above its own tracks in the snow.

An hour or two later the moon rose, silvering the open space. Then, one by one and two by two, the hares came leaping down the aisles of pine and fir. Hither and thither around the great birch-tree they played, every now and then stopping to sit up and thump challenges to their rivals. And because it was quite still, they never saw the body of their deadliest foe, hanging stark from the branch above them.

When Twilight Falls on the Stump Lots*

WHEN TWILIGHT FALLS
ON THE
STUMP LOTS

---

* From *The Kindred of the Wild* (Boston: L.C. Page, 1902), 273-84.

The wet, chill first of the spring, its blackness made tender by the lilac wash of the afterglow, lay upon the high, open stretches of the stump lots. The winter-whitened stumps, the sparse patches of juniper and bay just budding, the rough-mossed hillocks, the harsh boulders here and there upthrusting from the soil, the swampy hollows wherein a coarse grass began to show green, all seemed anointed, as it were, to an ecstasy of peace by the chrism of that paradisal colour. Against the lucid immensity of the April sky the thin tops of five or six soaring ram-pikes aspired like violet flames. Along the skirts of the stump lots a fir wood reared a ragged-crested wall of black against the red amber of the horizon.

Late that afternoon, beside a juniper thicket not far from the centre of the stump lots, a young black and white cow had given birth to her first calf. The little animal had been licked assiduously by the mother's caressing tongue till its colour began to show of a rich dark red. Now it had struggled to its feet, and, with its disproportionately long, thick legs braced wide apart, was beginning to nurse. Its blunt wet muzzle and thick lips tugged eagerly, but somewhat blunderingly as yet, at the unaccustomed teats; and its tail lifted, twitching with delight, as the first warm streams of mother milk went down its throat. It was a pathetically awkward, unlovely little figure, not yet advanced to that youngling winsomeness which is the heritage, to some degree and at some period, of the infancy of all the kindreds that breathe upon the earth. But to the young mother's eyes it was the most beautiful of things. With her head twisted far around, she nosed and licked its heaving flanks as it nursed; and between deep, ecstatic breathings she uttered in her throat low murmurs, unspeakably tender, of encouragement and caress. The delicate but pervading flood of sunset colour had the effect of blending the ruddy-hued calf into the tones of the landscape; but the cow's insistent blotches of black and white stood out sharply, refusing to harmonise. The drench of violet light was of no avail to soften their staring contrasts. They made her vividly conspicuous across the whole breadth of the stump lots, to eyes that watched her from the forest coverts.

The eyes that watched her—long, fixedly, hungrily—were small and red. They belonged to a lank she-bear, whose gaunt flanks and rusty coat proclaimed a season of famine in the wilderness. She could not see the calf, which was hidden by a hillock and some juniper scrub; but its presence was very legibly conveyed to her by the mother's solicitous watchfulness. After a motionless scrutiny from behind the screen of fir branches, the lean bear stole noiselessly forth from the shadows into the great wash of violet light. Step by step, and very slowly, with the patience that endures because confident of its object, she crept toward that oasis of mothering joy in the vast emptiness of the stump lots. Now crouching, now crawling, turning to this side and to that, taking advantage of every hollow, every thicket, every hillock, every aggressive stump, her craft succeeded in eluding even the wild and menacing watchfulness of the young mother's eyes.

The spring had been a trying one for the lank she-bear. Her den, in a dry tract of hemlock wood some furlongs back from the stumps lots, was a snug little cave under the uprooted base of a lone pine, which had somehow grown up among the alien hemlocks only to draw down upon itself at last, by its superior height, the fury of a passing hurricane. The winter had contributed but scanty snowfall to cover the bear in her sleep; and the March thaws, unseasonably early and ardent, had called her forth to activity weeks too soon. Then frosts had come with belated severity, sealing away the budding tubers, which are the bear's chief dependence for spring diet; and worst of all, a long stretch of intervale meadow by the neighbouring river, which had once been rich in ground-nuts, had been ploughed up the previous spring and subjected to the producing of oats and corn. When she was feeling the pinch of meagre rations, and when the fat which a liberal autumn of blueberries had laid up about her ribs was getting as shrunken as the last snow in the thickets, she gave birth to two hairless and hungry little cubs. They were very blind, and ridiculously small to be born of so big a mother; and having so much growth to make during the next few months, their appetites were immeasurable. They tumbled, and squealed, and tugged at their mother's teats, and grew astonishingly, and made huge haste to cover their bodies with fur of a soft and silken black; and all this vitality of theirs made a strenuous demand upon their mother's milk. There were no more bee-trees left in the neighbourhood.

The long wanderings which she was forced to take in her search for roots and tubers were in themselves a drain upon her nursing powers. At last, reluctant though she was to attract the hostile notice of the settlement, she found herself forced to hunt on the borders of the sheep pastures. Before all else in life was it important to her that these two tumbling little ones in the den should not go hungry. Their eyes were open now—small and dark and whimsical, their ears quaintly large and inquiring for their roguish little faces. Had she not been driven by the unkind season to so much hunting and foraging, she would have passed near all her time rapturously in the den under the pine root, fondling those two soft miracles of her world.

With the killing of three lambs—at widely scattered points, so as to mislead retaliation—things grew a little easier for the harassed bear; and presently she grew bolder in tampering with the creatures under man's protection. With one swift, secret blow of her mighty paw she struck down a young ewe which had strayed within reach of her hiding-place. Dragging her prey deep into the woods, she fared well upon it for some days, and was happy with her growing cubs. It was just when she had begun to feel the fasting which came upon the exhaustion of this store that, in a hungry hour, she sighted the conspicuous markings of the black and white cow.

It is altogether unusual for the black bear of the eastern woods to attack any quarry so large as a cow, unless under the spur of fierce hunger or fierce rage. The she-bear was powerful beyond her fellows. She had the strongest possible incentive to bold hunting, and she had lately grown confident beyond her wont. Nevertheless, when she began her careful stalking of this big game which she coveted, she had no definite intention of forcing a battle with the cow. She had observed that cows, accustomed to the protection of man, would at times leave their calves asleep and stray off some distance in their pasturing. She had even seen calves left all by themselves in a field, from morning till night, and had wondered at such negligence in their mothers. Now she had a confident idea that sooner or later the calf would lie down to sleep, and the young mother roam a little wide in search of the scant young grass. Very softly, very self-effacingly, she crept nearer step by step, following up the wind, till at last, undiscovered, she was crouching behind a thick patch of juniper, on the slope of a little hollow not ten paces distant from the cow and the calf.

By this time the tender violet light was fading to a grayness over hillock and hollow; and with the deepening of the twilight the faint breeze, which had been breathing from the northward, shifted suddenly and came in slow, warm pulsations out of the south. At the same time the calf, having nursed sufficiently, and feeling his baby legs tired of the weight they had not yet learned to carry, laid himself down. On this the cow shifted her position. She turned half round, and lifted her head high. As she did so a scent of peril was borne in upon her fine nostrils. She recognised it instantly. With a snort of anger she sniffed again; then stamped a challenge with her fore hoofs, and levelled the lance-points of her horns toward the menace. The next moment her eyes, made keen by the fear of love, detected the black outline of the bear's head through the coarse screen of the juniper. Without a second's hesitation, she flung up her tail, gave a short bellow, and charged.

The moment she saw herself detected, the bear rose upon her hindquarters; nevertheless she was in a measure surprised by the sudden blind fury of the attack. Nimbly she swerved to avoid it, aiming at the same time a stroke with her mighty forearm, which, if it had found its mark, would have smashed her adversary's neck. But as she struck out, in the act of shifting her position, a depression of the ground threw her off her balance. The next instant one sharp horn caught her slantingly in the flank, ripping its way upward and inward, while the mad impact threw her upon her back.

Grappling, she had her assailant's head and shoulders in a trap, and her gigantic claws cut through the flesh and sinew like knives; but at the desperate disadvantage of her position she could inflict no disabling blow. The cow, on the other hand, though mutilated and streaming with blood, kept pounding with her whole massive weight, and with short tremendous shocks crushing the breath from her foe's ribs.

Presently, wrenching herself free, the cow drew off for another battering charge; and as she did so the bear hurled herself violently down the slope, and gained her feet behind a dense thicket of bay shrub. The cow, with one eye blinded and the other obscured by blood, glared around for her in vain, then, in a panic of mother terror, plunged back to her calf.

Snatching at the respite, the bear crouched down, craving that invisibility which is the most faithful shield of the furtive kindred. Painfully, and leaving a drenched red trail behind her, she crept off from the disastrous neighbourhood. Soon the deepening twilight sheltered her. But she could not make haste; and she knew that death was close upon her.

Once within the woods, she struggled straight toward the den that held her young. She hungered to die licking them. But destiny is as implacable as iron to the wilderness people, and even this was denied her. Just a half score of paces from the lair in the pine root, her hour descended upon her. There was a sudden redder and fuller gush upon the trail; the last light of longing faded out of her eyes; and she lay down upon her side.

The merry little cubs within the den were beginning to expect her, and getting restless. As the night wore on, and no mother came, they ceased to be merry. By morning they were shivering with hunger and desolate fear. But the doom of the ancient wood was less harsh than its wont, and spared them some days of starving anguish; for about noon a pair of foxes discovered the dead mother, astutely estimated the situation, and then, with the boldness of good appetite, made their way into the unguarded den.

As for the red calf, its fortune was ordinary. Its mother, for all her wounds, was able to nurse and cherish it through the night; and with morning came a searcher from the farm and took it, with the bleeding mother, safely back to the settlement. There it was tended and fattened, and within a few weeks found its way to the cool marble slabs of a city market.

In Panoply of Spears*

There was a pleasant humming all about the bee-tree, where it stood solitary on the little knoll upon the sunward slope of the forest. It was an ancient maple, one side long since blasted by lightning, and now decayed to the heart; while the other side yet put forth a green bravery of branch and leaf. High up under a dead limb was a hole, thronged about with diligent bees who came and went in long diverging streams against the sun-steeped blue. A mile below, around the little, straggling backwoods settlement, the buckwheat was in bloom; and the bees counted the longest day too short for the gathering of its brown and fragrant sweets.

In fine contrast to their bustle and their haste was a moveless dark brown figure clinging to a leafy branch on the other and living side of the tree. From a distance it might easily have been taken for a big bird's-nest. Far out on the limb it sat, huddled into a bristling ball. Its nose, its whole head indeed, were hidden between its fore paws, which childishly but tenaciously clutched at a little upright branch. In this position, seemingly so precarious, but really, for the porcupine, the safest and most comfortable that could be imagined, it dozed away the idle summer hours.

From the thick woods at the foot of the knoll emerged a large black bear, who lifted his nose and eyed shrewdly the humming streams of workers converging at the hole in the bee-tree. For some time the bear stood contemplative, till an eager light grew in his small, cunning, half-humourous eyes. His long red tongue came out and licked his lips, as he thought of the summer's sweetness now stored in the hollow tree. He knew all about that prosperous bee colony. He remembered when, two years before, the runaway swarm from the settlement had taken possession of the hole in the old maple. That same autumn he had tried to rifle the treasure-house, but had found the wood about the entrance still too sound and strong

---

* From *The Kindred of the Wild* (Boston: L.C. Page, 1902), 349-74. "In Panolpy of Spears" also appeared in *The Independent* (May 8, 1902).

for even such powerfully rending claws as his. He had gone away surly with disappointment, to scratch a few angry bees out of his fur, and wait for the natural processes of decay to weaken the walls of the citadel.

On this particular day he decided to try again. He had no expectation that he would succeed; but the thought of the honey grew irresistible to him as he dwelt upon it. He lumbered lazily up the knoll, reared his dark bulk against the trunk, and started to climb to the attack.

But the little workers in the high-set hive found an unexpected protector in this hour of their need. The dozing porcupine woke up, and took it into his head that he wanted to go somewhere else. Perhaps in his dreams a vision had come to him of the lonely little oat-field in the clearing, where the young grain was plumping out and already full of milky sweetness. As a rule he preferred to travel and feed by night. But the porcupine is the last amid the wild kindreds to let convention interfere with impulse, and he does what seems good to the whim of the moment. His present whim was to descend the bee-tree and journey over to the clearing.

The bear had climbed but seven or eight feet, when he heard the scraping of claws on the bark above. He heard also the light clattering noise, unlike any other sound in the wilderness. He knew it at once as the sound of the loose-hung, hollow quills in a porcupine's active tail; and looking up angrily, he saw the porcupine curl himself downward from a crotch and begin descending the trunk to meet him.

The bear weighed perhaps four hundred or five hundred pounds. The porcupine weighed perhaps twenty-five pounds. Nevertheless, the bear stopped; and the porcupine came on. When he saw the bear, he gnashed his teeth irritably, and his quills, his wonderful panoply of finely barbed spears, erected themselves all over his body till his usual bulk seemed doubled. At the same time his colour changed. It was almost as if he had grown suddenly pale with indignation; for when the long quills stood up from among his blackish-brown fur they showed themselves all white save for their dark keen points. Small as he was in comparison with his gigantic opponent, he looked, nevertheless, curiously formidable. He grunted and grumbled querulously, and came on with confidence, obsti-

"THE BEAR EYED HIM FOR SOME MOMENTS."

nately proclaiming that no mere bear should for a moment divert him from his purpose.

Whether by instinct, experience, or observation, the bear knew something about porcupines. What would honey be to him, with two or three of those slender and biting spear-points embedded in his nose? As he thought of it, he backed away with increasing alacrity. He checked a rash impulse to dash the arrogant little hinderer from the tree and annihilate him with one stroke of his mighty paw,—but the mighty paw cringed, winced, and drew back impotent, as its sensitive nerves considered how it would feel to be stuck full, like a pin-cushion, with inexorably penetrating points. At last, thoroughly outfaced, the bear descended to the ground, and stood aside respectfully for the porcupine to pass.

The porcupine, however, on reaching the foot of the trunk, discovered an uncertainty in his mind. His whim wavered. He stopped, scratched his ears thoughtfully first with one fore paw and then with the other, and tried his long, chisel-like front teeth, those matchless gnawing machines, on a projecting edge of bark. The bear eyed him for some moments, then lumbered off into the woods indifferently, convinced that the bee-tree would be just as interesting on some other day. But before that other day came around, the bear encountered Fate, lying in wait for him, grim and implacable, beneath a trapper's deadfall in the heart of the tamarack swamp. And the humming tribes in the bee-tree were left to possess their honeyed commonwealth in peace.

Soon after the bear had left the knoll, the porcupine appeared to make up his mind as to what he wanted to do. With an air of fixed purpose he started down the knoll, heading for the oat-field and the clearing which lay some half-mile distant through the woods. As he moved on the ground, he was a somewhat clumsy and wholly grotesque figure. He walked with a deliberate and precise air, very slowly, and his legs worked as if the earth were to them an unfamiliar element. He was about two and a half feet long, short-legged, solid and sturdy looking, with a nose curiously squared off so that it should not get in the way of his gnawing. As he confronted you, his great chisel teeth, bared and conspicuous, appeared a most formidable weapon. Effective as they were, however, they were not a weapon which he was apt to call into use, save against inanimate and edible opponents; because he could not do so without exposing his weak points to attack,—his nose, his head, his soft, unprotected throat. His real weapon of offence was his short, thick tail, which was heavily armed with very powerful quills. With this he could strike slashing blows, such as would fill an enemy's face or paws with spines, and send him howling from the encounter. Clumsy and inert it looked, on ordinary occasions; but when need arose, its muscles had the lightning action of a strong steel spring.

As the porcupine made his resolute way through the woods, the manner of his going differed from that of all the other kindreds of the wild. He went not furtively. He had no particular objection to making a noise. He did not consider it necessary to stop every little while, stiffen himself to a monument of immobility, cast wary glances about the gloom, and sniff the air for the taint of enemies. He did not care who knew of his coming; and he did not greatly care who came. Behind his panoply of biting spears he felt himself secure, and in that security he moved as if he held in fee the whole green, shadowy, perilous woodland world

A wood-mouse, sitting in the door of his burrow between the roots of an ancient fir-tree, went on washing his face with his dainty paws as the porcupine passed within three feet of him. Almost any other forest traveller would have sent the timid mouse darting to the depths of his retreat; but he knew that the slow-moving figure, however terrible to look at, had no concern for wood-mice. The porcupine had barely passed, however, when a weasel came in view. In a flash the mouse was gone, to lie hidden for an hour, with trembling heart, in the furthest darkness of his burrow.

Continuing his journey, the porcupine passed under a fallen tree. Along the horizontal trunk lay a huge lynx, crouched flat, movelessly watching for rabbit, chipmunk, mink, or whatever quarry might come within his reach. He was hungry, as a lynx is apt to be. He licked his chaps, and his wide eyes paled with savage fire, as the porcupine dawdled by beneath the tree, within easy clutch of his claws. But his claws made no least motion of attack. He, too, like the bear, knew something about porcupines. In a few moments, however, when the porcupine had gone on some ten or twelve feet beyond his reach, his feelings overcame him so completely that he stood up and gave vent to an appalling scream of rage. All the other wild things within hearing trembled at the sound, and were still; and the porcupine, startled out of his equipoise, tucked his nose between his legs, and bristled into a ball of sharp defiance. The lynx eyed him venomously for some seconds, then dropped lightly from the perch, and stole off to hunt in other neighbourhoods, realising that his reckless outburst of bad temper had warned all the coverts for a quarter of a mile around. The porcupine, uncurling, grunted scornfully and resumed his journey.

Very still, and lonely and bright the clearing lay in the flooding afternoon sunshine. It lay along beside a deeply rutted, grass-grown backwoods road which had been long forgotten by the attentions of the road-master. It was enclosed from the forest in part by a dilapidated wall of loose stones, in part by an old snake fence, much patched with brush. The cabin which had once presided over its solitude had long fallen to ruin; but its fertile soil had saved it from being forgotten. A young farmer-lumberman from the settlement a couple of miles away held possession of it, and kept its boundaries more or less intact, and made it yield him each year a crop of oats, barley, or buckwheat.

Emerging from the woods, the porcupine crawled to the top of the stone wall and glanced about him casually. Then he descended into the cool, light-green depths of the growing oats. Here he was completely hidden, though his passage was indicated as he went by the swaying and commotion among the oat-tops.

The high plumes of the grain, of course, were far above the porcupine's reach; and for a healthy appetite like his it would have been tedious work indeed to pull down the stalks one by one. At this point, he displayed an ingenious resourcefulness with which he is seldom credited by observers of his kind. Because he is slow in movement, folk are apt to conclude that he is slow in wit; whereas the truth is that he has fine reserves of shrewdness to fall back on in emergency. Instead of pulling and treading down the oats at haphazard, he moved through the grain in a small circle, leaning heavily inward. When he had thus gone around the circle several times, the tops of the grain lay together in a convenient bunch. This succulent sheaf he dragged down, and devoured with relish.

When he had abundantly satisfied his craving for young oats, he crawled out upon the open sward by the fence, and carelessly sampled the bark of a seedling apple-tree. While he was thus engaged a big, yellow dog came trotting up the wood-road, poking his nose inquisitively into every bush and stump in the hope of finding a rabbit or chipmunk to chase. He belonged to the young farmer who owned the oat-field; and when, through the rails of the snake fence, he caught sight of the porcupine, he was filled with noisy wrath. Barking and yelping,—partly with excitement, and partly as a signal to his master who was trudging along the road far behind him,—he clambered over the fence, and bore down upon the trespasser.

The porcupine was not greatly disturbed by this loud onslaught, but he did not let confidence make him careless. He calmly tucked his head under his breast, set his quills in battle array, and awaited the event with composure.

Had he discovered the porcupine in the free woods, the yellow dog would have let him severely alone. But in his master's oat-field, that was a different matter. Moreover, the knowledge that his master was coming added to his zeal and rashness; and he had long cherished the ambition to kill a porcupine. He sprang forward, open-jawed,—and stopped short when his fangs were just within an inch or two of those bristling and defiant points. Caution had come to his rescue just in time.

For perhaps half a minute he ran, whining and baffled, around the not-to-be daunted ball of spines. Then he sat down upon his haunches, lifted up his muzzle, and howled for his master to come and help him.

As his master failed to appear within three seconds, his impatience got the better of him, and he again began running around the porcupine, snapping fiercely, but never coming within two or three inches of the militant points. For a few moments these two or three inches proved to be a safe distance. Such a distance from the shoulders, back, and sides was all well enough. But suddenly, he was so misguided as to bring his teeth together within a couple of inches of the armed but quiescent tail. This was the instant for which the porcupine had been waiting. The tail flicked smartly. The big dog jumped, gave a succession of yelping cries, pawed wildly at his nose, then tucked his tail between his legs, scrambled over the fence, and fled away to his master. The porcupine unrolled himself, and crawled into an inviting hole in the old stone wall.

About ten minutes later a very angry man, armed with a fence-stake, appeared at the edge of the clearing with a cowed dog at his heels. He wanted to find the porcupine which had stuck those quills into his dog's nose. Mercifully merciless, he had held the howling dog in a grip of iron while he pulled out the quills with his teeth; and now he was after vengeance. Knowing a little, but not everything, about porcupines, he searched every tree in the immediate neighbourhood, judging that the porcupine, after such an encounter, would make all haste to his natural retreat. But he never looked in the hole in the wall; and the yellow dog, who had come to doubt the advisability of finding porcupines, refused firmly to assist in the search. In a little while, when his anger began to cool, he gave over the hunt in disgust, threw away the fence-stake, bit off a goodly chew from the fig of black tobacco which he produced from his hip-pocket, and strode away up the grassy wood-road.

For perhaps half an hour the porcupine dozed in the hole among the stones. Then he woke up, crawled out, and moved slowly along the top of the wall.

There was a sound of children's voices coming up the road; but the porcupine, save for a grumble of impatience, paid no attention. Presently the children came in sight,—a stocky little boy of nine or ten, and a lank girl of perhaps thirteen, making their way homeward from school by the short cut over the mountain. Both were barefooted and barelegged, deeply freckled, and with long, tow-coloured locks. The boy wore a shirt and short breeches of blue-gray homespun, the breeches held up precariously by one suspender. On his head was a tattered and battered straw; and in one hand he swung a little tin dinner-pail. The girl wore the like blue-gray homespun for a petticoat, with a waist of bright red calico, and carried a limp pink sunbonnet on her arm.

"Oh, see the porkypine!" cried the girl, as they came abreast of the stone wall.

"By gosh! Let's kill it!" exclaimed the stocky little boy, starting forward eagerly, with a prompt efflorescence of primitive instincts. But his sister clutched him by the arm and anxiously restrained him.

"My lands, Jimmy, you musn't go near a porkypine like that!" she protested, more learned than her brother in the hoary myths of the settlements. "Don't you know he can fling them quills of his'n at you, an' they'll go right through an' come out the other side?"

"By gosh!" gasped the boy, eyeing the unconcerned animal with apprehension, and edging off to the furthermost ditch. Hand in hand, their eyes wide with excitement, the two children passed beyond the stone wall. Then, as he perceived that the porcupine had not seemed to notice them, the boy's hunting instinct revived. He stopped, set down the tin dinner-pail, and picked up a stone.

"No, you don't, Jimmy!" intervened the girl, with mixed emotions of kindliness and caution, as she grabbed his wrist and dragged him along.

"Why, Sis?" protested the boy, hanging back, and looking over his shoulder longingly. "Jest let me fling a stone at him!"

"No!" said his sister, with decision. "He ain't a-hurtin' us, an' he's mindin' his own business. An' I reckon maybe he can fling quills as fur as you can fling stones!"

Convinced by this latter argument, the boy gave up his design, and suffered his wise sister to lead him away from so perilous a neighbourhood. The two little figures vanished amid the green glooms beyond the clearing, and the porcupine was left untroubled in his sovereignty.

II.

That autumn, late one moonlight night, the porcupine was down by a little forest lake feasting on lily pads. He occupied a post of great advantage, a long, narrow ledge of rock jutting out into the midst of the lilies, and rising but an inch or two above the water. Presently, to his great indignation, he heard a dry rustling of quills behind him, and saw another porcupine crawl out upon his rock. He faced about, bristling angrily and gnashing his teeth, and advanced to repel the intruder.

The intruder hesitated, then came on again with confidence, but making no hostile demonstrations whatever. When the two met, the expected conflict was by some sudden agreement omitted. They touched blunt noses, squeaked and grunted together for awhile till a perfect understanding was established; then crawled ashore and left the lily pads to rest, broad, shiny, and unruffled in the moonlight, little platters of silver on the dark glass of the lake.

The newcomer was a female; and with such brief wooing the big porcupine had taken her for his mate. Now he led her off to show her the unequalled den which he had lately discovered. The den was high in the side of a heap of rocks, dry in all weathers, and so overhung by a half-uprooted tree as to be very well concealed from passers and prowlers. Its entrance was long and narrow, deterrent to rash investigators. In fact, just after the porcupine had moved in, a red fox had discovered the doorway and judged it exactly to his liking; but on finding that the occupant was a porcupine, he had hastily decided to seek accommodation elsewhere. In this snug house the two porcupines settled contentedly for the winter.

The winter passed somewhat uneventfully for them, though for the rest of the wood-folk it was a season of unwonted hardship. The cold was more intense and more implacable than had been known about the settlements for years. Most of the wild creatures, save those who could sleep the bitter months away and abide the coming of spring, found themselves face to face with famine. But the porcupines feared neither famine nor cold. The brown fur beneath their quills was thick and warm, and hunger was impossible to them with all the trees of the forest for their pasturage. Sometimes, when the cold made them sluggish, they would stay all day and all night in a single balsam-fir or hemlock, stripping one branch after another of leaf and twig, indifferent to the monotony of their diet. At other times, however, they were as active and enterprising as if all the heats of summer were loosing their sinews. On account of the starvation-madness that was everywhere ranging the coverts, they were more than once attacked as they crawled lazily over the snow; but on each occasion the enemy, whether lynx or fox, fisher or mink, withdrew discomfited, with something besides hunger in his hide to think about.

Once, in midwinter, they found a prize which added exquisite variety to their bill of fare. Having wandered down to the outskirts of the settlements, they discovered, cast aside among the bushes, an empty firkin which had lately contained salt pork. The wood, saturated with brine, was delicious to the porcupines. Greedily they gnawed at it, returning night after night to the novel banquet, till the last sliver of the flavoured wood was gone. Then, after lingering a day or two longer in the neighbourhood, expecting another miracle, they returned to their solitudes and their hemlock.

When winter was drawing near its close, but spring had not yet sent the wilderness word of her coming, the porcupines got her message in their blood. They proclaimed it abroad in the early twilight from the tops of the high hemlocks, in queer, half-rhythmical choruses of happy grunts and squeaks. The sound was far from melodious, but it pleased every one of the wild kindred to whose ears it came; for they knew that when the porcupines got trying to sing, then the spring thaws were hurrying up from the south.

At last the long desired one came; and every little rill ran a brawling brook in the fulness of its joy. And the ash-buds swelled rich purple; and the maples crimsoned with their misty blooms; and the skunk cabbage began to thrust up bold knobs of emerald, startling in their brightness, through the black and naked leaf-mould of the swamp. And just at this time, when all the wild kindred, from the wood-mouse to the moose, felt sure that life was good, a porcupine baby was born in the snug den among the rocks.

It was an astonishingly big baby,—the biggest, in proportion to the size of its parents, of all the babies of the wild. In fact it was almost as big as an average bear cub. It was covered with long, dark brown, silky fur, under which the future panoply of spear-points was already beginning to make way through the tender skin. Its mother was very properly proud, and assiduous in her devotion. And the big father, though seemingly quite indifferent, kept his place contentedly in the den instead of going off sourly by himself to another lair as the porcupine male is apt to do on the arrival of the young.

One evening about dusk, when the young porcupine was but three days old, a weasel glided noiselessly up to the door of the den, and sniffed. His eyes, set close together and far down toward his malignant, pointed nose, were glowing red with the lust of the kill. Fierce and fearless as he was, he knew well enough that a porcupine was something for him to let alone. But this, surely, was his chance to feed fat an ancient grudge; for he hated everything that he could not hope to kill. He had seen the mother porcupine feeding comfortably in the top of a near-by poplar. And now he made assurance doubly sure by sniffing at her trail, which came out from the den and did not return. As for the big male porcupine, the prowler took it for granted that he had followed the usage of his kind, and gone off about other business. Like a snake, he slipped in, and found the furry baby all alone. There was a strong, squeaking cry, a moment's struggle; and then the weasel drank eagerly at the blood of his easy prey. The blood, and the fierce joy of the kill, were all he wanted, for his hunting was only just begun.

The assassin stayed but a minute with his victim, then turned swiftly to the door of the den. But the door was blocked. It was filled by an ominous, bristling bulk, which advanced upon him slowly, inexorably, making a sharp, clashing sound with its long teeth. The big porcupinc had come home. And his eyes blazed more fiercely red than those of the weasel.

The weasel, fairly caught, felt that doom was upon him. He backed away, over the body of his victim, to the furthest depth of the den. But, though a ruthless murderer, the most cruel of all the wild kindred, he was no coward. He would evade the slow avenger if he could; but if not, he would fight to the last gasp.

Against this foe the porcupine scorned his customary tactics, and depended upon his terrible, cutting teeth. At the same time he knew that the weasel was desperate and deadly. Therefore he held his head low, shielding his tender throat. When he reached the wider part of the den, he suddenly swung sidewise, thus keeping the exit still blocked.

Seeing now that there was no escape, the weasel gathered his forces for one last fight. Like lightning he sprang, and struck; and being, for speed, quite matchless among the wild folk, he secured a deadly hold on the porcupine's jaw. The porcupine squeaked furiously and tried to shake his adversary off. With a sweep of his powerful neck, he threw the weasel to one side, and then into the air over his head.

The next instant the weasel came down, sprawling widely, full upon the stiffly erected spears of the porcupine's back. They pierced deep into his tender belly. With a shrill cry he relaxed his hold on the avenger's jaw, shrank together in anguish, fell to the ground, and darted to the exit. As he passed he got a heavy slap from the porcupine's tail, which filled his face and neck with piercing barbs. Then he escaped from the den and fled away toward his own lair, carrying his death with him. Before he had gone a hundred yards one of the quills in his belly reached a vital part. He faltered, fell, stretched his legs out weakly, and died. Then a red squirrel, who had been watching him in a quiver of fear and hate, shot from his hiding-place, ran wildly up and down his tree, and made the woods ring with his sharp, barking chatter of triumph over the death of the universal enemy.

In the midst of the squirrel's shrill rejoicings the porcupine emerged from his den. He seemed to hesitate, which is not the way of a porcupine. He looked at his mate, still foraging in the top of her poplar, happily unaware for the present of how her little world had changed. He seemed to realise that the time of partings had come, the time when he must resume his solitude. He turned and looked at his den,—he would never find another like it! Then he crawled off through the cool, wet woods, where the silence seemed to throb sweetly with the stir and fulness of the sap. And in a hollow log, not far from the bee-tree on the knoll, he found himself a new home, small and solitary.

The Little Wolf of the Pool*

The bottom of the pool (it was too small to be called a pond) was muddy, with here and there a thicket of rushes or arrow-weed stems. Down upon the windless surface streamed the noon sun warmly. Under its light the bottom was flecked with shadows of many patterns,—circular, heart-shaped, spear-shaped, netted, and barred. There were other shadows that were no more than ghosts of shadows, cast by faint, diaphanous films of scum which scarcely achieved to blur the clear downpour of radiance, but were nevertheless perceived and appreciated by many of the delicate larval creatures which made a large part of the life of the pool.

For all its surface tranquillity and its shining summer peace, the pool was thronged with life. Beneath the surface, among the weeds and stalks, the gleams and shadows, there was little of tranquillity or peace. Almost all the many-formed and strange-shaped inhabitants of the pool were hunting or being hunted, preying or being preyed upon,—from the goggle-eyed, green-throated bullfrog under the willow root, down to the swarming animalculae which it required a microscope to see. Small crawling things everywhere dotted the mud or tried to hide under the sticks and stones. Curled fresh-water snails moved up and down the stems of the lilies. Shining little black water-bugs scurried swiftly in all directions. In sheltered places near the surface, under the leaves, wriggled the slim gray larvae of the mosquitoes. And hither and thither, in flickering shoals, darted myriads of baby minnows, from half an inch to an inch and a half in length.

In a patch of vivid sunshine, about six inches from a tangle of arrow-weed stems, a black tadpole lay basking. Light to him meant not only growth, but life. Whenever, with the slow wheeling of the sun, the shadow of a lily leaf moved over him, he wriggled impatiently aside, and settled down again on the brightest part of the mud. Most of the time he seemed to be asleep; but in reality he was keeping that incessant sharp lookout which, for the pool-dwellers, was the price of survival.

---

* From *The Watchers of the Trails* (Boston: L.C. Page, 1904), 65-70.

Swimming slowly up toward the other side of the arrow-weed stems, came a fantastic-looking creature, something more than an inch and a half in length. It had a long, tapering, ringed and armoured body, ending in a spine; a thick, armoured thorax, with six legs attached; and a large head, the back of which was almost covered by two big, dully staring globes of eyes. The whole front of its head—part of the eyes, and all the face—was covered by a smooth, cleft, shieldlike mask, reaching well down under the breast, and giving the creature an expression both mysterious and terrible. On its back, folded close and obviously useless, were rigidly encased attempts at wings.

The little monster swam slowly by the motion of its long and strong legs, thrusting out two short, hornlike antennae over the top of its mask. It seemed to be eyeing a snail-shell on a stem above, and waiting for the snail's soft body to emerge from the citadel; when on a sudden, through the stems, it caught sight of the basking tadpole. Instantly it became motionless, and sank, like a waterlogged twig, to the level of the mud. It crept around, effacing itself against the brown and greenish roots, till it was just opposite the quarry. Then it sprang, propelling itself not only by its legs, but by the violent ejection of a little stream of water from the powerful breathing-valves near its tail.

The tadpole, as we have seen, was not asleep. With a convulsive wriggle of its tail it darted away in a panic. It was itself no mean swimmer, but it could not escape the darting terror that pursued. When the masked form was almost within reach of its victim, the mask dropped down and shot straight out, working on a sort of elbow-shaped lever, and at the same time revealed at its extremity a pair of powerful mandibles. These mandibles snapped firm hold of the victim at the base of its wriggling tail. The elbow-shaped lever drew back, till the squirming prize was held close against its captor's face. Then with swift jets from the turbine arrangement of its abdominal gills, the strange monster darted back to a retreat among the weed stems, where it could devour its prey in seclusion.

Under those inexorable jaws the tadpole soon disappeared and for a few minutes the monster rested, working its mandibles to and fro and rubbing them with its front legs before folding back that inscrutable mask over its savage face. Presently a plump minnow, more than an inch long, with a black stripe along its bronze and silver sides, swam down close by the arrow-weed stems. The big eyes of the monster never moved. But, suddenly, out shot the mask once more, revealing the face of doom behind it; and those hooked mandibles fixed themselves in the belly of the minnow. Inexorable as was the grip, it nevertheless for the moment left unimpeded the swimming powers of the victim; and he was a strong swimmer. With lashing tail and beating fins, he dragged his captor out from among the weed stems. For a few seconds there was a vehement struggle. Then the minnow was borne down upon the mud, out in the broad sheen where, a little before, the tadpole had been basking. Clutching ferociously with its six long legs, the conqueror crawled over the prey and bit its backbone in two.

Swift, strong, insatiably ravenous, immeasurably fierce, the larva of the dragon-fly (for such the little monster was) had fair title to be called the wolf of the pool. Its appearance alone was enough to daunt all rivals. Even the great black carnivorous water-beetle, with all its strength and fighting equipment, was careful to give wide berth to that dreadful, quick-darting mask. Had these little wolves been as numerous as they were rapacious, there would soon have been left no life at all in the pool but theirs and that of the frogs. Between these there would have been a long and doubtful struggle, the frogs hunting the larvae among the weed stems, and the larvae devouring the tadpoles on their basking-grounds.

It chanced that the particular larva whose proceedings we have noted was just on the eve of that change which should transport it to the world of air. After eating the minnow it somehow failed to recover its appetite, and remained, all the rest of the day and through the night, clinging to one of the weed stems. Next morning, when the sun was warm on the pool, it crawled slowly up, up, up, till it came out into a new element, and the untried air fanned it dry. Its great round eyes, formerly dull and opaque, had now grown transparent, and were gleaming like live jewels, an indescribable blend of emerald, sapphire, and amethyst. Presently its armour, now for the first time drying in the sun, split apart down the back, and a slender form, adorned with two pairs of crumpled, wet wings, struggled three-quarters of its length from the shell. For a short time it clung motionless, gathering strength. Then, bracing its legs firmly on the edges of the shell, it lifted its tail quite clear, and crawled up the weed a perfect dragon-fly, forgetful of that grim husk it was leaving behind. A few minutes later, the good sun having dried its wings, it went darting and hurtling over the pool, a gemlike, opalescent shining thing, reflected gloriously in the polished mirror beneath.

By the Winter Tide*

Behind the long, slow-winding barrier of the dyke the marshes of Tantramar lay secure, mile on mile of blue-white radiance under the unclouded moon. Outside the dyke it was different. Mile on mile of tumbled, mud-stained ice-cakes, strewn thickly over the Tantramar flats, waited motionless under the moon for the incoming tide. Twice in each day the far-wandering tide of Fundy would come in, to lift, and toss, and grind, and roll the ice-cakes, then return again to its deep channels; and with every tide certain of the floes would go forth to be lost in the open sea, while the rest would sink back to their tumbled stillness on the mud. Just now the flood was coming in. From all along the outer fringes of the flats came a hoarse, desolate roar; and in the steady light the edges of the ice-field began to turn and flash, the strange motion creeping gradually inland toward that impassive bulwark of the dyke. Had it been daylight, the chaotic ice-field would have shown small beauty, every wave-beaten floe being soiled and streaked with rust-coloured Tantramar mud. But under the transfiguring touch of the moon the unsightly levels changed to plains of infinite mystery—expanses of shattered, white granite, as it were, fretted and scrawled with blackness—reaches of loneliness older than time. So well is the mask of eternity assumed by the mutable moonlight and the ephemeral ice.

Nearer and nearer across the waste drew the movement that marked the incoming flood. Then from over the dyke-top floated a noiseless, winnowing, sinister shape which seemed the very embodiment of the desolation. The great white owl of the north, driven down from his Arctic hunting-grounds by hunger, came questing over the ragged levels. His long, soft-feathered wings moved lightly as a ghost, and almost touched the ice-cakes now and then as his round, yellow eyes, savagely hard and brilliant, searched the dark crevices for prey. With his black beak, his black talons protruding from the mass of snowy feathers which swathed his legs, and the dark bars on his

---

* From *The Watchers of the Trails* (Boston: L.C. Page, 1904), 121-27.

"HE STRUCK JUST TOO LATE."

plumage, one might have fancied him a being just breathed into menacing and furtive life by the sorcery of the scene.

Suddenly, with a motion almost as swift as light, the great owl swooped and struck. Swift as he was, however, this time he struck just too late. A spot of dark on the edge of an ice-cake vanished. It was a foraging muskrat who had seen the approaching doom in time and slipped into a deep and narrow crevice. Here, on the wet mud, he crouched trembling, while the baffled bird reached down for him with vainly clutching claws.

On either side of the two ice-cakes which had given thc muskrat refuge, was a space of open mud which he knew it would be death to cross. Each time those deadly black talons clutched at him, he flattened himself to the ground in panic; but there were several inches to spare between his throat and death. The owl glared down with fixed and flaming eyes, then gave up his useless efforts. But he showed no inclination to go away. He knew that the muskrat could not stay for ever down in that muddy crevice. So he perched himself bolt upright on the very edge, where he could keep secure watch upon his intended victim, while at the same time his wide, round eyes might detect any movement of life among the surrounding ice-cakes.

The great flood-tides of Fundy, when once they have brimmed the steep channels and begun to invade the vast reaches of the flats, lose little time. When the baffled owl, hungry and obstinate, perched himself on the edge of the ice-cake to wait for the muskrat to come out, the roar of the incoming water and the line of tossing, gleaming floes were half a mile away. In about four minutes the fringe of tumult was not three hundred yards distant,—and at the same time the vanguards of the flood, thin, frothy rivulets of chill water, were trickling in through the crevice where the little prisoner crouched. As the water touched his feet, the muskrat took heart anew, anticipating a way of escape. As it deepened he stood upright,—and instantly the white destruction cruelly watching struck again. This time the muskrat felt those deadly talons graze the long, loose fur of his back; and again he cowered down, inviting the flood to cover him. As much at home under water as on dry land, he counted on easy escape when the tide came in.

It happens, however, that the little kindreds of the wild are usually more wise in the general than in the particular. The furry prisoner at the bottom of the crevice knew about such regular phenomena as the tides. He knew, too, that presently there would be water enough for him to dive and swim beneath it, where his dreadful adversary could neither reach him nor detect him. What he did not take into account was the way the ice-cakes would grind and batter each other as soon as the tide was deep enough to float them. Now, submerged till his furry back and spiky tail were just even with the surface, his little, dark eyes glanced up with mingled defiance and appeal at the savage, yellow glare of the wide orbs staring down upon him. If only the water would come, he would be safe. For a moment his eyes turned longingly toward the dyke, and he thought of the narrow, safe hole, the long, ascending burrow, and the warm, soft-lined chamber which was his nest, far up in the heart of the dyke, high above the reach of the highest tides and hidden from all enemies. But here in the hostile water, with a cruel death hanging just above him, his valorous little heart ached with homesickness for that nest in the heart of the dyke; and though the water had no chill for his hardy blood, he shivered.

Meanwhile, the long line of clamour was rushing steadily inland. The roar suddenly crashed into thunder on the prisoner's ears and a rush of water swept him up. The white owl spread his wings and balanced himself on tiptoe, as the ice-cake on which he was perching lurched and rolled. Through all the clamour his ears, miraculously keen beyond those of other birds, caught an agonized squeak from below. The jostling ice had nipped the muskrat's hind quarters.

Though desperately hurt, so desperately that his strong hind legs were almost useless, the brave little animal was not swerved from his purpose. Straight from his prison, no longer now a refuge, he dived and swam for home through the loud uproar. But the muskrat's small forelegs are of little use in swimming, so much so that as a rule he carries them folded under his chin while in the water. Now, therefore, he was at a piteous disadvantage. His progress was slow, as in a nightmare,—such a nightmare as must often come to muskrats if their small, careless brains know how to dream. And in spite of his frantic efforts, he found that he could not hold himself down in the water. He kept rising toward the surface every other second.

Balancing had by this time grown too difficult for the great, white owl, and he had softly lifted himself on hovering wings. But not for an instant had he forgotten the object of his hunt. What were floods and cataclysms to him in the face of his hunger? Swiftly his shining eyes searched the foamy, swirling water. Then, some ten feet away, beside a pitching floe, a furry back appeared for an instant. In that instant he swooped. The back had vanished,—but unerringly his talons struck beneath the surface—struck and gripped their prey. The next moment the wide, white wings beat upward heavily, and the muskrat was lifted from the water.

As he rose into the air, though near blind with the anguish of that iron grip, the little victim writhed upward and bit furiously at his enemy's leg. His jaws got nothing but a bunch of fluffy feathers, which came away and floated down the moonlight air. Then the life sank out of his brain, and he hung limply; and the broad wings bore him inland over the dyke-top—straight over the warm and hidden nest where he had longed to be.

A Stranger to the Wild *

As the vessel, a big three-masted schooner, struck again and lurched forward, grinding heavily, she cleared the reef by somewhat more than half her length. Then her back broke. The massive swells, pounding upon her from the rear, over-whelmed her stern and crushed it down inescapably upon the rock; and her forward half, hanging in ten fathoms, began to settle sickeningly into the loud hiss and chaos. Around the reef, around the doomed schooner, the lead-coloured fog hung thick, impenetrable at half a ship's length. Her crew, cool, swift, ready,—they were Gaspé and New Brunswick fishermen, for the most part,—kept grim silence, and took the sharp orders that came to them like gunshots through the din. The boats were cleared away forward, where the settling of the bow gave some poor shelter.

At this moment the fog lifted, vanishing swiftly like a breath from the face of a mirror. Straight ahead, not two miles away, loomed a high, black, menacing shore—black, scarred rock, with black woods along its crest and a sharp, white line of surf shuddering along its base. Between that shore and the shattered schooner lay many other reefs, whereon the swells boiled white and broke in dull thunder; but off to the southward was clear water, and safety for the boats. At a glance the captain recognized the land as a cape on the south coast of the Gaspé peninsula, so far from her course had the doomed schooner been driven. Five minutes more, and the loaded boats, hurled up from the seething caldron behind the reef, swung out triumphantly on a long, oil-dark swell, and gained the comparative safety of the open. Hardly had they done so when the broken bow of the schooner, with a final rending of timbers, settled in what seemed like a sudden hurry, pitched nose downward into the smother, and sank with a huge, startling sigh. The rear half of the hull was left lodged upon the reef, a kind of gaping cavern, with the surf plunging over it in cataracts, and a mad mob of boxes, bales, and wine-casks tumbling out from its black depths.

---

* From *The Haunters of the Silences* (Boston: L.C. Page, 1907), 108-131. "A Stranger to the Wild" also appeared in *Century Illustrated Magazine* (Dec. 1906).

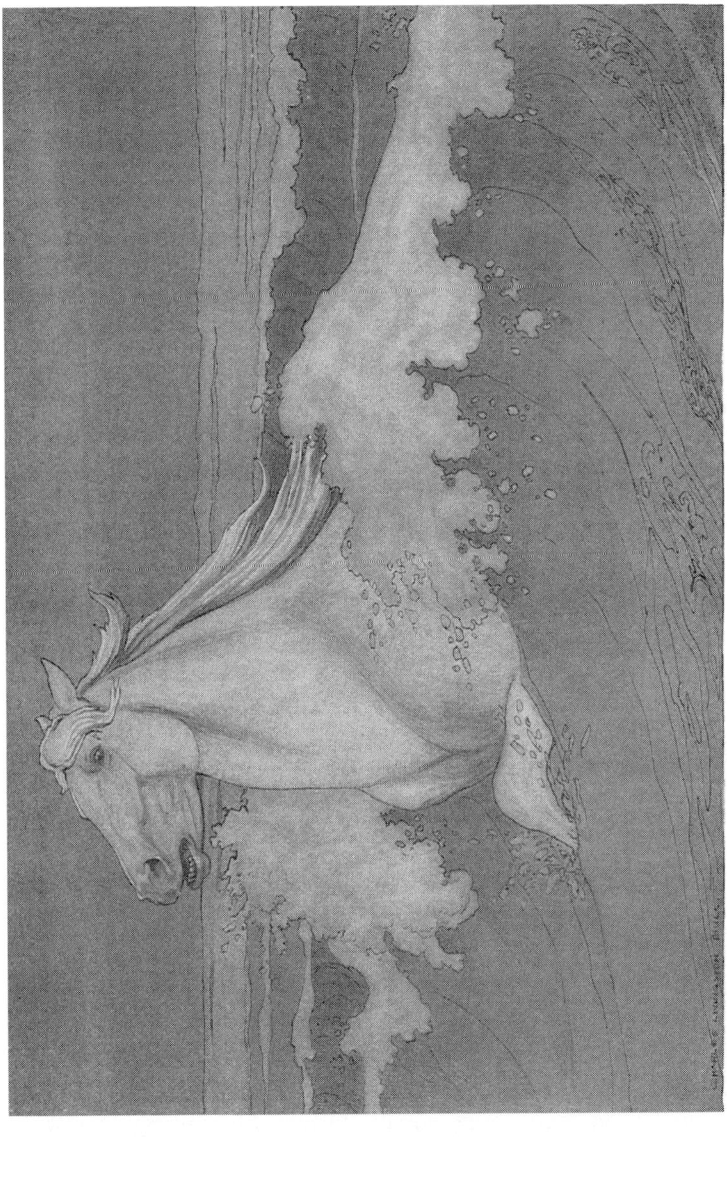

"HE STRUCK OUT DESPERATELY, AND SOON CLEARED THE TURMOIL OF THE BREAKERS."

Presently the torrent ceased. Then, in the yawning gloom, appeared the head and fore-quarters of a white horse, mane streaming, eyes starting with frantic terror at the terrific scene that met them. The vision sank back instantly into the darkness. A moment later a vast surge, mightier than any which had gone before, engulfed the reef. Its gigantic front lifted the remnant of the wreck half-way across the barrier, tipping it forward, and letting it down with a final shattering crash; and the white horse, hurled violently forth, sank deep into the tumult behind the reef.

The schooner which had fallen on such sudden doom among the St. Lawrence reefs had sailed from Oporto with a cargo, chiefly wine, for Quebec. Driven far south of her course by a terrific north-easter roaring down from Labrador, she had run into a fog as the wind fell, and been swept to her fate in the grip of an unknown tide-drift. On board, as it chanced, travelling as an honoured passenger, was a finely bred, white Spanish stallion of Barb descent, who had been shipped to Canada by one of the heads of the great house of Robin, those fishing-princes of Gaspé. When the vessel struck, and it was seen that her fate was imminent and inevitable, the captain had loosed the beautiful stallion from his stall, that at the last he might at least have a chance to fight his own fight for life. And so it came about that, partly through his own agile alertness, partly by the singular favour of fortune, he had avoided getting his slim legs broken in the hideous upheaval and confusion of the wreck.

When the white stallion came to the surface, snorting with terror and blowing the salt from his wide nostrils, he struck out desperately, and soon cleared the turmoil of the breakers. Over the vast, smooth swells he swam easily, his graceful, high head out of water. But at first, in his bewilderment and panic, he swam straight seaward. In a few moments, however, as he saw that he seemed to be overcoming disaster very well, his wits returned, and the nerve of his breeding came to his aid. Keeping on the crest of a roller, he surveyed the situation keenly, observed the land, and noted the maze of reefs that tore the leaden surges into tumult. Instead of heading directly shoreward, therefore,—for every boiling whiteness smote him with horror,—he shaped his course in on a long slant, where the way seemed clear.

Once well south of the loud herd of reefs, he swam straight inshore, until the raving and white convulsion of the surf along the base of the cliff again struck terror into his heart; and again he bore away southward, at a distance of about three hundred yards outside the breakers. Strong, tough-sinewed, and endowed with the unfailing wind of his far-off desert ancestors, he was not aware of any fatigue from his long swim. Presently, rounding a point of rock which thrust a low spur out into the surges, he came into a sheltered cove where there was no surf. The long waves rolled on past the point, while in the cove there was only a measured, moderate rise and fall of the gray water, like a quiet breathing, and only a gentle back-wash fringed the black-stoned, weedy beach with foam. At the head of the cove a shallow stream, running down through a narrow valley, emptied itself between two little red sand-spits.

Close beside the stream the white stallion came ashore. As soon as his feet were quite clear of the uppermost fringe of foam, as soon as he stood on ground that was not only firm, but dry, he shook himself violently, tossed his fine head with a whinny of exultation, and turned a long look of hate and defiance upon the element from which he had just made his escape. Then at a determined trot he set off up the valley, eager to leave all sight and sound of the sea as far as possible behind him.

Reared as he had been on the windy and arid plateau of Northern Spain, the wanderer was filled with great loneliness in these dark woods of fir and spruce. An occasional maple in its blaze of autumn scarlet, or a clump of white birch in shimmering, aërial gold, seen unexpectedly upon the heavy-shadowed green, startled him like a sudden noise. Nevertheless, strange though they were, they were trees, and so not altogether alien to his memory. And the brook, with its eddying pools and brawling, shallow cascades, that seemed to him a familiar, kindly thing. It was only the sea that he really feared and hated. So long as he was sure he was putting the huge surges and loud reefs farther and farther behind him, he felt a certain measure of content as he pushed onward deeper and deeper into the serried gloom and silence of the spruce woods. At last, coming to a little patch of brookside meadow where the grass kept short and sweet and green even at this late season, he stopped his flight, and fell to pasturing.

Late in the afternoon, the even gray mass of cloud which for days had veiled the sky thinned away and scattered, showing the clear blue of the north. The sun, near setting, sent long rays of cheerful light down the narrow valley, bringing out warm, golden bronzes in the massive, dull green of the fir and spruce and hemlock, and striking sharp flame on the surfaces of the smooth pools. Elated by the sudden brightness, the white stallion resumed his journey at a gallop, straight toward the sunset, his long mane and tail, now dry, streaming out on the light afternoon breeze that drew down between the hills. He kept on up the valley till the sun went down, and then, in the swiftly deepening twilight, came to a little grassy point backed by a steep rock. Here where the rippling of the water enclosed him on three sides, and the rock, with a thick mass of hemlocks surmounting it, shut him in on the fourth, he felt more secure, less desolate, than when surrounded by the endless corridors of the forest; and close to the foot of the rock he lay down, facing the mysterious gloom of the trees across the stream.

Just as he was settling himself, a strange voice, hollow yet muffled, cried across the open space "*Hoo-hoo, hoo-hoo, woo-hoo-hoo!*" and he bounded to his feet, every nerve on the alert. He had never in his life before heard the voice of the great horned owl, and his apprehensive wonder was excusable. Again and yet again came the hollow call out of the deep dark of the banked woods opposite. As he stood listening tensely, eyes and nostrils wide, a bat flitted past his ears, and he jumped half around, with a startled snort. The ominous sound, however, was not repeated, and in a couple of minutes he lay down again, still keeping watchful eyes upon the dark mass across the stream. Then, at last, a broad-winged bird, taking shape softly above the open, as noiseless as a gigantic moth, floated over him, and looked down upon him under his rock with round, palely luminous eyes. By some quick intuition he knew that this visitor was the source of the mysterious call. It was only a bird, after all, and no great thing in comparison with the eagles of his own Pyrenean heights. His apprehensions vanished, and he settled himself to sleep.

Worn out with days and nights of strain and terror, the exile slept soundly. Soon, under the crisp autumn starlight, a red fox crept down circumspectly to hunt mice in the tangled dry grasses of the point. At sight of the strange white form sleeping carelessly at the foot of the rock he bounded back into cover, startled quite out of his philosophic composure. He had never before seen any such being as that; and the smell, too, was mysterious and hostile to his wrinkling fastidious nostrils. Having eyed the newcomer for some time from his hiding-place under the branches, he crept around the rock and surveyed him stealthily from the other side. Finding no enlightenment, or immediate prospect of it, he again drew back, and made a careful investigation of the stranger's tracks, which were quite unlike the tracks of any creature he knew. Finally he made up his mind that he must confine his hunting to the immediate neighbourhood, keeping the stranger under surveillance till he could fine out more about him.

Soon after the fox's going a tuft-eared lynx came out on the top of the rock, and with round, bright, cruel eyes glared down upon the grassy point, half-hoping to see some rabbits playing there. Instead, she saw the dim white bulk of the sleeping stallion. In her astonishment at this unheard-of apparition, her eyes grew wider and whiter than before, her hair stood up along her back, her absurd little stub of a tail fluffed out to a fussy pompon, and she uttered a hasty, spitting growl as she drew back into the shelter of the hemlocks. In the dreaming ears of the sleeper this angry sound was only a growl of the seas which had for days been clamouring about the gloom of his stall on the ship. It disturbed him not at all.

At about two o'clock in the morning, at that mystic hour when Nature seems to send a message to all her animate children, preparaing them for the advent of dawn, the white stallion got up, shook himself, stepped softly down to the brook's edge for a drink, and then fell to cropping the grass wherever it remained green. The forest, though to a careless ear it might have seemed as silent as before, had in reality stirred to a sudden, ephemeral life. Far off, from some high rock, a she-fox barked sharply. Faint, muffled chirps from the thick bushes told of junkos and chickadees waking up to see if all was well with the world. The mice set up a scurrying in the grass. And presently a high-antlered buck stepped out of the shadows and started across the open toward the brook.

The dark buck, himself a moving shadow, saw the stallion first, and stopped with a loud snort of astonishment and defiance. The stallion wheeled about, eyed the intruder for a moment doubtfully, then trotted up with a whinny of pleased interrogation. He had no dread of the antlered visitor, but rather a hope of companionship in the vast and overpowering loneliness of the alien night.

The buck, however, was in anything but a friendly mood. His veins aflame with the arrogant pugnacity of the rutting season, he saw in the white stranger only a possible rival, and grew hot with rage at his approach. With an impatient stamping of his slim fore hoofs, he gave challenge. But to the stallion this was an unknown language. Innocently he came up, his nose stretched out in question, till he was within a few feet of the motionless buck. Then, to his astonishment, the latter bounced suddenly aside like a ball, stood straight up on his hind legs, and struck at him like lightning with those keen-edged, slim fore hoofs. It was a savage assault, and two long, red furrows—one longer and deeper than the other—appeared on the stallion's silky, white flank.

In that instant the wanderer's friendliness vanished, and an avenging fury took its place. His confidence had been cruelly betrayed. With a harsh squeal, his mouth wide open and lips drawn back from his formidable teeth, he sprang at his assailant. But the buck had no vain idea of standing up against this whirlwind of wrath which he had evoked. He bounded aside, lightly but hurriedly, and watched for an opportunity to repeat his attack.

The stallion, however, was not to be caught again; and the dashing ferocity of his rushes kept his adversary ceaselessly on the move, bounding into the air and leaping aside to avoid those disastrous teeth. The buck was awaiting what he felt sure would come, the chance to strike again; and his confidence in his own supreme agility kept him from any apprehension as to the outcome of the fight.

But the buck's great weakness lay in his ignorance, his insufficient knowledge of the game he was playing. He had no idea that his rushing white antagonist had any other tactics at command. When he gave way, therefore, he went just far enough to escape the stallion's teeth and battering fore feet.

The stallion, on the other hand, soon realized the futility of his present method of attack against so nimble an adversary. On his next rush, therefore, just as the buck bounced aside, he wheeled in a short half-circle, and lashed out high and far with his steel-shod heels. The buck was just within the most deadly range of the blow. He caught the terrific impact on the base of the neck and the forward point of the shoulder, and went down as if an explosive bullet had struck him. Before he could even stir to rise, the stallion was upon him, trampling, battering, squealing, biting madly; and the fight was done. When the wanderer had spent his vengeance, and paused, snorting and wild-eyed, to take breath, he look down upon a mangled shape that no longer struggled or stirred or even breathed. Then the last of his righteous fury faded out. The sight and smell of the blood sickened him, and in a kind of terror he turned away. For a few hesitating moments he stared about his little retreat and then, finding it had grown hateful to him, he forsook it, and pushed onward up the edge of the stream, between the black, impending walls of the forest.

About daybreak he came out on the flat, marshy shores of a shrunken lake, the unstirred waters of which gleamed violet and pale-gold beneath the twisting coils and drifting plumes of white vapour. All around the lake stood the grim, serried lines of the firs, under a sky of palpitating opal. The marshes, in their autumn colouring of burnt gold and pinky olive, with here and there a little patch of enduring emerald, caught the wanderer's fancy with a faint reminder of home. Here was pasture, here was sweet water, here was room to get away from the oppressive mystery of the woods. He halted to rest and recover himself; and in the clear, tonic air, so cold that every morning the edges of the lake were crisped with ice, the aching red gashes on his flank speedily healed.

He had been at the lake about ten days, and was beginning to grow restlessly impatient of the unchanging solitude, before anything new took place. A vividly conspicuous object in his gleaming whiteness as he roamed the marshes, pasturing or galloping up and down the shore with streaming mane and tail, he had been seen and watched and wondered at by all the wild kindreds who had their habitations in the woods about the lake. But they had all kept carefully out of his sight, regarding him with no less terror than wonder; and he imagined himself utterly alone, except for the fish-hawks, and the southward journeying ducks, which would drop with loud quacking and splashing into the shallows after sunset, and the owls, the sombre hooting of which disturbed him every night. Several times, too, from the extreme head of the lake he heard a discordant call, a great braying bellow, which puzzled him, and brought him instantly to his feet by a note of challenge in it; but the issuer of this hoarse defiance never revealed himself. Sometimes he heard a similar call, with a difference—a longer, less harshly blatant cry, the under note of which was one of appeal rather than of challenge. Over both he puzzled in vain; for the moose, bulls and cows alike, had no wish to try the qualities of the great white stranger who seemed to have usurped the lordship of the lake.

At last, one violet evening in the close of the sunset, as he stood fetlock-deep in the chill water, drinking, a light sound of many feet caught his alert ear. Lifting his head quickly, he saw a herd of strange-looking, heavy-antlered, whitish-brown deer emerging in long line from the woods and crossing the open toward the foot of the lake. The leader of the caribou herd, a massive bull, nearly white, with antlers almost equal to those of a moose, returned the stallion's inquiring stare with a glance of mild curiosity, but did not halt an instant. It was plain that he considered his business urgent; for the caribou, as a rule, are nothing if not curious when confronted by any strange sight. But at present the whole herd, which journeyed, in the main, in single file, seemed to be in a kind of orderly haste. They turned questioning eyes upon the white stallion as they passed, then looked away indifferently, intent only upon following their leader on his quest. The stallion stood watching, his head high and his nostrils wide, till the very last of the herd had disappeared into the woods across the lake. Then the loneliness of his spacious pasture all at once quite overwhelmed him. He did not want the company of the caribou, by any means, or he might have followed them as they turned their backs toward the sunset; but it was the dwellings of men he wanted, the human hand on his mane, the provendered stall, the voice of kindly command, and the fellowship of his kindred of the uncleft hoof. In some way he had got it into his head that men might be found most readily by travelling toward the south-west. Toward the head of the lake, therefore, and just a little south of the sunset's deepest glow, he now took his way. He was done with the lake and the empty marshes.

From the head of the lake he followed up a narrow still-water for perhaps half a mile, crashing his way through a difficult tangle of fallen, rotting trunks and dense underbrush, till he came out upon another and much smaller lake, very different from the one he had just left. Here were no meadowy margins; but the shores were steep and thick-wooded to the water's edge. Diagonally thrust out across the outlet, and about a hundred yards above it, ran a low, bare spit of white sand, evidently covered at high water. Over the black line of the woods hung a yellow crescent moon, only a few nights old and near setting.

Coming suddenly from the difficult gloom of the woods, where the noise of his own movements kept his senses occupied to the exclusion of all else, the wanderer stopped and stood quite still for a long time under the shadow of a thick hemlock, investigating this new world with ear and eye and nostril. Presently, a few hundred yards around the lake shore, to his left, almost opposite the jutting sand-spit, arose a noisy crashing and thrashing of the bushes. As he listened in wonder, his ears erect and eagerly interrogative, the noise stopped, and again the intense silence settled down upon the forest. A minute or two later a big, high-shouldered, shambling, hornless creature came out upon the sand-spit, stood blackly silhouetted against the moonlight, stretched its ungainly neck, and sent across the water that harsh, bleating cry of appeal which he had been hearing night after night. It was the cow moose calling for her mate. And in almost instant answer arose again that great crashing among the underbrush on the opposite shore.

With a certain nervousness added to his curiosity, the white stallion listened as the crashing noise drew near. At the same time something in his blood began to tingle with the lust of combat. There was menace in the approaching sounds, and his courage arose to meet it. All at once, within about fifty yards of him, and just across the outlet, the noise ceased absolutely. For perhaps ten minutes there was not a sound,—

"IT WAS THE COW MOOSE CALLING FOR HER MATE."

not the snap of a twig or the splash of a ripple,—except that twice again came the call of the solitary cow standing out against the moon. Then, so suddenly that he gave an involuntary snort of amazement at the apparition, the wanderer grew aware of a tall, black bulk with enormous antlers which took shape among the undergrowth not ten paces distant.

The wanderer's mane rose along his arched neck, his lips drew back savagely over his great white teeth, fire flamed into his eyes, and for a score of seconds he stared into the wicked, little, gleaming eyes of the bull moose. He was eager for the fight, but waiting for the enemy to begin. Then, as noiselessly and miraculously as he had come, the great moose disappeared, simply fading into the darkness, and leaving the stallion all a-tremble with apprehension. For some minutes he peered anxiously into every black thicket within reach of his eyes, expecting a rushing assault from some unexpected quarter. Then, glancing out again across the lake, he saw that the cow had vanished from the moonlit point. Bewildered, and in the grasp of an inexplicable trepidation, he waded out into the lake belly-deep, skirted around the south shore, climbed the steep slope, and plunged straight into the dark of the woods. His impulse was to get away at once from the mysteries of that little, lonely lake.

The deep woods, of course, for him were just as lonely as the lake, for his heedless trampling and conspicuous colouring made a solitude all about him as he went. At last, however, he stumbled upon a trail. This he adopted gladly as his path, for it led away from the lake and in a direction which his whim had elected to follow.

Moving now on the deep turf, with little sound save the occasional swish of branches that brushed his flanks, he began to realize that the woods were not as empty as he had thought. On each side, in the soft dark, he heard little squeaks and rustlings and scurryings. Rabbits went bounding across the trail, just under his nose. Once a fox trotted ahead of him, looking back coolly at the great, white stranger. Once a small, stripe-backed animal passed leisurely before him, and a whiff of pungent smell annoyed his sensitive nose. Wide wings winnowed over him now and then, making him jump nervously; and once a pouncing sound, followed by a snarl, a squeal, and a scuffle, moved him to so keen an excitement that he swerved a few steps from the trail in his anxiety to see what it was all about. He failed to see anything, however, and after much stumbling was relieved to get back to the easy trail again. With all these unusual interests the miles and the hours seemed short to him; and when the gray of dawn came filtering down among the trees, he saw before him a clearing with two low-roofed cabins in the middle of it. Wild with delight at this evidence of man's presence, he neighed shrilly, and tore up to the door of the nearest cabin at full gallop, his hoofs clattering on the old chips which strewed the open.

To his bitter disappointment, he found the cabin, which was simply an old lumber-camp, deserted. The door being ajar, he nosed it open and entered. The damp, cheerless interior, with no furnishing but a rusty stove, a long bench hewn from a log, and a tier of bunks along one side, disheartened him. The smell of human occupation still lingered about the bunks, but all else savoured of desertion and decay. With drooping head he emerged, and crossed over to the log stable. That horses had occupied it once, though not recently, was plain to him through various unmistakable signs; but it was more in the hope of sniffing the scent of his own kind than from any expectation of finding the stable occupied that he poked his nose in through the open doorway.

It was not scent of horses, however, which now greeted his startled nostrils. It was a scent quite unfamiliar to him, but one which, nevertheless, filled him with instinctive apprehension. At the first whiff of it he started back. Then, impelled by his curiosity, he again looked in, peering into the gloom. The next instant he was aware of a huge black shape leaping straight at him. Springing back with a loud snort, he wheeled like lightning, and lashed out madly with his heels.

The bear caught the blow full in the ribs, and staggered against the door-post with a loud, grunting cough, while the stallion trotted off some twenty yards across the chips and paused, wondering. The blow, in all probability, had broken several of the bear's ribs, but without greatly impairing his capacity for a fight; and now, in a blind rage, he rushed again upon the intruder who had dealt him so rude a buffet. The stallion, however, was in no fighting mood. Depressed as he was by the desolation of the cabin, and daunted by the mysterious character of this attack from the dark of the stable, he was now like a child frightened of ghosts. Not the bear alone, but the whole place, terrified him. Away he went at full gallop across the clearing, by good fortune struck the continuation of the loggers' road, and plunged onward into the shadowy forest.

For a couple of miles he ran, then he slowed down to a trot, and at last dropped into a leisurely walk. This trail was much broader and clearer than the one which had led him to the camp, and a short, sweet grass grew along it, so that he pastured comfortably without much loss of time. The spirit of his quest, however, was now so strong upon him that he would not rest after feeding. Mile after mile he pressed on, till the sun was high in the clear, blue heavens, and the shadows of the ancient firs were short and luminous. Then suddenly the woods broke away before him.

Far below he saw the blue sea sparkling. But it was not the beauty of the sea that held his eyes. From his very feet the road dropped down through open, half-cleared burnt lands, a stretch of rough pasture-fields, and a belt of sloping meadow, to a little white village clustering about an inlet. The clutter of roofs was homelike to his eyes, hungry with long loneliness; the little white church, with shining spire and cross, was very homelike. But nearer, in the very first pasture-field, just across the burnt land, was a sight that came yet nearer to his heart. There, in a corner of the crooked snake-fence, stood two bay mares and a foal, their heads over the fence as they gazed up the hill in his direction. Up went mane and tail, and loud and long he neighed to them his greeting. Their answer was a whinny of welcome, and down across the fields he dashed at a wild gallop that took no heed of fences. When, a little later in the day, a swarthy French-Canadian farmer came up from the village to lead his mares down to water, he was bewildered with delight to find himself the apparent master of a splendid white stallion, which insisted on claiming him, nosing him joyously, and following at his heels like a dog.

The Iron Edge of Winter *

The glory of the leaves was gone; the glory of the snow was not yet come; and the world, smitten with bitter frost, was grey like steel. The ice was black and clear and vitreous on the forest pools. The clods on the ploughed field, the broken hillocks in the pasture, the ruts of the winding backwoods road, were hard as iron and rang under the travelling hoof. The silent, naked woods, moved only by the bleak wind drawing through them from the north, seemed as if life had forgotten them.

Suddenly there came a light thud, thud, thud, with a pattering of brittle leaves; and a leisurely rabbit hopped by, apparently on no special errand. At the first of the sounds, a small, ruddy head with bulging, big, bright eyes had appeared at the mouth of a hole under the roots of an ancient maple. The bright eyes noted the rabbit at once, and peered about anxiously to see if any enemy were following. There was no danger in sight.

Within two or three feet of the hole under the maple the rabbit stopped, sat up as if begging, waved its great ears to and fro, and glanced around inquiringly with its protruding, foolish eyes. As it sat up, it felt beneath its whitey fluff of a tail something hard which was not a stone, and promptly dropped down again on all fours to investigate. Poking its nose among the leaves and scratching with its fore-paws, it uncovered a pile of beech-nuts, at which it began to sniff. The next instant, with a shrill, chattering torrent of invective, a red squirrel whisked out from the hole under the maple, and made as if to fly in the face of the big, good-natured trespasser. Startled and abashed by this noisy assault, the rabbit went bounding away over the dead leaves and disappeared among the desolate grey arches.

The silence was effectually dispelled. Shrieking and scolding hysterically, flicking his long tail in spasmodic jerks, and calling the dead solitudes to witness that the imbecile intruder had uncovered one of his treasure-heaps, the angry

* From *The Backwoodsmen* (New York: Macmillan, 1909), 193-98. "The Iron Edge of Winter" also appeared in *The Windsor Magazine* (Dec. 1908).

squirrel ran up and down the trunk for at least two minutes. Then, his feelings somewhat relieved by this violent outburst, he set himself to gathering the scattered nuts and bestowing them in new and safer hiding-places.

In this task he had little regard for convenience, and time appeared to be no object whatever. Some of the nuts he took over to a big elm fifty paces distant, and jammed them one by one, solidly and conscientiously, into the crevices of the bark. Others he carried in the opposite direction, to the edge of the open where the road ran by. These he hid under a stone, where the passing wayfarer might step over them, indeed, but would never think of looking for them. While he was thus occupied, an old countryman slouched by, his heavy boots making a noise on the frozen ruts, his nose red with the harsh, unmitigated cold. The squirrel, mounted on a fence stake, greeted him with a flood of whistling and shrieking abuse; and he, not versed in the squirrel tongue, muttered to himself half enviously: "Queer how them squur'ls can keep so cheerful in this weather." The tireless little animal followed him along the fence rails for perhaps a hundred yards, seeing him off the premises and advising him not to return, then went back in high feather to his task. When all the nuts were once more safely hidden but two or three, these latter he carried to the top of a stump close beside the hole in the maple, and proceeded to make a meal. The stump commanded a view on all sides; and as he sat up with a nut between his little, handlike, clever fore-paws, his shining eyes kept watch on every path by which an enemy might approach.

Having finished the nuts, and scratched his ears, and jumped twice around on the stump as if he were full of erratically acting springs, he uttered his satisfaction in a long, vibrant chir-r-r-r, and started to re-enter his hole in the maple-roots. Just at the door, however, he changed his mind. For no apparent reason he wisked about, scurried across the ground to the big elm, ran straight up the tall trunk, and disappeared within what looked like a mass of sticks perched among the topmost branches.

The mass of sticks was a deserted crow's nest, which the squirrel, not content with one dwelling, had made over to suit his own personal needs. He had greatly improved upon the architecture of the crows, giving the nest a tight roof of twigs and moss, and lining the snug interior with fine dry grass and soft fibres of cedar-bark. In this secure and softly swaying refuge, far above the reach of prowling foxes, he curled himself up for a nap after his toil.

He slept well, but not long; for the red squirrel has always something on his mind to see to. In less than half an hour he whisked out again in great excitement, jumped from branch to branch till he was many yards from his own tree, and then burst forth into vehement chatter. He must have dreamed that some one was rifling his hoards, for he ran eagerly from one hiding-place to another and examined them all suspiciously. As he had at least two-score to inspect, it took him some time; but not till he had looked at every one did he seem satisfied. Then he grew very angry, and scolded and chirruped, as if he thought some one had made a fool of him. That he had made a fool of himself probably never entered his confident and self-sufficient little head.

While indulging this noisy volubility he was seated on the top of his dining-stump. Suddenly he caught sight of something that smote him into silence and for the space of a second turned him to stone. A few paces away was a weasel, gliding toward him like a streak of baleful light. For one second only he crouched. Then his faculties returned, and launching himself through the air he landed on the trunk of the maple and darted up among the branches.

No less swiftly the weasel followed, hungry, bloodthirsty, relentless on the trail. Terrified into folly by the suddenness and deadliness of this peril, the squirrel ran too far up the tree and was almost cornered. Where the branches were small there was no chance to swing to another tree. Perceiving this mistake, he gave a squeak of terror, then bounded madly right over his enemy's head, and was lucky enough to catch foothold far out on a lower branch. Recovering himself in an instant, he shot into the next tree, and thence to the next and the next. Then, breathless from panic rather than from exhaustion, he crouched trembling behind a branch and waited.

The weasel pursued more slowly, but inexorably as doom itself. He was not so clever at branch-jumping as his intended prey, but he was not to be shaken off. In less than a minute he was following the scent up the tree wherein the squirrel was hiding; and again the squirrel dashed off in his desperate flight. Twice more was this repeated, the squirrel each time more panic-stricken and with less power in nerve or muscle. Then wisdom forsook his brain utterly. He fled straight to his elm and darted into his nest in the swaying top. The weasel, running lithely up the ragged trunk, knew that the chase was at an end. From this *cul de sac* the squirrel had no escape.

But Fate is whimsical in dealing with the wild kindreds. She seems to delight in unlooked-for interventions. While the squirrel trembled in his dark nest, and the weasel, intent upon the first taste of warm blood in his throat, ran heedlessly up a bare stretch of the trunk, there came the chance which a foraging hawk had been waiting for. The hawk, too, had been following this breathless chase, but ever baffled by intervening branches. Now he swooped and struck. His talons had the grip of steel. The weasel, plucked irresistibly from his foothold, was carried off writhing to make the great bird's feast. And the squirrel, realizing at last that the expected doom had been somehow turned aside, came out and chattered feebly of his triumph.

The Grip in Deep Hole*

The roar of the falls, the lighter and shriller raging of the rapids, had at last died out behind the thick masses of the forest, as Barnes worked his way down the valley. The heat in the windless underbrush, alive with insects, was stifling. He decided to make once more for the bank of the stream, in the hope that its character might by this time have changed, so as to afford him an easier and more open path. Pressing aside to his left, he presently saw the green gloom lighten before him. Blue sky and golden light came low through the thinning trees, and then a gleam of unruffled water. He was nearing the edge now; and because the underbrush was so thick about him he began to go cautiously.

All at once, he felt his feet sinking; and the screen of thick bushes before him leaned away as if bowed by a heavy gust. Desperately he clutched with both hands at the undergrowth and saplings on either side; but they all gave way with him. In a smother of leafage and blinding, lashing branches he sank downwards—at first, as it seemed, slowly, for he had time to think many things while his heart was jumping in his throat. Then, shooting through the lighter bushy companions of his fall, and still clutching convulsively at those upon which he had been able to lay his grasp, he plunged feet first into a dark water.

The water was deep and cold. Barnes went down straight, and clear under, with a strangled gasp. His feet struck, with some force, upon a tangled, yielding mass, from which he rose again with a spring. His head shot up above the surface, above the swirl of foam, leafage, and débris; and splutteringly he gulped his lungs full of air. But before he could clear his eyes or his nostrils, or recover his self-possession, he was stealthily dragged down again. And with a pang of horror he realized that he was caught by the foot.

A powerful swimmer, Barnes struck out mightily with his arms and came to the surface again at once, rising beyond the

---

* From *The Backwoodsmen* (New York: Macmillan, 1909), 199-210. "The Grip in Deep Hole" also appeared in *Chamber's Journal* (Feb. 1909), *Hampton's Magazine* (Nov. 1909), and *Canadian Magazine* (Sept. 1913).

shoulders. But by so much the more was he violently snatched back again, strangling and desperate, before he had time to empty his lungs and catch breath. This time the shock sobered him, flashing the full peril of the situation before his startled consciousness. With a tremendous effort of will he stopped his struggling, and contented himself with a gentle paddling to keep upright. This time he came more softly to the surface, clear beyond the chin. The foam and débris and turbulence of little waves seethed about his lips, and the sunlight danced confusingly in his streaming eyes; but he gulped a fresh lungful before he again went under.

Paddling warily now, he emerged again at once, and, with arms outspread, brought himself to a precarious equilibrium, his mouth just above the surface so long as he held his head well back. Keeping very still, he let his bewildered wits clear, and the agitated surface settle to quiet.

He was in a deep, tranquil cove, hardly stirred by an eddy. Some ten paces farther out from shore the main current swirled past sullenly, as if weary from the riot of falls and rapids. Across the current a little space of sand-beach, jutting out from the leafy shore, shone golden in the sun. Up and down the stream, as far as his extremely restricted vision would suffer him to see, nothing but thick, overhanging branches, and the sullen current. Very cautiously he turned his head—though to do so brought the water over his lips—and saw behind him just what he expected. The high, almost perpendicular bank was scarred by a gash of bright, raw, reddish earth, where the brink had slipped away beneath his weight.

Just within reach of his hand lay, half submerged, the thick, leafy top of a fallen poplar sapling, its roots apparently still clinging to the bank. Gently he laid hold of it, testing it, in the hope that it might prove solid enough to enable him to haul himself out. But it came away instantly in his grasp. And once more, in this slight disturbance of his equilibrium, his head went under.

Barnes was disappointed, but he was now absolutely master of his self-possession. In a moment he had regained the only position in which he could breathe comfortably. Then, because the sun was beating down too fiercely on the top of his head, he carefully drew the bushy top of the poplar sapling into such a position that it gave him shade. As its roots were still aground, it showed no tendency to float off and forsake him in his plight.

A very little consideration, accompanied by a cautious investigation with his free foot, speedily convinced Barnes, who was a practical woodsman, that the trap in which he found himself caught could be nothing else than a couple of interlaced, twisted branches, or roots, of some tree which had fallen into the pool in a former caving-in of the bank. In that dark deep wherein his foot was held fast, his mind's eye could see it all well enough—the water-soaked, brown-green, slimy, inexorable coil, which had yielded to admit the unlucky member, then closed upon the ankle like the jaws of an otter trap. He could feel that grip—not severe, but uncompromisingly firm, clutching the joint. As he considered, he began to draw comfort, however, from the fact that his invisible captor had displayed a certain amount of give and take. This elasticity meant either that it was a couple of branches slight enough to be flexible that held him, or that the submerged tree itself was a small one, not too steadfastly anchored down. He would free himself easily enough, he thought, as soon as he should set himself about it cooly and systematically.

Taking a long breath he sank his head under the surface, and peered downward through the amber-brown but transparent gloom. Little gleams of brighter light came twisting and quivering in from the swirls of the outer current. Barnes could not discern the bottom of the pool, which was evidently very deep; but he could see quite clearly the portion of the sunken tree in whose interwoven branches he was held. A shimmering golden ray fell just on the spot where his foot vanished to the ankle between two stout curves of what looked like slimy brown cable or sections of a tense snake body.

It was, beyond question, a nasty-looking trap; and Barnes could not blink the fact that he was in a tight place. He lifted his face above the surface, steadied himself carefully, and breathed deeply and quietly for a couple of minutes, gathering strength for a swift and vigorous effort. Then, filling his lungs very moderately, the better to endure a strain, he stooped suddenly downward, deep into the yellow gloom, and began wrenching with all his force at those oozy curves, striving to drag them apart. They gave a little, but not enough to release the imprisoned foot. Another moment, and he had to lift his head again for breath.

After some minutes of rest, he repeated the choking struggle, but, as before, in vain. He could move the jaws of the trap just enough to encourage him a little, but not enough to gain his release. Again and again he tried it, again and again to fail just as he imagined himself on the verge of success; till at last he was forced, for the moment, to acknowledge defeat, finding himself so exhausted that he could hardly keep his mouth above water. Drawing down a stiffish branch of the sapling, he gripped it between his teeth and so held himself upright while he rested his arms. This was a relief to nerves as well as muscles, because it made his balance, on which he depended for the chance to breathe, so much the less precarious.

As he hung there pondering, held but a bare half-inch above drowning, the desperateness of the situation presented itself to him in appalling clearness. How sunny and warm and safe, to his woods-familiar eyes, looked the green forest world about him. No sound broke the mild tranquillity of the solitude, except, now and then, an elfish gurgle of the slow current, or the sweetly cheerful *tsic-a-dee-dee* of an unseen chicadee, or, from the intense blue overhead, the abrupt, thin whistle of a soaring fish-hawk. To Barnes it all seemed such a safe, friendly world, his well-understood intimate since small boyhood. Yet here it was, apparently, turned smooth traitor at last, and about to destroy him as pitilessly as might the most scorching desert or blizzard-scourged ice-field. A silent rage burned suddenly through all his veins—which was well, since the cold of that spring-fed river had already began to finger stealthily about his heart. A delicate little pale-blue butterfly, like a periwinkle-petal come to life, fluttered over Barnes's grim, upturned face, and went dancing gaily out across the shining water, joyous in the sun. In its dancing it chanced to dip a hair's-breath too low. The treacherous, bright surface caught it, held it; and away it swept, struggling in helpless consternation against this unexpected doom. Before it passed out of Barnes's vision a great trout rose and gulped it down. Its swift fate, to Barnes's haggard eyes, seemed an analogue in little to his own.

But it was not in the woodsman's fibre to acknowledge himself actually beaten, either by man or fate, so long as there remained a spark in his brain to keep his will alive. He presently began searching with his eyes among the branches of the poplar sapling for one stout enough to serve him as a lever. With the right kind of a stick in his hand, he told himself, he might manage to pry apart the jaws of the trap and get his foot free. At last his choice settled upon a branch that he thought would serve his turn. He was just about to reach up and break it off, when a slight crackling in the underbrush across the stream caught his ear.

His woodman's instinct kept him motionless as he turned his eyes to the spot. In the thick leafage there was a swaying, which moved down along the bank, but he could not see what was causing it. Softly he drew over a leafy branch of the sapling till it made him a perfect screen, then he peered up the channel to find out what the unseen wayfarer was following.

A huge salmon, battered and gashed from a vain struggle to leap the falls, was floating, belly-upward, down the current, close to Barnes's side of the stream. A gentle eddy caught it, and drew it into the pool. Sluggishly it came drifting down toward Barnes's hidden face. In the twigs of the popular sapling it came to a halt, its great scarlet gills barely moving as the last of life flickered out of it.

Barnes now understood quite well that unseen commotion which had followed, along shore, the course of the dying salmon. It was no surprise to him whatever when he saw a huge black bear emerge upon the yellow sandspit and stand staring across the current. Apparently, it was staring straight at Barnes's face, upturned upon the surface of the water. But Barnes knew it was staring at the dead salmon. His heart jumped sickeningly with sudden hope, as an extravagant notion flashed into his brain. Here was his rescuer—a perilous one, to be sure—vouchsafed to him by some whim of the inscrutable forest-fates.

He drew down another branchy twig before his face, fearful lest his concealment should not be adequate. But in his excitement he disturbed his balance, and with the effort of his recovery the water swirled noticeably all about him. His heart sank. Assuredly, the bear would take alarm at this and be afraid to come for the fish.

But to his surprise the great beast, which had seemed to hesitate, plunged impetuously into the stream. Nothing, according to a bear's knowledge of life, could have made that sudden disturbance in the pool but some fish-loving otter or mink, intent upon seizing the booty. Indignant at the prospect of being forestalled by any such furtive marauder, the bear hurled himself forward with such force that the spray flew high into the branches, and the noise of his splashing was a clear notification that trespassers and meddlers had better keep off. That salmon was his, by right of discovery; and he was going to have it.

The bear, for all the seeming clumsiness of his bulk, was a redoubtable swimmer; and almost before Barnes had decided clearly on his proper course of action those heavy, grunting snorts and vast expulsions of breath were at his ear. Enormously loud they sounded, shot thus close along the surface of the water. Perforce, Barnes made up his mind on the instant.

The bunch of twigs which had arrested the progress of the floating salmon lay just about an arm's length from Barnes's face. Swimming high, his mighty shoulders thrusting up a wave before him which buried Barnes's head safely from view, the bear reached the salmon. Grabbing it triumphantly in his jaws, he turned to make for shore again.

This was Barnes's moment. Both arms shot out before him. Through the suffocating confusion his clutching fingers encountered the bear's haunches. Sinking into the long fur, they closed upon it with a grip of steel. Then, instinctively, Barnes shut his eyes and clenched his teeth, and waited for the shock, while his lungs felt as if they would burst in another moment.

But it was no long time he had to wait—perhaps two seconds, while amazement in the bear's brain translated itself through panic into action. Utterly horrified by this inexplicable attack, from the rear and from the depths, the bear threw himself shoulder high from the water, and hurled himself forward with all his strength. Barnes felt those tremendous haunches heaving irresistibly beneath his clutching fingers. He felt himself drawn out straight, and dragged ahead till he thought his ankle would snap. Almost he came to letting go, to save the ankle. But he held on, as much with his will as with his grip. Then, the slimy thing in the depths gave way. He felt himself being jerked through the water—free. His fingers relaxed their clutch on the bear's fur—and he came to the surface, gasping, blinking, and coughing.

For a moment or two he paddled softly, recovering his breath and shaking the water from nostrils and eyes. He had an instant of apprehensiveness, lest the bear should turn upon him and attack him at a disadvantage; and by way of precaution he gave forth the most savage and piercing yell that his labouring lungs were capable of. But he saw at once that on this score he had nothing to fear. It was a well-frightened bear, there swimming frantically for the sandspit; while the dead salmon, quite forgotten, was drifting slowly away on the sullen current.

Barnes's foot was hurting fiercely, but his heart was light. Swimming at leisure, so as to just keep head against the stream, he watched the bear scuttle out upon the sand. Once safe on dry land, the great beast turned and glanced back with a timid air to see what manner of being it was that had so astoundingly assailed him. Man he had seen before—but never man swimming like an otter; and the sight was nothing to reassure him. One longing look he cast upon the salmon, now floating some distance away; but that, to his startled mind, was just a lure of this same terrifying and perfidious creature whose bright grey eyes were staring at him so steadily from the surface of the water. He turned quickly and made off into the woods, followed by a loud, daunting laugh which spurred his pace to a panicky gallop.

When he was gone, Barnes swam to the sandspit. There he wrung out his dripping clothes, and lay down in the hot sand to let the sun soak deep into his chilled veins.

The Nest of the Mallard*

When the spring freshet went down, and the rushes sprang green all about the edges of the shallow, marshy lagoons, a pair of mallards took possession of a tiny, bushy island in the centre of the broadest pond. Moved by one of those inexplicable caprices which keep most of the wild kindreds from too perilous an enslavement to routine, this pair had been attracted by the vast, empty levels of marsh and mere, and had dropped out from the ranks of their northward-journeying comrades. Why should they beat on through the raw, blustering spring winds to Labrador, when here below them was such a nesting-place as they desired, with solitude and security and plenty. The flock went on, obeying an ancestral summons. With heads straight out before, and rigid, level necks—with web feet folded like fans and stretched straight out behind, rigid and level—they sped through the air on short, powerful, swift-beating wings at the rate of sixty or seventy miles an hour. Their flight, indeed, and their terrific speed were not unlike those of some strange missile. The pair who had dropped behind paid no heed to their going; and in two minutes they had faded out against the pale saffron morning sky.

These two were the only mallards in this whole wide expanse of grass and water. Other kinds of ducks there were, in plenty, but the mallards at this season kept to themselves. The little island which they selected for their peculiar domain was so small that no other mating couples intruded upon its privacy. It was only about ten feet across; but it bore a favourable thicket of osier-willow, and all around it the sedge and bulrush reared an impenetrable screen. Its highest point was about two feet above average water level; and on this highest point the mallard duck established her nest.

The nest was a mere shallow pile of dead leaves and twigs and dry sedges, scraped carelessly together. But the inside was not careless. It was a round smooth hollow, most softly lined with down from the duck's own breast. When the first pale,

* From *The Backwoodsmen* (New York: Macmillan, 1909), 211-18.

greenish-tinted egg was laid in the nest, there was only a little of this down; but the delicate and warm lining accumulated as the pale green eggs increased in number.

In the construction of the nest and the accumulation of the eggs no interest whatever was displayed by the splendid drake. He never, unless by chance, went near it. But as a lover the lordly fellow was most gallant and ardent. While his mate was on the nest laying, he was usually to be seen floating on the open mere beyond the reed-fringe, pruning his plumage in the cold pink rays of the first of the sunrise.

It was plumage well worth pruning, this of his, and fully justified his pride in it. The shining, silken, iridescent dark green of the head and neck; the snowy, sharply defined, narrow collar of white, dividing the green of the neck from the brownish ash of the back and the gorgeous chestnut of the breast; the delicate pure grey of the belly finely pencilled with black lines; the rich, glossy purple of the broad wing-bars shot with green reflections; the jaunty, recurved black feathers of the tail; the smart, citron-yellow of the bill and feet;—all these charms were ample excuse for his coxcombry and continual posings. They were ample excuse, too, for the admiration bestowed upon him by his mottled brown mate, whose colours were obviously designed not for show but for concealment. When sitting on her nest, she was practically indistinguishable from the twigs and dead leaves that surrounded her.

Having laid her egg, the brown duck would cover the precious contents of the nest with twigs and leaves, that they might not be betrayed by their conspicuous colour. Then she would steal, silently as a shadow, through the willow stems to the water's edge, and paddle cautiously out through the rushes to the open water. On reaching her mate all this caution would be laid aside, and the two would set up an animated and confidential quacking. They would sometimes sail around each other slowly in circles, with much arching of necks and quaint stiff bowing of heads; and sometimes they would chase each other in scurrying, flapping rushes along the bright surface of the water. Both before and after these gay exercises they would feed quietly in the shallows, pulling up water-weed sprouts and tender roots, or sifting insects and little shellfish from the mud by means of the sensitive tips and guttered edges of their bills.

The mallard pair had few enemies to dread, their island being so far from shore that no four-footed marauder, not even the semi-amphibious mink himself, ever visited it. And the region was one too remote for the visits of the pot-hunter. In fact, there was only one foe against whom it behoved them to be on ceaseless guard. This was that bloodthirsty and tireless slayer, the goshawk, or great grey henhawk. Where that grim peril was concerned, the brown duck would take no risks. For the sake of those eggs among the willow stems, she held her life very dear, never flying more than a short circle around the island to stretch her wings, never swimming or feeding any distance from the safe covert of the rushes.

But with the glowing drake it was different. High spirited, bold for all his wariness, and magnificently strong of wing, from sheer restlessness he occasionally flew high above the ponds. And one day, when some distance from home, the great hawk saw him and swooped down upon him from aërial heights.

The impending doom caught the drake's eye in time for him to avoid the stroke of that irresistible descent. His short wings, with their muscles of steel, winnowed the air with sudden, tremendous force, and he shot ahead at a speed which must have reached the rate of a hundred miles an hour. When the swooping hawk had rushed down to his level, he was nearly fifty yards in the lead.

In such a case most of the larger hawks would have given up the chase, and soared again to abide the chance for a more fortunate swoop. But not so the implacable goshawk. His great pinions were capable not only of soaring and sailing and swooping, but of the rapid and violent flapping of the short-winged birds; and he had at his command a speed even greater than that of the rushing fugitive. As he pursued, his wings tore the air with a strident, hissing noise; and the speed of the drake seemed as nothing before that savage, inescapable onrush. Had the drake been above open water, he would have hurled himself straight downward, and seized the one chance of escape by diving; but beneath him at this moment there was nothing but naked swamp and sloppy flats. In less than two minutes the hiss of the pursuing wings was close behind him. He gave a hoarse squawk, as he realized that doom had overtaken him.

Then one set of piercing talons clutched his outstretched neck, cutting clean through his wind-pipe; and another set bit deep into the glossy chestnut of his breast.

For several days the widowed duck kept calling loudly up and down the edges of the reeds—but at a safe distance from the nest. When she went to lay, she stayed ever longer and longer on the eggs, brooding them. Three more eggs she laid after the disappearance of her mate, and then, having nine in the nest, she began to sit; and the open water beyond the reed fringes saw her no more.

At first she would slip off the nest for a few minutes every day, very stealthily, to feed and stretch and take a noiseless dip in the shallow water among the reeds; but as time went on she left the eggs only once in two days. Twice a day she would turn the eggs over carefully, and at the same time change their respective positions in the nest, so that those which had been for some hours in the centre, close to her hot and almost naked breast, might take their turn in the cooler space just under her wings. By this means each egg got its fair share of heat, properly distributed, and the little life taking shape within escaped the distortion which might have been caused by lying too long in one position. Whenever the wary brown mother left the nest, she covered the eggs with down, now, which kept the warmth in better than leaves could. And whenever she came back from her brief swim, her dripping feathers supplied the eggs with needed moisture.

It is a general law that the older an egg is the longer it takes to hatch. The eggs of the mallard mother, of course, varied in age from fifteen days to one before she began to sit. This being the case, at the end of the long month of incubation they would have hatched at intervals covering in all, perhaps, a full day and a half; and complications would have arisen. But the wise mother had counteracted the working of the law by sitting a little while every day. Therefore, as a matter of fact, the older eggs got the larger share of the brooding, in exact proportion; and the building of the little lives within the shells went on with almost perfect uniformity.

During the long, silent month of her patient brooding, spring had wandered away and summer had spread thick green and yellow lily blooms all over the lonely meres. A bland but heavy heat came down through the willow tops, so that the brown duck sometimes panted at her task, and sat with open bill, or with wings half raised from the eggs. Then, one night, she heard faint tappings and peepings beneath her. Sturdy young bills began chipping at the inside of the shells, speedily breaking them. Each duckling, as he chipped the shell just before the tip of his beak, would turn a little way around in his narrow quarters; till presently the shell would fall apart, neatly divided into halves; and the wet duckling, tumbling forth, would snuggle up against the mother's hot breast and thighs to dry. Whenever this happened, the wise mother would reach her head beneath, and fit the two halves of shell one within the other, or else thrust them out of the nest entirely, lest they should get slipped over another egg and smother the occupant. Sometimes she fitted several sets of the empty shells together, that they might take up less room; and altogether she showed that she perfectly understood her business. Then, late in the morning, when the green world among the willows and rushes was still and warm and sweet, she led her fluffy, sturdy brood straight down to the water, and taught them to feed on the insects that clung to the bulrush stalks.

The Sentry of the Sedge Flats*

Pale, shimmering green, and soaked in sun, the miles of sedge-flats lay outspread from the edges of the slow bright water to the foot of the far, dark-wooded purple hills. Winding through the quiet green levels came a tranquil little stream. Where its sleepy current joined the great parent river, a narrow tongue of bare sand jutted out into the golden-glowing water. At the extreme tip of the sand-spit towered, sentry-like, a long-legged grey-blue bird, as motionless as if he had been transplanted thither from the panel of a Japanese screen.

The flat narrow head of the great heron, with its long, javelin-like, yellow beak and two slender black crest-feathers, was drawn far back by a curious undulation of the immensely long neck, till it rested between the humped blue wing-shoulders. From the lower part of the neck hung a fine fringe of vaporous rusty-grey plumes, which lightly veiled the chestnut-coloured breast. The bird might have seemed asleep, like the drowsy expanses of green sedge, silver-blue water, and opalescent turquoise sky, but for its eyes. Those eyes, round, unwinking, of a hard, glassy gold with intense black pupils, were unmistakably and savagely wide awake.

Over the tops of the sedges, fluttering and zig-zagging waywardly, came a big butterfly, its gorgeous red-brown wings pencilled with strange hieroglyphs in black and purple. It danced out a little way over the water; and then, as if suddenly terrified by the shining peril beneath, came wavering back toward shore. A stone's throw up the channel of the little stream lay a patch of vivid green, the leaves of the arrow-weed, with its delicate, pallid blooms dreaming in the still air above them. The butterfly saw these blossoms, or perhaps smelt them, and fluttered in their direction to see if those pure chalices held honey. But on his way he noted the moveless figure of the heron, conspicuous above the ranks of the sedge. Perhaps he took the curious shape for a post or a stump. In any

* From *Neighbours Unknown* (London: Ward, Lock, 1910), 45-63. "The Sentry of the Sedge Flats" also appeared in *The Windsor Magazine* (July 1910) and *Sunday Magazine* (May 8, 1910).

case, it seemed to offer an alluring place of rest, where he might pause for a moment and flaunt his glowing wings in the sun before dancing onward to the honey-blossoms. He flickered nearer. To him those unwinking jewels of eyes had no menace. He hovered an instant about two feet above them. In that instant, like a flash of light, the long, pale neck and straight yellow beak shot out; and the butterfly was caught neatly. Twisting his head shoreward, without shifting his feet, the heron struck the glowing velvet wings of the insect sharply on the sand. Then, having swallowed the morsel leisurely, he drew his head down again between his shoulders, and resumed his moveless waiting.

The next matter of interest to come within the vision of those inscrutable eyes was a dragon-fly chase. Hurtling low over the sedge-tops, and flashing in the sunlight like a lace-pin of rubies, came a small rose-coloured dragon-fly, fleeing for its life before a monster of its species which blazed in emerald and amethyst. The chase could have but one ending, for the giant had the speed as well as the voracious hunger. The glistening films of his wings rustled crisply as he overtook the shining fugitive and caught its slender body in his jaws. The silver wings of the victim vibrated wildly. The chase came to a hovering pause just before that immobile shape on the point of the sand-spit. Again the long yellow beak darted forth. And the radiant flies, captive and captor together, disappeared.

But such flimsy fare as even the biggest of butterflies and dragon-flies was not contenting to the sharp appetite of the heron. He took one stiff-legged stride forward, and stood in about six inches of water. Here he settled himself in a somewhat altered position, his back more awkwardly hunched, his head held lower, and his dagger of a bill pointing downward. His wicked golden eyes were not indifferent to the possibilities of the air above him, but they were now concerning themselves more particularly with the water which flowed about his feet.

If any one stands at the brink of a quiet summer stream, and keeps still enough, and watches intently enough, however deserted the landscape may appear, he will see life in many furtive forms go by. The great blue heron kept still enough. The water at this point went softly over a shoal half sand, half mud, and in the faint movement of the clear amber-brown current the sunlight wove a shimmering network on the bottom. Across this darted a shadow. The heron's beak shot downward with an almost inaudible splash, transfixing the shadow, and emerged with a glittering green and silver perch, perhaps five inches in length. The quivering body of the fish had its knife-edged gills wide open, and every spine of its formidable, armed fins threateningly erect. But the triumphant fisherman strode ashore with it and proceeded to hammer it into unconsciousness on the hard sand. Then he swallowed it head first, thus effectually disarming every weapon of fin and gill-cover. The progress of this substantial mouthful could be traced clearly down the bird's slim length of gullet, accompanied as it was by several seconds of contortions so violent that they made the round yellow eyes wink gravely. As soon as the morsel was fairly down the bird stretched its neck to its full length, with a curious hitch of the base as if to assure himself the process was completed. Then he resumed his post of watching. He had no more than taken his place than a huge black tadpole wriggled by over the gold-meshed bottom. It was speared and swallowed in an eye-wink. Soft, slippery, and spineless, it made but a moment's incident.

A little after, on the smooth surface of the smaller stream, some fifty feet up-channel, a tiny ripple appeared. Swiftly it drew near. It was pointed, and with a long fine curve of oily ripple trailing back from it on either side, like the outline of a comet's tail. As it approached, in the apex of the parabola could be seen a minute black nose, with two bright, dark little eyes just behind it. It was a small water-rat, voyaging adventurously out from its narrow inland haunts among the lilies.

The great heron eyed its approach. To the swimmer, no doubt, the blue-grey, immobile shape at the extremity of the sand-spit looked like some weather-beaten post, placed there by man for his inexplicable convenience in regard to hitching boats. But presently, something strange in the shape of the post seemed to strike the little voyager's attention. He stopped. Perhaps he saw the menacing glitter of that yellow, unwinking stare. After a moment of wavering irresolution, he changed his course, swam straight across channel, scrambled out upon the wet mud of the further shore, and vanished among the pale root-stalks of the sedge. The heron was savage with disappointment; but no slightest movement betrayed his anger, save that the pinkish film of the lower lid blinked up once, as it were with a snap, over each implacable eye. His time would come—which faith is that which supports all those who know how to wait. He peered up stream for the coming of another and less wary water-rat.

Instead of the expected ripple, however, he now caught sight of a shadow which flickered across the surface of the water and in an instant had vanished over the pale sea of the grass-tops. He looked up. In the blue above hung poised, his journeying flight just at that moment arrested, a wide-winged duck-hawk, boldest marauder of the air. The heron threw his head far back, till his beak pointed straight skyward. At the same time he half lifted his strong wings, poising himself to deliver a thrust with all the strength that was in him. On the instant the hawk dropped like a wedge of steel out of the sky, his rigid, half-closed pinions hissing with the speed of his descent. The heron never flinched. But within ten feet of him the hawk, having no mind to impale himself on that waiting spear-point, opened his wings, swerved upward, and went past with a harsh hum of wing-feathers. Wheeling again, almost instantly, he swooped back to the attack, buffeting the air just above the heron's head, but taking care not to come within range of the deadly beak. The heron refused to be drawn from his position of effective defence, and made no movement except to keep the point of his lance ever toward the foe. And presently the hawk, seeing the futility of his assaults, winged off sullenly to hunt for some unwary duck or gosling.

As he went the heron stretched himself to his full gaunt height and stared after him in triumph. Then, turning his head slowly, he scanned the whole expanse of windless grass and sunlit water. One sight fixed his attention. Far up the windings of the lesser stream he marked a man in a boat. The man was not rowing, but sitting in the stern and propelling the boat noiselessly with an Indian paddle. From time to time he halted and examined the shore minutely. Once in a while, after such an examination, he would get out, kneel down, and be occupied for several minutes among the weeds of the shallows along the stream's edge. He was looking at the musquash holes in the bank, and setting traps before those which showed signs of present occupancy. The heron watched the process, unstirring as a dead stump, till he thought the man was coming too near. Then, spreading a vast, dark pair of wings, he arose indignantly and flapped heavily away up river, trailing his length of black legs just over the sedge tops.

Not far above the mouth of the stream the man set the last of his musquash traps. Then he paddled back leisurely by the way he had come, his dingy yellow straw hat appearing to sail close over the grass as the boat followed the windings of the stream. When the yellow hat had at length been swallowed up in the violet haze along the base of the uplands, the great blue heron reappeared, winging low along the river shore. Arriving at the sand-spit he dropped his feet to the shallow water, closed his wings, and settled abruptly into a rigid pose of watching, with his neck outstretched and his head held high in the air.

The most searching scrutiny revealed nothing in all the tranquil summer landscape to disturb him. Nevertheless, he seemed to have lost conceit of his sentry post on the tip of the sand-spit. Instead of settling down to watch for what might come to him, he decided to go and look for what he waned. With long, ungainly, precise, but absolutely noiseless strides, he took his slow way up along the shore of the little river, walking on the narrow margin of mud between the grass-roots and the water. As he went his long neck undulated sinuously at each stride, his head was held low, and his eyes glared under every drooping leaf. The river margin, both in the water and out of it, was populous with insect life and the darting bill took toll of it at every step. But the most important game was frogs. There were plenty of them, small, greenish ochre fellows, who sat on the lily leaves and stared with foolish goggle-eyes till that stalking blue doom was almost upon them. Then they would dive head-foremost into the water, quick almost as the fleeting of a shadow. But quicker still was the stroke of the yellow beak—and the captive, pounded into limpness, would vanish down his captor's insatiable throat. This was better hunting than he had had upon the sand-spit, and he followed it up with great satisfaction. He even had the triumph of capturing a small water-rat, which had darted out of the grass-roots just as he came by. The little beast was tenacious of life, and had to be well hammered on the mud before it would consent to lie still enough to be swallowed comfortably. This pleasant task, however, was presently accomplished; and the great bird, as he stretched his head upward to give his neck that final hitch which drove the big mouthful home, took a careless step backward into the shallow water. There was a small sinister sound, and something closed relentlessly on his leg. He had stepped into a steel trap.

Stung by the sharp pain, astounded by the strangeness of the attack, and panic-stricken, as all wild creatures are by the sudden forfeit of their freedom, the great bird lost all his dignified self-possession. First hc nearly broke his beak with mad jabs at the inexplicable horror that had clutched him. Then, with a hoarse squawk of terror, he went quite wild. His huge wings flapped frantically, beating down the sedges and the blossoms of the arrow-weed, as he struggled to wrench himself free. He did succeed in lifting the trap above water; but it was securely anchored, and after a minute or two of insane, convulsive effort, it dragged him down again. Again and again he lifted it; again and yet again it dragged him down inexorably. And so the blind battle went on, with splashing of water and heavy buffeting of wings, till at last the bird fell back utterly beaten. In the last bout the trap had turned and got itself wedged in a slanting position, so that it was impossible for the captive to hold himself upright. He lay sprawling on his thighs, one wing outspread over the mud and leaves, the other on the water. His deadly beak was half open, from exhaustion. Only his indomitable eyes, still round, gold-and-black, glittering like gems, showed no sign of his weakness or his fear.

For a long time he lay there motionless, half numbed by the sense of defeat and by that gnawing anguish in his leg. Unheeded, the gleaming dragon-flies hurtled and darted, flashed and poised quivering, just above his head. Unheeded, the yellow butterflies, and the pale blue butterflies, alighted near him on the blooms of the arrow-weed. A big green bullfrog swam up and clambered out upon the mud close before him—to catch sight at once of that bright, terrible eye and fall back into the water almost paralysed with fright; but still he made no movement. His world had fallen about him, and there was nothing for him to do but wait and see what would happen next—what shape his doom would take.

Meanwhile, down along the margin mud, still hidden from view by a bend of the stream, another stealthy hunter was approaching. The big brown mink, who lived far up-stream in a musk-rat hole whose occupants he had cornered and devoured, was out on one of his foraging expeditions. Nothing in the shape of flesh, fish, or insect came amiss to him; but having ever the blood-lust in his ferocious veins, so that he loved to slaughter even when his appetite was well-sated, he preferred, of course, big game—something that could struggle, and suffer, and give him the sense of killing. A nesting duck or plover, for example, or a family of musquash—that was something worth while. On this day he had caught nothing but insects and a few dull frogs. He was savage for red blood.

Very short in the legs, but extraordinarily long in the body, lithe, snake-like in his swift darting movements, every inch of him a bundle of tough elastic muscles, with a sharp triangular head and incredibly malevolent eyes, the mink was a figure to be dreaded by creatures many times his size. As he came round the bend of the stream, and saw the great blue bird lying at the water's edge with wings outstretched, the picture of helplessness, his eyes glowed suddenly like live coals blown upon. He ran forward without an instant's hesitation, and made as if to spring straight at the captive's throat.

This move, however, was but a feint; for the big mink, though his knowledge of herons was by no means complete, knew nevertheless that the heron's beak was a weapon to beware of. He swerved suddenly, sprang lightly to one side, and tried to close in from the rear. But he didn't know the flexibility of the heron's neck. The lightning rapidity of his attack almost carried it through; but not quite. He was met by a darting stroke of the great yellow beak, which hurled him backward and ploughed a deep red furrow across his shoulder. Before he could recover himself the bird's neck was coiled again like a set spring, the javelin beak poised for another blow.

Most of the wild creatures would have been discouraged by such a reception, and slunk away to look for easier hunting. But not so the mink. His fighting blood now well up, for him it was a battle to the death. But for all his rage he did not lose his cunning. Making as if to run away, he doubled upon himself with incredible swiftness and flew at his adversary's neck. Quick as he was, however, he could not be so quick as that miracle of speed, which the eye can scarcely follow, the heron's thrust. The blow caught him this time on the flank, but slantingly, leaving a terrible gash, and at the same time a lucky buffet from the elbow of one great wing dashed him into the water. With this success the heron strove to rise to his feet—a position from which he could have fought to greater advantage. But the lay of the trap pulled him down again irresistibly. As he sank back the mink clambered out upon the shore and crouched straight in front of him, just a little beyond the reach of his stroke.

The mink was now a picture of battle fury, every muscle quivering, blood pulsing from his gashes, his white teeth showing in a soundless snarl, his eyes seeming to throb with crimson fire. The heron, on the other hand, seemed absolutely composed. His head, immobile, alert, in perfect readiness, was drawn back between his shoulders. His eyes were as wide, and fixed, and clear, and glassily staring, as the jewelled eyes of an idol.

For some seconds the mink crouched, as if trying to stare his adversary out of countenance. Then he launched himself straight at the bird's back. The movement had all the impetuosity of a genuine attack, but with marvellous control it was checked on the instant. It had been enough, however, to draw the heron's counter-stroke, which fell just short of its object. With the bird's recovery the mink shot in to close quarters. He received a second blow, which laid open the side of his face, but it was a short stroke, with not enough force behind it to repulse him. Ignoring it, he closed, fixed his teeth in the bird's neck, and flung his lithe length over the back, where it would be out of reach of the buffeting wings.

The battle was over; for the mink's teeth were long and strong. They cut deep, straight into the life; and, undisturbed by the windy flopping of the great, helpless wings, the victor lay drinking the life-blood which he craved. A black whirling shadow sailed over the scene, but it passed a little behind the mink's tail and was not noticed. It paused, seeming to hover over a patch of lily leaves. A moment more, and it vanished. There was a hiss; and the great duck-hawk, the same one whom the heron had driven off earlier in the day, dropped out of the zenith. The mink had just time to raise his snarling and dripping muzzle in angry surprise when the hawk's talons closed upon him. One set fastened upon his throat, cutting straight through windpipe and jugular; the other set gripped and pierced his tender loins. The next moment he was jerked from the body of his prey, and carried—head, legs, and tail limply hanging—away far over the green wastes of the sedge to the great hawk's eyrie, in the heart of the cedar-swamp beyond the purple uplands.

Some ten minutes later a splendid butterfly, all glowing orange and maroon, came and settled on the back of the dead heron, and waved its radiant wings in the tranquil light.

The Black Fisherman*

Along the grim cliffs that guard, on the north, the gates of tide-vext Fundy, the green seas foamed and sobbed beneath the surge of the tremendous flood. There was no wind; and out from shore the slow swells, unfrothed by rock or shoal, heaved gently, smooth as glass. The sky, of that intensely pure, vibrant blue which seems to hold sparks of sharp light enmeshed in it, carried but two or three small clouds, floating far and high, clean-edged, and white as new snow.

Close above the water, and closely followed by his shadow, flew slowly a large and sinister-looking black bird, about midway in size between a duck and a goose, but very unlike either in shape and mien. Its head, neck, breast, and underbody, and lower part of the back, next the tail, were glossy black, with a sharp iridescence flashing green and jewelled in the sun. Its short, square, rigid tail was ink black, as were its legs and strong, webbed feet. Ink black, too, was its long, straight, hook-tipped beak—even longer than the sharp, savage head, which was strangely adorned by a thin, backward-sweeping black crest on either side. At the base of the beak and on the throat just beneath it was a splash of orange; and the piercing eyes, hard as a hawk's, were surrounded each by a vivid orange patch of naked skin. In somber contrast to this impressive coloring, the back and wings were brown, the feathers trimly laced with black.

As the dark shape flew, almost skimming the transparent swells, its fierce, flame-circled eyes peered downward, taking note of the fish that swam at varying depths. These fruitful waters of Fundy teemed with fish, of many varieties and sizes, and the great cormorant, for all his insatiable appetite, could afford to pick and choose among them those most convenient to handle. As far as his taste was concerned there was little to choose, for quantity, rather than quality, was what appealed to him in fish.

---

* From *Wisdom of the Wilderness* (New York: Macmillan, 1923), 28-44. "The Black Fisherman" also appeared in *The Windsor Magazine* (August 1922).

Suddenly he made his choice. His tail went up, his head went down, his wings closed tight to his body, and he shot beneath the beryl surface. At first, he missed his quarry. But that was nothing to him. More fish than bird himself, now, he gave chase to it, at a depth of several feet below the water. Propelled by the drive of his powerful thighs and broad webs, by the screwing twist of his stern and his stiff tail, he darted through the alien element at a speed which very few of its natives could pretend to rival. From his wake a few bright bubbles escaped and flew upwards, to break in flashes of sharp light upon the silvery mirror of the under surface. The quarry, a gleaming and nimble "gaspereau," doubled frantically this way and that, its round, fixed eyes astare as if painted. But it could not shake off its implacable pursuer. In a dozen seconds or so it was overtaken. That long, hook-tipped beak snapped upon it inexorably, and paralyzed its writhings.

Shooting forth upon the surface, the cormorant sat motionless for a few moments, carrying his prize crosswise in his beak. Then with a sudden jerk tossing it in the air, he caught it dexterously head first as it fell, and gulped it down—but not all the way down. The black fisherman's stomach was, as it chanced, already full. The present capture, therefore, was lodged in the sac of loose skin below his throat, where its size and shape were clearly revealed.

For a short while—for a very few minutes, indeed, since the cormorant's digestion is swift and indefatigable, and has no objection to working overtime—the black fisherman sat floating complacently on the swells. Then suddenly, with a convulsive movement that to an onlooker would have seemed agonizing, but which to him was a satisfying delight, he swallowed the prize in his gullet, stretching up and straightening his neck, till its trim outlines were quite restored. Immediately the hunting light flamed again into his savage eyes. With a heavy flapping rush along the surface he rose into the air and fell once more to quartering the liquid field for a new prey.

Meanwhile, from far up in the blinding blue where he wheeled slowly on wide, motionless wings, a white-headed eagle, most splendid and most shameless of robbers, had been watching the insatiable fisherman. Now he dropped swiftly to a lower level, where he again hung poised, his gem-bright, implacable eyes peering downward expectantly. It was not often that he interfered with the cormorants, whom he regarded as obstinate, ill-tempered birds, with an insistent regard for their rights and remarkable precision in the use of their long beaks. But hunting had been bad that day, and he was hungry. The complacent success of the black fisherman was galling to watch while his own appetite was so unsatisfied.

The cormorant, absorbed in his quest, and never dreaming of any interference, did not notice the long-winged shape circling high overhead. He marked a fine whiting—rather bigger than he usually troubled with, but too tempting to resist. He dived, pursued it hither and thither for a breathless minute or more, captured it, and shot to the surface again triumphantly, with the captive still squirming between his deadly mandibles. In the same instant, before he had time to dive or dodge, there was a hissing rush, the air above his head was buffeted by tremendous wings; and great talons, closing like a trap on one half of the fish projecting from his beak, strove to snatch it from him. Startled and furious, he hung on like a bulldog, stiffening his broad tail and backing water with his powerful webs. He was almost lifted clear of the surface, but his weight, and his passionate resistance, were too much for even those mighty pinions to overcome. The fish was torn in half, and the eagle sprang upwards with his spoils. The cormorant swallowed the remaining fragment in fierce haste, blinking with the effort, and then sat and glared at the kingly marauder beating upwards into the blue.

After a few minutes of sullen meditations—and swift digestion—the untiring but still angry fisherman resumed his game. This time, however, he did not rise into the air, but swam slowly onward, searching the crystal tide beneath him till he marked a likely prey. Then once more he dived, once more he chased the quarry through its native element, and captured it. But now, instead of shooting out boldly upon the surface, he rose cautiously and showed only his head above the water. There was his foe, already swooping again to the attack, but still high in air. In a lightning gulp he swallowed his prey, down into the halfway-house of his throat sac, and dived again, disappearing just as the robber, dropping like a thunderbolt, spread sudden wing and struck angrily at the spot where he had vanished.

As the eagle hovered for a moment, giving vent to his feelings in a sharp yelp of disappointment, the black fisherman reappeared some twenty or thirty paces away, and sat there eyeing his enemy with mingled triumph and defiance. He held his vicious-looking head slightly down between the shoulders, ready for a lightning stroke; and his long, efficient beak was half open. His sturdy spirit was not going to be browbeaten even by the king of the air.

The eagle, with snowy head stretched downwards, eyes gleaming bright as glass, and great talons menacingly outstretched, sailed backwards and forwards over him several times at a height of not more than four or five feet, hoping to frighten him into disgorging the prey. Had the royal robber cared to push matters to a conclusion, he would certainly have been more than a match for the cormorant, but he knew well enough that he would not emerge without scars from the encounter; and he was not ready to pay any such price for a mouthful of fish. Presently, realizing that the surly fisherman was not going to be bluffed, he slanted aloft disdainfully, and went winnowing away over the cliffs to seek less troublesome hunting.

A few minutes later the cormorant, well pleased with himself, flew up to rejoin his nesting mate, on a grassy ledge just below the crest of the cliff.

Arriving at the nest he alighted close beside it, and immediately sat up, supported by his stiff, square tail, as rigidly erect as a penguin. His vigilant gaze scanning rock and sky and sea, the polished, black armor of his hard plumage radiant in the sunlight, he looked a formidable sentinel. His dark mate, hungry and weary after long brooding, slipped from the nest and plunged downward to refresh herself in the fruitful gleaming pastures of the tide, leaving the nest and eggs to his guardianship.

It was a crude affair, this nest—a haphazard, messy structure of dry, black seaweed and last year's grey mullein stalks. Within the nest were four big eggs of a dirty pale-green color, partly covered with a whitish, limey film. These treasures the black fisherman watched proudly, ready to do battle for them against any would-be thief that might approach.

In truth the nest was in a somewhat exposed position. At

this point the ledge was only about four feet wide, and just behind the nest the cliff face was so crumbled away that any sure-footed marauder might easily make his way down from the cliff top, some thirty feet above. In front of the nest, on the other hand, the cliff face dropped a sheer three hundred feet to the surges that seethed and crashed along its base. Some twenty paces to the right the ledge widened to a tiny plateau, carpeted with close, light-green turf and dotted with half a dozen dark juniper bushes. A most desirable nesting place, this, but already occupied to the last available inch of space by the earlier arrivals of the cormorant migration. The black fisherman and his spouse, tardy in their wooing and their mating, had lingered overlong in the warm waters of the south and been obliged to content themselves with such accommodation as was left to them. To their courageous and rather unsociable spirits, however, this was a matter of small concern. They had the companionship of their kind—but not too close, not too intimate; just where they wanted it, in fact. They were well fitted to hold the post of danger—to guard the gateway to the cormorant colony. Few other birds there were in that colony who would have had the mettle, bold as they were, to face the eagle as the black fisherman had done.

Those dirty-green eggs in the slovenly nest were now near their time of hatching, so the mother hurried back from the sea as soon as possible, to cover them with her hot and dripping breast, setting her mate free to pursue his one engrossing pastime. A day or two later, however, when faint cries and the sound of tapping beaks began to be heard within the shells, then the devoted mother would not leave the nest even for a moment, so the black fisherman had to fish for her as well as for himself. His pastime now became a heavy task, made doubly hard by the fact that the eagle returned from time to time to harass him. His method of foraging, at first, was to fill his own stomach, then his neck pouch till it would hold no more, and then fly home with a big fish held crosswise in his beak. This was the eagle's opportunity. When the cormorant was in mid-air, half way between cliff and sea, and flying heavily with his load, the crafty robber would swoop down and catch him at a hopeless disadvantage. Unable either to strike back or to resist, and mindful of his responsibilities, he would relinquish the prize and fly back home to feed his mate on what he could disgorge from his crop. After two experiences of this sort he gave up attempting to carry anything home in his beak and contented himself with what his pouch would hold. Thereupon the eagle, no longer tempted by the sight of an actually visible prey and marking the long, black beak all in readiness to strike, gave up molesting him. But the rest of the colony, less wary and quick-witted than the black fisherman, were continually being forced to pay tribute to the robber king. When their eggs were hatched, both parents were kept busy, the four youngsters being voracious beyond even the usual voracity of nestlings. At first they were but blind, stark-naked, ink-black, sprawling bundles of skin and bone, their great beaks ever wide open in demand for more, more, more. Their tireless parents had not only to catch, but also to half digest their food for them, pumping it into their throats from their own stomachs, which were thus kept working at high pressure.

As the nestlings grew—which they did with great rapidity—their appetites increased in proportion and when their eyes opened there was an added emphasis to the demand of their ever open beaks. The father and mother began to grow thin with their exertions. Then one day the fickle Fates of the Sea came very near to closing the mother's career and throwing the whole responsibility upon the black fisherman's shoulders. The mother was down, far down below the surface, chasing a nimble sprat through the green transparency, when a swift and hungry dogfish with jaws like those of his great cousin, the shark, came darting in her wake. Fortunately for her the sprat dodged—and she, in turning to pursue, caught sight of her own terrible pursuer. Straight as an arrow she shot to the surface; and then, with sure instinct, she flashed aside at right angles, thus evading, though only by a hair's breadth, her enemy's upward rush. Flapping desperately along the water for a few feet she sprang into the air with a frantic effort; and the jaws of the dogfish snapped just below her vanishing feet. Somewhat shaken she started homeward. But before she had gone halfway she regained her self-possession. She would not return empty to her nestlings, confessing defeat. Whirling abruptly she flew off far to the left, and resumed her fishing in a deep cove where that particular dogfish, at least, was not likely to pursue her. But the adventure had warned her to keep her eyes open, and on her return to the nest she managed to convey to her mate the news that dogfish were about. It was information which that wary bird was not likely to forget.

Shortly after this incident the overworked parents were afforded a certain measure of relief, but in a form which was very bitter to them. One morning when they were both absent from the nest, and the nestlings, full-fed for the moment, sprawled comfortably in the sun, a slender, long-tailed, grey-and-buff chicken hawk came slanting down over the crest of the cliff. Its swift, darting flight carried it low above the crowded nests of the cormorant colony, but, audacious slaughterer though it was, discretion kept it from coming within reach of the menacing beaks uplifted to receive it. The lonely nest of the black fisherman, however, left unguarded for the moment, caught its eye. It pounced like lightning, struck its talons into the tender body of one of the nestlings, despatched it with a single blow, dragged it forth upon the edge of the nest, and fell to tearing it greedily. A moment more and another of the nestlings would have been served in the same fashion; but just in the nick of time the black fisherman himself arrived. The hawk saw his ominous form shoot up over the rim of the ledge. With one thrust of its fine pinions it sprang into the air, evading the onslaught by a splendid side sweep far out over the depths. Then it beat upwards and over the crest of the cliff, its bleeding victim dangling from its talons. With a croak of fury the cormorant gave chase. For half a mile in over the downs he followed, lusting for vengeance. But his heavy flight, though strong and straight, was no match for the speed of that beautiful and graceful slayer. The hawk presently vanished with its prey among the dark tree tops of an inland valley, and the black fisherman flapped back sullenly to his nest.

The three remaining nestlings throve all the better for the loss of their companion. They were nearly half feathered before any further misadventure befell the nest. Then it came in an unexpected guise.

A wandering fox, far out of his accustomed range, came to the crest of the cliff and stood staring curiously out into the vast space of air and sea. There was a wind that day, and his bushy, red brush of a tail was blown almost over his back. The cormorant colony was just below him. At the sight of it his eyes narrowed cunningly. Sinking flat in the grass he thrust his sharp face over the edge, in the shelter of an overhanging rose-bush, and peered down upon the novel scene. What a lot of nests! What a tempting array of plump younglings! His lean jaws slavered with greed.

The fox knew nothing about cormorants. But he could see the black, fine-plumaged guardians of the nests were very helfty, self-confident birds, with bold, fierce eyes and extraordinarily efficient-looking beaks. He speedily came to the conclusion that the immediate vicinity of those beaks would be bad for his health. Decidedly those grapes were sour. Being a sagacious beast and not given to wasting effort on the unattainable, he was just about to curb his appetite and turn away when his glance fell upon the black fisherman's nest, lying far apart and solitary. To be sure, both parents were beside the nest at the moment. But they were only two; and after all they were only birds. This looked more promising. He crept nearer, and waited, it being his wise custom to look before he leaped.

Both parents were busy feeding the gaping mouths of their young, and the fox watched with interest the unusual process. It seemed to him absurd, and unnecessary; and his respect for the great, black birds began to diminish. Presently the larger of the two, the black fisherman himself, having disgorged all the food he could spare, plunged downward from the ledge and disappeared.

This was the red watcher's opportunity. With a rushing leap down the steep slope he sprang upon the nest. Never dreaming that the one lone guardian would dare to face him, and craving the tender flesh of the young rather than the tough adult, he made the mistake of ignoring the mother bird. He seized one of the nestlings and crushed the life out of it in a single snap of his jaws. But at the same instant the stab of a steel-hard mandible struck him full in one eye, simply obliterating it, and a mighty buffeting of wings forced him off the nest.

With a yelp of rage and anguish the fox turned upon his assailant, and seized her by one wing, high up and close to the body. As his fangs ground through the bone the dauntless mother raked his flank with her stabbing beak and threw herself backwards, frantically struggling, toward the lip of the ledge. Her instinctive purpose was twofold—first, to drag the fox from the precious nest; second to seek escape from this land enemy in either the air or the water, where she would be more at home. The fox, his one remaining eye for the moment veiled by his opponent's feathers, could not see his peril, but resisted instinctively whatever she seemed trying to do.

From the first moment of the battle the mother bird had sent out her harsh cries for help. And now, while the unequal combat went on at the very brink of the abyss, the black fisherman arrived. With a mighty shock he landed on the fox's back, striking and stabbing madly. Bewildered, and half stunned, the fox jerked up his head to seize his new antagonist; but, met by a demoralizing thrust fair on the snout, he missed his aim, and caught the throat of the mother bird instead. The next instant, in a mad confusion of pounding wings and yelpings and black feathers and red fur, the three went over the brink together in an awful plunge.

Immediately the black fisherman, who was unhurt, flew clear. He could do nothing but follow the other two downwards, as they fell rolling over each other in the death grip. Half way down they crashed upon a jutting point of rock, and fell apart as they bounced off. With two tremendous splashes they struck the water. The body of the fox sank from sight, whirled away by an undercurrent and probably caught in some deep crevice, there to be devoured by the crabs and other sea scavengers. The dead cormorant, supported by her feathers and her hollow bones, lay floating, belly upward, with sprawled wings, on the surface. Her mate, alighting beside her, swam around her several times, eyeing her with an intense gaze. Then, realizing that she was dead, he slowly swam away to take up the double duties now thrust upon him. After all, as there were now but two mouths left in the nest to feed, there was no doubt but that he would be equal to the task.

Starnose of the Under Ways *

He was in a darkness that dense, absolute, palpable. And his eyes were shut tight—though it made no difference, under the circumstances, whether they were shut or open. But if his sense of sight was for the moment off duty, its absence was more than compensated for by the extreme alertness of his other senses. To his supersensitive nostrils the black, peaty soil surrounding him was full of distinct and varying scents. His ears could detect and locate the wriggling of a fat grub, the unctuous withdrawal of a startled earthworm. Above all, his sense of touch—that was so extraordinarily developed that it might have served him for eyes, ears, and nostrils all in one. And it came about that, there in the blackness of his close and narrow tunnel, deep in the black soil of the swamp, he was not imprisoned, but free and at large as the swift hares gamboling overhead—far freer, indeed, because secure from the menace of prowling and swooping foes.

Starnose was a mole. But he was not an ordinary mole of the dry uplands and well-drained meadows, by any means, or he would not have been running his deep tunnel here in the cool, almost swampy soil within a few yards of the meandering channel of the Lost Water. In shape and color he was not unlike the common mole—with his thick, powerful neck of about the same size as his body, his great, long-clawed, immensely strong, handlike forefeet, and his mellow, velvety, shadowy, gray-brown fur. But his tail was much longer, and thicker at the base, than that of his plebeian cousin of the lawns. And his nose—*that* was something of a distinction which no other beast in the world, great or small could boast of. From all round its tip radiated a fringe of feelers, no less than twenty-two in number, naked, flexible, miraculously sensitive, each one a little nailless, interrogating finger. It entitled him, beyond question, to the unique title of Starnose.

This tireless worker in the dark was driving a new tunnel—partly, no doubt, for the sake of worms, grubs, and *pupae*

---

* From *Wisdom of the Wilderness* (New York: Macmillan, 1923), 45-62. “Starnose of the Under Ways” also appeared in *The Windsor Magazine* (Dec. 1920) and *Sunset* (May 1922).

which he might find on the way, and partly for purposes known only to himself. At the level where he was digging, a scant foot below the surface, the mould, though damp, was fairly light and workable, owing to the abundance of fine roots and decayed leafage mixed through it; and his progress was astonishingly rapid.

His method of driving his tunnel was practical and effective. With back arched so as to throw the full force of it into his foreshoulders, with his hind feet wide apart and drawn well up beneath him, he dug mightily into the damp soil straight before his nose with the long, penetrating claws of his exaggerated and powerful forepaws. In great, swift, handfuls (for his forepaws were more like hands than feet), the loosened earth was thrown behind him, passing under his body and out between his roomily straddling hind legs. And as he dug he worked in a circle, enlarging the tunnel head to a diameter of about two and a half inches, at the same time pressing the walls firm and hard with his body, so that they should not cave in upon him. This compacting process further enlarged the tunnel to about three inches, which was the space he felt he needed for quick and free movement. When he had accumulated behind him as much loose earth as he could comfortably handle, he turned round, and with his head and chest and forearms pushed the mass before him along the tunnel to the foot of his last dump hole—an abrupt shaft leading to the upper air. Up this shaft he would thrust his burden, and heave it forth among the grass and weeds, a conspicuous and contemptuous challenge to would-be pursuers. He did not care how many of his enemies might thus be notified of his address, for he knew he could always change it with baffling celerity, blocking up his tunnels behind him as he went.

And now, finding that at his present depth the meadow soil, at this point, was not well stocked with such game—grubs and worms—as he chose to hunt, he slanted his tunnel slightly upward to get among the grass roots near the surface. Almost immediately he was rewarded. He cut into a pipelike canal of a large earthworm just in time to intercept its desperate retreat. It was one of those stout, dark-purplish lobworms that feed in rich soil, and to him the most toothsome of morsels. In spite of the eagerness of his appetite he drew it forth most delicately and gradually from its canal, lest it should break in two and the half of it escape him. Dragging it back into his tunnel he held it with his big, inexorable "hands," and felt it over gleefully with that restless star of fingers which adorned the tip of his nose. Then he tore it into short pieces, bolted it hurriedly, and fell to work again upon his tunnelling. But now, having come among the grass roots, he was in a good hunting ground and his work was continually interrupted by feasting. At one moment it would be a huge, fat, white grub as thick as a man's little finger, with a hard, light-copper-colored head; at the next a heavy, liver-colored lobworm. His appetite seemed insatiable; but at last he felt he had enough, for the moment. He stopped tunneling, turned back a few inches, drove a short shaft to the surface as a new exit, and heaved forth a mighty load of débris.

In the outer world it was high morning, and the strong sunlight glowed softly down through the tangled grasses of the water meadow. The eyes of Starnose were but two tiny, black beads almost hidden in fur, but after he had blinked them for a second or two in the sudden light he could see quite effectively—much better, indeed, than his cousin, the common mole of the uplands. Though by far the greater part of his strenuous life was spent in the palpable darkness of his tunnels in the underworld, daylight, none the less, was by no means distasteful to him, and he was not averse to a few minutes of basking in the tempered sun. As he sat stroking his fine fur with those restless fingers of his nose, and scratching himself luxuriously with his capable claws, a big grasshopper, dropping from one of its aimless leaps, fell close beside him, bearing down with it a long blade of grass which it had clutched at in its descent. Starnose seized the unlucky hopper in a flash, tore off its hard inedible legs, and started to eat it. At that instant, however, a faint swish of wings caught his ear and a swift shadow passed over him. At the touch of that shadow—as if it had been solid and released an oiled spring within his mechanism—he dived back into his hole; and the swooping marsh hawk, after a savage but futile clutch at the vanishing tip of his tail, wheeled off with a yelp of disappointment.

It was certainly a narrow shave; and for perhaps a whole half minute Starnose, with his heart thumping, crouched in his refuge. Then, remembering the toothsome prize which he had been forced to abandon, he put forth his head warily to reconnoitre. The hawk was gone; but the dead grasshopper was still there, green and glistening in the sun, and a burly bluebottle had just alighted upon it. Starnose crept forth cautiously to retrieve his prey.

Now at this same moment, as luck would have it, gliding along one of the tiny runways of the meadow mice, came a foraging mole shrew, a pugnacious cousin of the starnose tribe. The mole shrew was distinctly smaller than Starnose, and handicapped with such defective vision that he had to do all his hunting by scent and sound and touch. He smelt the dead grasshopper at once, and came straight for it, heedless of whatever might stand in the way.

Under the circumstances Starnose might have carelessly stood aside, not through lack of courage, but because he had no special love of fighting for its own sake. And he knew that his cousin, though so much smaller and lighter than himself, was much to be respected as an opponent by reason of his blind ferocity and dauntless tenacity. But he was no weakling, to let himself be robbed of his lawful prey. He whipped out of his hold, flung himself upon the prize, and lifted his head just in time to receive the furious spring of his assailant.

Between two such fighters there was no fencing. The mole shrew secured a grip upon the side of the immensely thick and muscular neck of his antagonist, and immediately began to worry and tear like a terrier. But Starnose, flexible as an eel, set his deadly teeth into the side of his assailant's head, a little behind the ear, and worked in deeper and deeper, after the manner of a bulldog. For a few seconds, in that death grapple, the two rolled over and over, thrashing the grass stems. Then the long teeth of Starnose bit in to the brain; and the mole shrew's body, after a convulsive stiffening, went suddenly limp.

But the disturbance in the grass—there being no wind that golden morning—had not escaped the eyes of the foraging marsh hawk. She came winnowing back to learn the cause of it. The sun being behind her, however, her ominous shadow swept over the grass before her, and Starnose, unfailingly vigilant even in the moment of victory, caught sight of it coming.

He loosened his hold on his dead adversary and plunged for the hole. At least, he tried to plunge for it. But the plunge was little more than a crawl, for the teeth of the mole shrew, set deep in his neck, had locked themselves fast in death, and all that Starnose could do was to drag the body with him. This however, he succeeded in doing, so effectively that he was in time to back down into the hole, out of reach, just as the hawk swooped and struck.

The clutching talons of the great bird fixed themselves firmly into the protruding hind quarters of the mole shrew, and she attempted to rise with her capture. But to her amazed indignation the prize resisted. Starnose was holding on to the walls of his tunnel with all the strength of his powerful claws, while at the same time struggling desperately to tear himself loose from the grip of those dead teeth in his neck. The contest, however, was but momentary. The strength of Starnose was a small thing against the furious beating of those great wings; and in two or three seconds, unable either to hold on or to free himself from the fatal incubus of his victim, he was dragged forth ignominiously and swept into the air, squirming and dangling at the tip of the dead mole shrew's snout.

Starnose was vaguely conscious of a chill rush of air, of a sudden, dazzling glare of gold and blue, as the victorious hawk flapped off toward the nearest tree top with her prize. Then suddenly, the grip of the dead jaws relaxed and he felt himself falling. Fortunately for him the hawk had not risen to any great height—for the marsh hawk, hunter of meadow mice and such secretive quarry, does not, as a rule, fly high. He felt himself turn over and over in the air, dizzily, and then landed, with a stupefying swish, in a dense bed of wild parsnips. He crashed right through, of course, but the strong stems broke his fall and he was little the worse for the stupendous adventure. For a few moments he lay half stunned. Then, pulling himself together, he fell to digging with all his might, caring only to escape from a glaring outer world which seemed so full of tumultuous and altogether bewildering perils. He made the earth fly in a shower, and in an unbelievable brief space of time he had buried himself till even the tip of his tail was out of sight. But even then he was not content. He dug on frantically, till he was a good foot beneath the surface and perhaps a couple of feet more from the entrance. Then, leaving he passage safely blocked behind him, he enlarged the tunnel to a small chamber, and curled himself up to lick his wounds and recover from his fright.

It was perhaps half an hour before Starnose completely regained his composure and his appetite. His appetite—that was the first consideration. And second to that, a poor second, was his need of tunneling back to his familiar maze of underground passages. Resuming his digging with full vigor, he first ran a new dump shaft to the surface, gathering in several fat grubs in his progress through the grass roots. Then, at about six inches below the surface—a depth at which he could count upon the best foraging—he began to drive his tunnel. His sense of direction was unerring, which was the more inexplicable as there in the thick dark he could have no landmarks to guide him. He headed straight for the point which would, by the shortest distance, join him up with his own under ways.

It happened, however, that in that terrible journey of his through the upper air the swift flight of the hawk had carried him some distance, and across the course of a sluggish meadow brook, a tributary of the Lost Water. Suddenly and unexpectedly his vigorous tunneling brought him to this obstacle. The darkness before him gave way to a glimmer of light. He hesitated, and then burrowed on more cautiously. A screen of matted grass roots confronted him, stabbed through with needles of sharp gold which quivered dazzlingly. Warily he dug through the screen, thrust forth his nose, and found himself looking down upon a shimmering glare of quiet water, about a foot below him.

Glancing upward to see if there were any terrible wings in the air above, Starnose perceived, to his deep satisfaction, that the steep bank was overhung by a mat of pink-blossomed wild roses, humming drowsily with bees. The concealment, from directly overhead, was perfect. Reassured upon this point he crawled forth, intending to swim the bright channel and continue his tunnel upon the other side. The water itself was no obstacle to him, for he could swim and dive like a muskrat. He was just about to plunge in, when under his very nose popped up a black, triangular, furry head with fiercely bright, hard eyes and lips curled back hungrily from long and keen white fangs.

With amazing dexterity he doubled back upon himself straight up the slope and dived into his burrow; and the mink, springing after him, was just in time to snap vainly at the vanishing tip of his tail.

The mink was both hungry and bad-tempered, having just missed a fish which he was hunting amid the tangle of water weeds along the muddy bottom of the stream. Angrily he jammed his sharp snout into the mouth of the tunnel, but the passage was much too small for him and Starnose was well out of reach. He himself could dig a burrow when put to it, but he knew that in this art he was no match for the expert little fugitive. Moreover, keen though was his appetite, he was not overanxious to allay it with the rank and stringy flesh of the Underground One. He shook his head with a sniff and a snarl, brushed the earth from his muzzle, and slipped off swiftly and soundlessly to seek more succulent prey.

It was ten or fifteen minutes before Starnose again ventured forth into the perilous daylight. His last adventure had not in the least upset him—for to his way of thinking a miss was as good as a mile. But he was hungry, as usual, and he had found good hunting in the warm light soil just under the roots of the wild rosebushes along the bank. At length his desires once more turned toward the home tunnels. He poked his starry nose out through he hole in the bank, made sure that there were no enemies in sight, slipped down to the water's edge, and glided in as noiselessly as if he had been oiled. He had no mind to make a splash, lest he should advertise his movements to some voracious pike which might be lurking beneath that green patch of water-lily leaves a little further upstream.

Deep below the shining surface he swam, straight and strong through a world of shimmering and pellucid gold, roofed by a close, flat, white sky of diaphanous silver, upon which every fallen rose petal or drowning fly or moth was shown with amazing clearness. As he reached the opposite shore and clambered nimbly up through that flat, silver sky he glanced back, and saw a long, gray shadow, with terrible jaws and staring, round eyes, dart past the spot from which he had just emerged. The great pike beneath the lily pads had caught sight of him, after all—but too late! Starnose shook himself, and sat basking for a few moments in the comfortable warmth, complacently combing his face with his nimble forepaws. He had an easy contempt for the pike, because it could not leave the water to pursue him.

Some fifty yards away, on the side of the brook from which Starnose had just come, beside a tiny pool in the deeps of the grass stood an immense bird of a pale bluish-gray color, motionless as a stone, on the watch for unwary frogs. Though the rich grasses were about two feet in height, the blue heron towered another clear two feet above them. He was all length—long stiltlike legs, long snakelike neck, long dagger-like bill, and a firm, arrogant crest of long, slim delicate plumes. All about him spread the warm and sun-steeped sea of the meadow grass—starred thick with blooms of purple vetch and crimson clover and sultry orange lilies—droning sleepily with bees and flies, steaming with summer scents and liquidly musical with the songs of the fluttering, black-and-white bobolinks, like tangled peals of tiny, silver bells. But nothing of this intoxicating beauty did the great heron heed. Rigid and decorative as if he had just stepped down from a Japanese screen, his fierce, unwinking, jewel-bright eyes were intent upon the pool at his feet. His whole statuesque being was concentrated upon the subject of frogs.

But the frogs in that particular pool had taken warning. Not one would show himself so long as that inexorable blue shape of death remained in sight. Nor did a single meadow mouse stir amid the grass roots for yards about the pool; for word of the watching doom had gone abroad. And presently the great heron, grown tired of such poor hunting, lifted his broad wings, sprang lazily into the air, and went flapping away slowly over the grass tops, trailing his long legs stiffly behind him. He headed for the other side of the brook and fresh hunting grounds.

At the first lift of those great, pale wings Starnose had detected this new and appalling peril. By good luck he was sitting on a patch of bare earth, where the overhanging turf had given way some days before. Frantically he began to dig himself in. The soft earth flew from under his desperate paws. The piercing eyes of the heron detected the curious disturbance, and he winged swiftly for the spot.

But Starnose, in his vigilance, had gained a good start. In about as much time as it takes to tell it, he was already buried to his own length. And then, to his terror, he came plump upon an impenetrable obstacle—an old mooring stake driven deep into the soil. In a sweat of panic he swerved off to the left and tunneled madly almost at right angles to the entrance.

And just this it was—a part of his wonderful luck on this eventful day—that turned to his salvation. Dropping swiftly to the entrance of the all too shallow tunnel, the great heron, his head bent sideways, peered into the hold with one implacable eye. Then drawing back his neck till it was like a coiled spring, he darted his murderous bill deep into the hole.

Had it not been for the old mooring stake, which compelled him to change directions, Starnose would have been neatly impaled, plucked forth, hammered to death, and devoured. As it was, the dreadful weapon merely grazed the top of his rump—scoring, indeed, a crimson gash—and struck with a terrifying thud upon the hard wood of the stake. The impact gave the heron a nasty jar. He drew his head back abruptly and shook it hard in his indignant surprise. Then, trying to look as if nothing unusual had happened, he stepped down into the water with lofty deliberation and composed himself to watch for fish. At this moment the big pike came swimming past again, hoping for another chance at the elusive Starnose. He was much too heavy a fish for the heron to manage, of course; but the heron, in his wrath, stabbed down upon him vindictively. There was a moment's struggle which made the quiet water boil. Then the frightened fish tore himself free and darted off, with a great red wound in his silver-gray side, to hide and sulk under the lily pads.

In the meantime Starnose, though smarting from that raw but superficial gash upon his hind quarters, was burrowing away with concentrated zeal. He had once more changed directions, and was heading, as true as if by compass, for the nearest point of the home galleries. He was not even taking time to drive dump shafts at the customary intervals, but was letting the tunnel fill up behind him, as if sure he was going to have no further use for it. He just wanted to get home. Of course he might have traveled much faster above ground; but the too exciting events of the past few hours had convinced him that, for this particular day at least, the upper world of sun and air was not exactly a health resort for a dweller in the under ways. Through all his excitement, however, and all his eagerness for the safe home burrows, his unquenchable appetite remained with him; and, running his tunnel as close to the surface as he could without actually emerging, he picked up plenty of worms and grubs and fat, helpless *pupae* as he went.

It was past noon, and the strong sunshine, beating straight down through the grass and soaking through the matted roots, was making a close but sweet and earthy-scented warmth in the tunnel, when at last Starnose broke through into one of his familiar passages, well trodden by the feet of his tribe. Not by sight, of course—for the darkness was black as pitch—but by the comfortable smell he knew exactly where he was. Without hesitation he turned to the left and scurried along as fast as he could, for the big, central burrow, or lodge, where his tribe had their headquarters and their nests. The path forked and re-forked continually, but he was never for one instant at a loss. Here and there he passed little, short side galleries ending in shallow pockets, which served for the sanitation of the tribe. Here and there a ray of green-and-gold light flashed down upon him as he ran past one of the exit shafts. And then, his heart beating with his haste and his joy he came forth into a roomy, lightless chamber, thick with warmth and musky smells, and filled with the pleasant rustlings and small, contented squealings of his own gregarious tribe.

The Winged Scourge of the Dark *

OPPRESSORS, DEVOURERS OF THE WEAK, ARE NOT CONFINED TO HUMANITY

The windless, gray-violet dusk, soft as a mole's fur, brooded low over the bushy upland pasture. In the shallow valley below, a gleam of yellow lamplight shone steadily from the kitchen window of the little backwoods farmhouse. Faint, comfortable sounds floated up on the still air from the low-roofed barn, where the two horses, resting after a hard day's work, reveled in their generous feed of oats. There was a soft creaking, a rattle, and a splash, as the farmer's wife, a dim, gray figure, drew a bucket of water from the deep well in the center of the farmyard. From a patch of alder swamp beyond the brook which threaded the valley a bullfrog uttered his hoarsely mellow croak, repeating it several times with subtle variations as if trying to improve the note. Twilight and the dewfall hushed the world to peace.

In the rough, upland pasture, among the scattered stumps and patches of juniper and young fir seedlings, some five or six brown rabbits were at play in the sheltering dusk like carefree children. They went leaping softly this way and that, passing and repassing each other in what looked almost like the set figures of a dance. At intervals one of the furry little players would stop short and thump heavily with his strong hind paws upon the firm, close-cropped turf, producing a curious, dully resonant sound. At the signal all the other players would turn about, as if on drill, and continue the game with what looked like a new figure.

In the midst of this furry merrymaking, from the dark woods which overhung the back and northern side of the pasture, came a strange and ominous voice. *Whuh-whoo-oo,—Whuh-whoo-oo,*—deep-toned, long-drawn, sonorous, and thrilling with an indescribable menace, it sounded, twice, across the quiet dusk.

---

* From *Wisdom of the Wilderness* (New York: Macmillan, 1923), 63-82. "The Winged Scourge of the Dark" also appeared in *The Windsor Magazine* (Feb. 1921).

At first the note of the play of the rabbits stopped short, as if all the players had been smitten instantaneously into stone. In the next half second the majority of them darted frantically into the shelter of the nearest bushes, with a momentary flicker of white tail fluffs as they vanished. The rest, as if too panic-stricken to move, or else fearing the revelation of movement, simply crouched flat where they were, motionless save for the wild pounding of their frightened hearts. Their shadowy fur melting perfectly into the dusk and the shadowy turf, so long as they kept still they were as invisible as their companions who had found refuge under the bushes. And they kept still, as if frozen.

It was perhaps half a minute later when a great, dim form, as noiseless as the passing of a cloud shadow, came winnowing low, on downy wings, over the bushes of the silent pasture. It seemed but a fragment of denser dusk come alive—except for its dreadful eyes. These eyes—great, round, palely shining globes—searched the thickets and the open spaces with deadly intentness, as their owner swept hither and thither with his head stooped low, on the watch for any slightest motion or sign of life. But nothing stirred.

Then, just as the dim shape drifted over the open space where the rabbits were crouching, it opened its sickle-shaped beak and gave forth a sudden, piercing cry, terrible and startling. This was too much for the overstrung nerves of the crouching rabbits. They sprang into the air as if shot, and leaped frantically for the bushes. The dim form swooped, struck; and the nearest fugitive felt himself clutched in neck and back by knife-edged talons, hard as steel. He gave one short scream of terror, strangled on the instant. Then he was swept into the air, kicking spasmodically. And the dim shape bore him off into the deeps of the woods, to the hollow where its fierce mate and savage nestlings had their home.

The great horned owl alighted with his prey on a stout, naked branch which stood out conveniently beside the spacious hole in the ancient, half-dead maple tree which formed his dwelling. He laid the limp body of the rabbit across the edge of the nest, half in the hole and half out of it, and with a curious, formal bobbing of his fiercely tufted head he sidled up close to his mate, softly snapping his hooked beak by way of greeting, and giving utterance to a low, twittering sound that seemed ridiculously unsuitable to such a ferocious countenance as his. His mate, larger than he and even more savage-looking, had herself just returned from a successful hunt, laden with a luckless duck from some backwoods farmyard. Her two owlets, nearly half-grown but still downy, were tearing greedily at the duck and bolting huge mouthfuls of it, feathers and all. She herself had already satisfied her appetite—having probably gulped down two or three mice and small birds, captured on the edge of twilight, before bringing home the duck to her brood. She was not so unselfish as her mate, who, bloodthirsty and insatiable marauder though he was, could boast, nevertheless, of no small domestic virtue. A model spouse and father, he seldom consulted his own needs till he was sure that his mate and his young were fed. Now, having assured himself that all were supplied, he turned again to his prey. Holding it down with both feet, securely, he tore the skull apart with his sharp and powerful beak, and devoured first the head, which he considered the choicest morsel, bolting it bones and all. In the meantime his mate, moved purely by the hunting lust, had sailed noiselessly from her perch and winnowed off between the dark and silent tree trunks to seek for other prey.

Having swiftly and voraciously satisfied his appetite, the great owl wiped his crimsoned beak on the edge of the nest, sat up very erect, and for a few moments solemnly watched his youngsters still tearing at the carcass of the duck. He was massively built, broad-breasted, and about two feet in length from the tip of his short, broad tail to the crown of his big, round head with its two fierce, hornlike ear tufts. In color he was a mixture of soft browns, grays, and fawns, above, distributed irregularly in vague bars and splashes, while below he was of a creamy buff, delicately barred with deep chocolate. The wide, circular discs of flat feathering which surrounded his eyes were cream-white, shading into fawn, and between them came down a frowning, pointed brow of darker feathers. His eyes, extraordinarily bright and cruel, were enormous, as round as full moons, of a gemlike yellow with great, staring pupils of jetty black. They were fixed in their sockets—as with all owls—so that when he wished to turn them he had to turn his whole head with them. His look was always a full-faced stare, challenging and tamelessly savage. His legs and feet were thickly and softly feathered in white, right down to those inexorable horn-colored talons whose clutch could throttle a full-grown goose in a few seconds.

To ordinary ears, of man or beast, the silence of the forest, at this hour, was absolute. But to the great owl's supersensitive eardrums—veritable microphones, they were—the darkness was filled with innumerable furtive sounds. A far-off beech leaf, suddenly unburdening itself of a gathering load of dew, spoke loudly, though without significance, to him. He caught the infinitesimal whisper of crowded young twigs as they occasionally stretched themselves in their growth. Down in the thick earth-darkness close to the ground, perhaps fifty feet away, he detected the stealthy, padded footfalls of a prowling lynx, so light as to be scarcely audible to their owner himself. Without moving his body he turned his head in the direction of the sound, and stared intently. The lynx, a brilliant tree climber, was one of the very few wild creatures whom he feared; and hc held himself in tense readiness to signal for his absent mate to do battle, if necessary, for his nest and young. But the sinister footfalls crept off in another direction, and he knew that his home—which was well concealed from the ground by a bushy growth of Indian pea and wild viburnum—had not been discovered.

A minute or two later the grim listener on his high listening post detected a fairy rustling which was not of stretching twigs or dew-laden leaves. It came from under a fir thicket some fifty or sixty yards away; and so faint it was that other ears than his could scarce have caught it at a distance of ten paces. But he knew it at once for the scurrying of the shy little wood mice over the floor of the dead and crisp fir needles. On downy wings he dropped from his perch and sailed, swift and soundless as thought, straight in beneath the overhanging fir branches. His outstretched talons struck, like lightning, in two directions at once—and in one successfully. In that annihilating clutch a furry little life went out, without time for even a squeak of protest. The unerring hunter swept on without a pause, and rose to the nearest convenient limb. Settling himself there for a moment he lifted his tiny victim in one claw—like a parrot eating a biscuit—bit off its head daintily and swallowed it with an air of one appreciating a titbit, and then bolted the body at one careless gulp. A few seconds later he was back again upon his home perch, sitting upright as stiffly as a sentry at salute, his great eyes flaming spectrally through the dark.

And now thin pencils of pale light began to penetrate the uppermost branches of the trees, giving an ink-black edge to the shadow below. As the first slender ray reached him the great owl opened his beak and ruffled up the feathers about his neck.

Whuh-whoo-oo, Whuh-whoo-oo-oo, he called, a hollow, long-drawn cry all on one deep note, which seemed to come from several different quarters of the darkness at once. It was impossible, indeed, for any of the timid lurkers in the coverts, who listened to it with quivering hearts, to make out just where it did come from. But his far-off mate heard it, and knew. And from somewhere away beyond the other side of the pasture, came the response, muffled by distance and ghostly dim—*Whuh-whoo-oo-oo*. It signified to him that she was on her way back to the nest. He waited motionless perhaps half a minute, glanced at the two owlets who sat solemnly in the doorway of the nest digesting their heavy meal, and then sailed off through the silvering tree tops to hunt fresh victims about the pasture lands and clearings.

As he emerged into the open country, his soundless passing, through the strange, distorting light of the low moon, was like that of a specter—but unlike a specter he swept along with him a twisting and writhing shadow which gave warning of his approach. Mice, rabbits, chipmunks, even the dauntless and furious weasels, slipped to cover. The field was as empty as a desert, except for one big, black-and-white striped skunk which glanced up at him, unconcernedly, and went on digging up a mouse net. Tyrant and assassin though he was, and audacious as he was murderous, and more than a match in beak and talons for several skunks at once, he had no inclination to come to close quarters with this self-assured little creature which carried such an armory of choking poison under its tail. He swerved sullenly off to the edge of the woods again, and continued his flight along beneath their shadow till he reached the edge of the brook which flowed behind the farmyard. Here he dropped upon a momentarily unwary frog which was sitting, half-submerged, at the water's edge. He carried it to a near-by stump, and swallowed it whole. Then his ears caught a soft, sleepy twittering from among the branches of a straggling thorn bush some twenty or thirty yards downstream. A sudden ray from the moon, just rising over the hill, had awakened a sleeping song sparrow, and he had murmured some drowsy endearments to his mate who sat brooding her half-fledged nestlings close beside him. The next instant a monstrous, shadowy form with blazing eyes had burst in upon them. Both tiny parents were clutched simultaneously and squeezed to death before they had time to realize what doom had overtaken them. They were promptly gulped down, in quick succession; and then, sitting erect and solemn close beside the nest, the grim marauder proceeded to pick the half-naked nestlings from the nest one by one and to swallow them with deliberation. Though so small, they were the tastiest morsels he had sampled for a long time—since the nestful of partridge eggs, just beginning to hatch, which he had ravaged some weeks earlier in the season.

Up to this point, knowing that his greedy family was well supplied, the great owl had had no thought but for his own feasting. Now, however, he felt it was time to hunt for bigger game—for something substantial to carry home to the nest. He winged swiftly across to the farmstead, where the barn and house and woodshed stood black against the low moon. No living thing was astir in the farmyard, except a big, white cat prowling for mice along the edge of the barn. Though she was dangerous game he swooped at her without a moment's hesitation. But the cat had seen him, just in time; and with an indignant spitting she whisked in under the barn. He snapped his beak angrily, made a tour of the buildings, and found the window of the chicken house. But it was closed with wire netting. Glaring in through the wide meshes he saw the hens all asleep on their perches, some with half-grown chickens beside them. But the vigilant red cock was awake and, eyeing him defiantly, gave utterance to a sharp *kut-ee-ee-ee* of warning. The marauder tore savagely at the meshes with his mighty talons; but the wire was too strong for him, and in an instant the place was in an uproar of frightened squawks and cacklings.

The kitchen door flew open with a bang. A stream of yellow lamplight flooded across the shadowy yard. The farmer ran out, shouting and swearing fluently, and the would-be assassin, furious at being barred from such a luxury of slaughter, flew off to seek some less well-guarded prey.

About a quarter of a mile farther down the valley lay another little backwoods farm, whose owner, when clearing the land, had had the good taste to leave several fine elms standing beside the house and barns. The valley was by this time full-flooded with moonlight, and the great owl, to avoid observation, flew low beside the willow and alder bushes which fringed the brook. Across the open meadow that divided the barns from the brook he skimmed, almost brushing the grass tops, then rose noiselessly into the deep shadows which clung among the branches of the thick-leaved elms. And here, as luck would have it, he found two turkey hens, roosting upon one of the topmost boughs.

The turkeys, being light sleepers, detected him at once; but all they did was to stretch out their long necks inquiringly and cry *Kwit-kwit, kwit-kwit.* They were acquainted with the harmless, little, mouse-hunting barn owl, but this great bird was something they had never seen before; and they were full of curiosity. In one moment he had risen above them. In the next he had fallen upon the nearest, clutched her by the neck, and choked her foolish noise. Beating her wings convulsively, she toppled off her perch. Her captor strove to bear her up and fly off with her, but she was too heavy a burden for him, and with a mighty flapping the two came slowly to the ground.

This was not exactly what the marauder wanted, but he was not one to lose any opportunity for destruction. He bit and tore with that deadly sickle of his beak till he had decapitated his massive prize; and though he was by no means hungry, he broke up and swallowed most of the head, for the sake of the brains. In the meantime the other turkey, still resting on her perch, had kept on uttering her foolish *Kwit-kwit, kwit-kwit*, as if begging to know what all the excitement meant. She all too soon found out. Glancing up from his sanguinary meal, as if angered by her stupid noise, the great owl fixed her for a second or two with his glassy stare. Then he shot up through the gloom till her was a few feet above the anxious chatterer, pounced upon her vindictively, and swept her, strangled and futilely fluttering, from her perch. Her life promptly went out through her gaping beak; but she, too, proved too heavy for her destroyer's wing power; and despite his determined flapping, he was borne slowly to the ground. He tore off her silly head, in sheer wantonness of destruction. Then, wiping his beak on her still quivering body, he bounced into the air and flew away to seek other quarry, sailing close to the ground to avoid making himself conspicuous, and glaring fiercely under every bush as he passed.

It chanced that an indiscreet hen, impatient of the safe nests in the barn and fowl house where, in return for her security, her precious eggs were always taken from her, had found a secret spot under a clump of lilacs at the back of the garden. Here she had accumulated a clutch of eggs, which she had now been happily brooding for close upon the allotted three weeks. The chicks within were stirring, and just beginning to tap with tiny bills at the walls of their shell prisons. The proud mother was answering these taps with low, crooning sounds of encouragement and content.

It was those soft utterances of mother love that betrayed her to her doom. She saw a pair of wide, dreadful eyes glaring in upon her through the leafage. With a shrill screech of defiance she ruffled up all her feathers, threw back her head, and faced the enemy with threatening, wide-open beak. But of scant avail was all her devoted courage against such a foe as this. In a moment she was gripped by irresistible talons, jerked, valiantly battling, from her nest, strangled, and tossed aside, a heap of feebly-kicking feathers. And the slaughterer fell to gorging himself with the just-hatching eggs. Full-fed though he was, such supreme delicacies as these could not be left behind; and he managed somehow to put away the whole nestful. Then he grasped the body of the mother in his claws, hopped awkwardly out of the bushes with it, bore it somewhat heavily into the air, and headed his flight direct for the hollow tree in the woods.

He flew high now, having no care to conceal his coming, and the backwoods world of forest and scattered farms, rough, stump-strewn pastures and raw, new clearings, with the silver coils of the slow brook brightly threading them, lay outspread sharp-edged below him in the white flood of the moonlight. The robber flew more slowly than was his wont, his limp booty being a massive-bodied Brahma of some six or seven pounds dead weight, and he himself somewhat sluggish from his over-hearty feast. But there was no need for haste; so he did not exert himself, but winnowed on through the blue-silver night, well satisfied with his list of slain.

Suddenly, from far over the tree tops came a hollow call. *Whuh-whoo; whuh-whuh, whuh-whu*—not long-drawn, but staccato, hurried, urgent. It was his mate's voice, summoning him, crying for help. He woke instantly from his lethargy, dropped his booty, answered with one sonorous *Whoo-oo-oo*, and shot homeward with the utmost speed.

During his absence that prowling lynx, which had caused him apprehension an hour before, had crept back on the trail of a rabbit, to the neighborhood of the hollow tree. She had missed the rabbit; but happening to glance upward, with cruel eyes as round and moonlike as those of the great owl himself, she had detected the big, black hole in the age-whitened trunk. Such a hole, she knew well enough, would be sure to be occupied by something—most probably by something young and defenseless, and good to eat. She was hungry; and, moreover, she had a pair of sturdy kittens to feed at home in her own well-hidden lair. She ran nimbly up the huge, gnarled trunk to investigate.

At the first rattling sound of her claws upon the bark, the mother owl, who had been snuggling her owlets, shot forth angrily from the hole to see what creature was so bold as to invade her realm. But at the sight of the lynx—a gigantic, tuft-eared cat as big as a fox hound—her wrath changed to frantic terror for her young, who were not yet sufficiently fledged for effective flight. Though even more bloodthirsty and wastefully murderous than her mate, her courage was of the finest, and she knew no such thing as shirking where the defense of her round-eyed nestlings was concerned. With that one sharp cry for help—which her homing mate had heard—she swooped from her branch and struck the lynx heavily in the face with wing and claw.

Taken by surprise, the lynx was almost jolted from her hold. With a harsh spitting she cowered, and shielded her face between her paws, while the frantic mother raked her back savagely. Then, furious at being so handled by an adversary whom she despised, the lynx scrambled on upward, and gained the branch beside the nest. From this vantage point she struck out like lightning with her great, armed paw, just as the desperate mother was swooping upon her again. Had the blow got fairly home it would have been final; but the agile bird swerved backward in time, and it struck her but glancingly, with its force half spent, on the breast. Her dense, elastic armor of feathers saved her; but a shower of feathers flew, and she was hurled halfway to the ground before she could recover from the shock.

Imagining that her adversary was disposed of, the lynx thrust her head into the hole. The hardy owlets bit and clawed her face valiantly, but she snatched one in her jaws, crunched its neck, and plucked it forth upon the branch. Holding it comfortably between her huge forepaws she lay flat along the branch and proceeded to devour it. As she did so the desperate mother, shaken but undaunted, returned to the attack and struck her again in the face with rending talons.

Holding her prey firmly with one paw the lynx, with an ear-splitting yowl of pain and rage, lashed out again at her resolute assailant, but missed her aim completely. And at this juncture the male bird arrived.

In silence he shot downward and struck at the great, gray beast. The latter had caught sight of him as he swooped. She let go of the dead owlet—which dropped to the ground—and rose slightly on her hind quarters in order to meet this new attack with the full armory of her fore-claws. By a fortunate stroke she caught him by one wing; and the next moment her long fangs were buried in his thigh. Held thus at close quarters he pounded madly with his wings, and tore in a frenzy at his enemy's face with his beak and his free talons. He was pulled down, however, and borne backward, for all his indomitable struggles; and getting her claws set into one wing, near the shoulder, the lynx fairly tore it from its socket. But undaunted even in that hopeless strait, he went on fighting to the death.

The mother owl, meanwhile, had been tearing and clawing viciously at the lynx's neck, from above. Unable any longer to endure this torment, the latter tried to double back upon the narrow branch and defend herself. The male bird heaved up valiantly beneath, and with a last effort fixed his beak in the side of her throat. She lost her balance, and the two toppled off into space together. Over and over they turned, closed locked, and then fell apart. The owl, all but dead and with one wing hanging useless from its tendons, continued to roll over and over in his descent, and landed with a thud which finished him. The lynx, on the other hand, turning herself right-side up and spreading all four legs apart so as to make a sort of parachute of herself, landed lightly on the powerful elastic springs of her paws. The mother owl had been on top of her all the way down, and was still frantically tearing at her back. But the lynx had had enough. With a screech of panic she darted under some low branches, scraping off her assailant, and sped away, belly to earth like a terrified cat, through the densest thickets she could find.

The victorious mother owl did not pursue. She circled twice, very slowly, above the sprawled bodies of her mate and her nestling, staring down upon them with wide, unwinking, expressionless eyes. Then she winnowed soundlessly up to her perch, and hurried into the nest to see if her other fledgeling had escaped unharmed.

The Citadel in the Grass*

In a sunny fence corner at the foot of the pasture, partly overhung by a pink-blossomed bush of wild rose and palisaded by a thin fringe of slender, pallid grass stems, lay the ants' nest. In outward appearance it was a shallow, flattened, tawny-colored mound, this citadel in the grass, about a foot and a half across and eight or ten inches high, its whole surface covered with particles of dry earth mixed with and lightened by bitten fragments of dead grass and spruce needles, and pitted irregularly with round black holes from an eighth to a quarter of an inch in diameter. These were the easily guarded gateways to the tunnels leading to the dark and mysterious interior of the citadel. For some feet all around the base of the mound the grass roots were threaded by faint trails, made by the ants in bringing home supplies and booty to the nest.

On this bland blue morning of early summer, when the unclouded sunshine was not too hot to be gracious and stimulating, the tawny dome of the citadel was alive with workers. They were a sturdy species of ant, this tribe, somewhere about a half inch in length, with powerful mandibles and broad heads, the head and thorax of a rusty-red color and the abdomen blackish brown. Some were busy opening up the tunnel entrances, which had been closed during the night, and letting fresh air into the interior. They carefully removed the pellets of dry earth and bits of dead grass which had formed the stoppers, and seemed to give themselves much unnecessary work by carrying their burdens about in their jaws before making up their minds just where to lay them down. Others ran around aimlessly, as if they had lost something and had no idea of where to look for it. Possibly these had been on night duty in the deep underground nurseries, and were merely taking the air before getting back to their helpless charges. But the majority acted quite differently. On emerging to the light they would pause and wave their antennae for a few seconds, as if signaling, and would then hurry straight ahead, with an air of set

* From *Wisdom of the Wilderness* (New York: Macmillan, 1923), 162-84. "The Citadel in the Grass" also appeared in *Saturday Evening Post* (July 8, 1922).

purpose, down the steep of the citadel and out through a forest of grass stems. They were the foragers and hunters, seeking their booty or their prey in the weedy wilderness along the fence.

In a few minutes certain of these began to straggle back, early successful in their quest and carrying their prizes; perhaps a small dead fly, or a tiny grub still squirming inconvenient protest against his fate, or the head or leg or wing of some victim so bulky as only to be dealt with piecemeal; while here and there some triumphant forager would come struggling homeward inch by slow inch, dragging a prize many times bigger and heavier than herself—perhaps a fat spider or a sprawling little dead grasshopper—which she had feared to dissect for transport lest the pieces should be stolen in her absence. Working her way backwards and tugging the prize along by the head or leg or wing, held up for minutes at a time by the obstacle of a root or a pebble, she would drag and pull and worry like a terrier on a rope, till at last the precious burden was brought to the foot of the mound, where it could safely be cut up at leisure.

Among these eager foragers was one whom, as typical of her species, we may distinguish by the name Formica. A strenuous and experienced worker in the prime of her powers, on leaving the nest she had speedily struck off aside from the trails of her fellows, desirous of fresh hunting grounds in the miniature jungle of grass and weeds. Having come across a head of red-clover bloom trodden down and crushed by the pasturing cattle, she was now filling herself greedily with honey from the bottom of the broken flower tubes. This red-clover honey was a delicacy which, though she might sniff its perfume longingly, she could never hope to taste except by lucky accident; for at the base of those deep, narrow-tubed blossoms it was beyond the reach of all despoilers but the long-tongued bumblebees. Now, in the golden warmth, hummed over by tiny, envious flies who were careful not to come within reach of her mandibles, she was lapping up the nectar and enjoying herself as if she had not a duty or responsibility in the world.

But Formica, though much more independent, more conscious of her individual right than, for instance, that communistic automaton, the bee, was a most responsible little personage, aware of all her duties to the state. When she had absorbed all the clover honey she could hold she climbed down from the ruined blossom and glanced about, waving her antennae, in the hope of finding something worth taking home to the state larder. At this moment there was a rustling among the grass stems, and a tiny, grayish-brown shrewmouse, looking to Formica as huge as an elephant, came scurrying by with a shining bluebottle fly gripped in his jaws. As he crossed the open space where the clover was trodden down there came a fierce rush of wind that nearly swept Formica from her feet; and a sparrow hawk, who had been watching from her perch on the nearest fence stake, swooped down upon the luckless shrew and bore him off. As he opened his jaws in a squeak of anguish the bluebottle dropped from them and fell beside Formica.

Though almost overwhelmed by that gust from the sparrow hawk's wings, Formica pounced instantly upon the rich and unexpected prize. The bluebottle was not quite dead. It was on its back and too severely wounded to turn over, but it could still kick and move its wings with an embarrassing degree of vigor. The great, many-faceted eyes of the crippled insect glared upon its assailant with shifting, many-colored flame; but Formica was herself well equipped in the way of eyes and refused to be impressed. Forcing herself in between the waving legs, she sank her mandibles deep into the victim's thorax; and then, arching her body to bring the tip of her abdomen well beneath, like the attitude of a wasp in stinging, she injected into the wound a dose of formic acid from the poison glands which served her in place of a sting. Whether by good luck or intuitive knowledge, she had struck upon a great nerve center for her injection, and the dose worked swiftly. The twitching wings and waving legs grew still. The unfortunate fly was not yet dead, for it could still move its head, and the opalescent fires still flamed and fleeted in its great eyes. But as long as it could not struggle Formica was satisfied, and she set herself valiantly to the task of dragging her booty home.

The distance from the crushed clover bloom to the citadel in the grass was only about fifteen feet, but it took Formica a full hour of furious effort to accomplish it. For a good half the distance the jungle was dense and trackless; and the captive, though utterly unresisting, had a way of getting its wings tangled up with the grass roots or of wedging itself between a couple of stiff stems that would drive Formica frantic with exasperation. Under these circumstances she would always waste many minutes and a vast amount of energy in striving to master the obstacle by main force before she could bring herself to take a new grip and try an easier path.

When at last she had come to the frequented trail and was continually meeting her friends, she never demanded help and seldom received any offer of it; and this was just as well, seeing that whenever a passer-by paused to lend a hand—or a mandible—the result was only confusion. The newcomer was pretty sure to go about the job in a casual, absent-minded fashion, and as often as not to pull in quite the wrong direction, till Formica, in a rage, would rush at her and unceremoniously hustle her away.

Arrived at last safely at the citadel with her splendid trophy, Formica seemed to consider her labors for the moment at an end. That gleaming blue bulk was much too heavy for her to drag it up the slope of the dome. She handed it over, with a hasty waving of antennae, to a knot of her comrades, and wandered up the steep slope with the air of one who has earned a bit of leisure but does not quite know what to do with it. She made a tour of the top of the mound, occasionally wandering into one of the entrances, but always coming out again in a few seconds. And every now and then she would stop to touch antennae with an acquaintance. Presently she came face to face with a disheveled friend who was evidently just home from a rough-and-tumble fight of some sort. Weary, wounded, and covered with dirt, the newcomer seemed to convey some sorry tale to Formica, who straightway fell to stroking and cleansing her with every mark of sympathy.

The ant hill, as we have seen at the beginning of this narrative, was partly overhung by the branches of a wild rosebush which grew against the fence. The rosebush at this season was in full bloom, and the pale-pink, golden-centered blossoms were thronged with pollen hunters and hummed about with innumerable wings. Sober brown bees dusted over with the lemon-colored rose pollen, darting iridescent flies, irresponsible yellow butterflies and black-and-yellow wasps, swift and fiercely intent on their hunting—all found the glowing rosebush their focus of interest or of fate.

A black-and-white dog from the farmhouse on the hillside above the pasture came trotting up to the fence sniffing for rabbit tracks, and as he passed the rosebush one of the busy wasps buzzed close at his ear. Thoughtlessly—mistaking it, in his absorption, for a big fly—he snapped at it and caught it. With a yelp of surprise he spat it out again violently and began to paw at his smarting muzzle. Finding this quite ineffective to allay the fiery torment in his tongue, he raced off, whimpering, with his tail between his legs, to plunge his mouth into the soothing chill of the horse trough in the farmyard.

The wasp, meanwhile, her wings disabled and daubed with saliva, but still very much alive and furiously angry, had fallen upon the very center of the teeming ant hill, and almost, so to speak, under Formica's nose. Formica, with a courage and a self-sacrifice beyond all praise, instantly seized the dreadful monster by a wing. Her career would have come to an end there and then, but that, in the same lightning fraction of a second, three other ants, equally brave and reckless of destruction, flung themselves into the struggle. The wasp had fallen on her back. Now, curving her muscular black-and-yellow body nearly double, she brought into play her long, terrible sting—a bitter red flame which flickered in and out, this way and that, like a lightning flash, and whose least touch meant death. Two of her small assailants dropped instantly, stiffened out as if struck by a thunderbolt; but in the next moment she was literally covered. Fighting not only with that fatal sting but also with her feet, like a boxer, and with her powerful jaws, like a terrier, she was presently surrounded by a ring of dead or crippled foes; but for every one that fell there were a dozen more eager to rush in, till she was almost buried from view.

Formica, by worrying at her like a bulldog, having succeeded in biting off the wing which she had first seized, now drew away for a moment to consider. An experienced and resourceful fighter, she liked to spend herself to the best advantage. Suddenly she darted in and secured a grip upon the slender but powerful tubelike joint which connected the wasp's abdomen with her thorax. Here, though almost crushed by her victim's frantic lashings, she bit and sawed with her tireless mandibles till she succeeded in dividing the great trunk nerve. Instantly the abdomen lost its rigid curve, ceased its lashing, and straightened out. Formica continued her operation, however, till the whole tube was severed; and the disjointed abdomen rolled aside, its sting still flickering in and out, but no longer directed, and dangerous only to those who were careless enough to get it its way.

The battle being now over, certain of the ants set themselves to dragging the spoils down into the nest by one of the larger tunnels, while others began to clear up the field, carrying the bodies of the slain away from the citadel and dropping them among the grass roots. Yet others fell to caring for the wounded, carrying them into the cool, dark passages and cleansing them and tenderly licking their wounds. But Formica, feeling that she had done enough for the moment, left all these duties to the others and betook herself into the interior of the citadel in search of rest and refreshment.

About an inch below the surface the narrow passage by which she had entered made a sharp turn, almost doubling upon itself; and immediately she was in what would have seemed to our human eyes thick darkness. But to her, with her highly complex and many-faceted organs of vision, it was only a cool gloom, very soothing to her sensitive nerves after the glare of the outside world. Still descending—and passing on the way, with a touch of the antennae, many acquaintances and comrades—she came to the doorway of a wide but low-roofed chamber, with a watchful guard at the entrance. Here were about a hundred of the whitish so-called ant eggs—in reality pupae, almost mature, in their frail cocoons—all ranged carefully in the centre of the chamber and with a couple of guardians walking about among them. They had been brought up from the safe depths of the citadel to absorb the tempered but vitalizing warmth in this apartment near the surface, and were being watched with special solicitude because they were very near the time for their emergence as full-grown ants.

Formica merely glanced in upon them, exchanging greetings with the guards, and continued her way down to the cooler and moister depths. Here she turned into another spacious chamber, its low ceiling supported by several irregular columns of compacted earth. Here and there about the center of the chamber were little clusters of the ant grubs, or larvae, sorted carefully according to their age and size, each cluster attended by several diligent nurses who were kept busy feeding the hungry but legless and quite helpless young. To all these Formica paid no attention whatever. One of the older, more highly experienced members of the community, she had long ago graduated from the simple routine duties of the nurseries. These fell, for the most part, upon the very young ants, or upon a few smaller, blackish ants of another race which the community kept as slaves.

Around the walls of the chamber were a number of little, chubby, squat-built insects, each placidly pasturing on the tips of grass roots which had penetrated the foundations of the citadel. It was these tiny creatures—a species of aphis, or plant louse, carefully kept and tended by the ants as we keep our herds of cows—that Formica was now seeking in her desire for refreshment. Going up to one of them she began to stroke and caress it coaxingly with her antennae, till presently the little creature, in response, exuded a sticky drop of honeydew, which Formica lapped up greedily. From one to another she passed, getting always a sweet contribution, except from such as had already been milked, until her appetite was satisfied. Then she made a hasty inspection of the rest of the flock, as if to assure herself that all were duly supplied with provender. This done, she ran across to one of the slaves and tapped her gently with her antennae; whereupon the latter, dutifully and with the utmost good will, set herself to the task of making her mistress' toilet, licking and polishing her from head to foot, and ending up by feeding her with a drop of honey just as she would have fed one of the helpless larvae.

Thoroughly refreshed, Formica now passed gayly through several galleries and presently entered the great central chamber of the citadel—an apartment some five or six inches across, nearly circular, and supported by half a dozen stout pillars. This chamber was thronged. It was the life center of the citadel. Every here and there were clusters of eggs, or groups of larvae and pupae, surrounded by their guards. Active little pallid-colored wood lice, the scavengers of the nest, scurried busily hither and thither, as completely ignored as the street cleaners are in the thoroughfares of a busy human city.

At the very center of the chamber was the great queen mother of the tribe, a huge ant more than double the size of any of her subjects. She was surrounded by a dense crowd of attendants, all with their heads turned toward her as if in respectful homage, waiting to feed her or cleanse her or carry away her eggs whenever she saw fit to lay them, or to perform eagerly any service which she might require. Three or four idle males, gentlemen of leisure, much smaller and slenderer than the queen, strolled about among the busy throng, occasionally caressing a complaisant worker or a slave, and generally receiving a taste of honey in return.

Formica went straight up to the crowd surrounding the queen mother and stood there for perhaps a half minute, waving her antennae and paying her respects. It would seem, however, that some sort of a council was being held at the moment, presumably under the guidance of the queen, and that decisions of importance to the tribe were being reached. For all at once there was a great stir and shifting, and a number of the ants, hurriedly extricating themselves from the press, formed themselves in an orderly file and hastened from the chamber. Among the foremost of these, already recovered and prepared for adventure in spite of her strenuous morning, was Formica.

As it started from the state chamber the detachment was a small one, of not more than eighty or a hundred; but as it went it was swelled by fresh adherents flocking out from every gallery, for word had gone all through the citadel that a slave-raiding expedition was afoot. Filing forth upon the surface of the dome, the detachment was joined by squads from other tunnel exits; and when it formed up into a compact column and marched off down the side of the nest it was perhaps from five to six hundred strong.

It was obvious that this expedition had been fully prepared for in advance and all necessary scouting carried out. Prudent forethought and a fine directing intelligence, as distinguished from mere instinct, or what the scientists call reflex action, were most unmistakably stamped upon it. The little army knew where it was going and why it was going. The line of march had been selected, and the leaders knew the route; and there was no hesitation or delay. In spite of obstacles, for there was no clear trail, the column kept its array in most disciplined fashion, and there were no stragglers.

Fully a hundred feet away from the citadel, in the grass, on the other side of the fence, and just upon the open fringe of the forest, stood another ant hill, upreared from the short turf between the roots of an old weather-bleached stump. This nest was occupied by a strong tribe of blackish-brown ants, similar to the slaves in Formica's community. Though slightly smaller than Formica, they were a sturdy, industrious, intelligent race, making the best of slaves; and Formica's people had decided that they must have a fresh supply of them. Hence this warlike and altogether unprovoked invasion. Whatever the virtues to be observed in the world of the ant folk, a regard for the rights of strangers is not among them. The ants' morality begins and ends with the interests of their own community.

The approach of the enemy was observed by the dark ants while the hostile column was yet several feet away, or possibly the alarm had been given by terrified scouts. However that may be, a swarm of defenders gathered swiftly on the summit of the threatened nest. They rushed down the slope and hurled themselves desperately upon the invaders. Their courage and devotion were beyond reproach; but in strength, in the effectiveness of their weapons, and in military skill they were no match for Formica and her fellows. After five minutes or less of furious mêlée they were routed and fled back into the depths of their nest, leaving half their number dead or mortally stricken on the field, while the casualties among the invading ranks were hardly worth mentioning.

The battle once decided, the victors were not vindictive. They had come not to slaughter needlessly but to procure slaves. For this purpose adult captives were of no use to them. They wanted larvae and pupae of the vanquished, whom they could rear in captivity and who—knowing no other state and not regarding their captors as foes—would be contented and unaware of their bondage. At the doorway to each tunnel guards were placed, while strong parties dashed down through all the galleries. At the narrow entrances to the nurseries and to the great central chamber there were brief but sharp struggles with the guards, who all died on the spot rather than betray their trusts.

But, entrance once gained, there was practically no more fighting, as the thoroughly beaten black army had disappeared into the underground passages beneath the stump.

The actions of the invaders within the nest were deliberate, disciplined, and swift. To the big black queen, whom they regarded less as an enemy than as a potential mother of a future supply of slaves, they paid no heed whatever. The scattered piles of eggs, too, they ignored, though they would have been glad to devour such succulent fare had there been time. But for some reason the order had gone forth that there was to be no delay and no divergence from the one supreme object of the expedition.

In the main chamber and the several subsidiary nurseries there were almost enough pupae to burden the whole army of the invaders. The remainder had to content themselves with larvae, who, being able to wriggle, were less convenient to carry, especially as they had to be gripped without wounding their delicate skins. As soon as each marauder had secured her prize she hastened with it to the surface of the nest. There the column again formed up, but this time rather loosely and irregularly, as there was no longer any fear of attack; and the triumphant red warriors, each bearing aloft in her mandibles, very tenderly and without apparent effort, a captive as big and heavy as herself, were soon streaming back homeward in long procession through the grass roots.

This expedition, however, hitherto so triumphantly successful, was not destined to reach home without a measure of ill luck to dull the brightness of its triumph. A sharp-eyed, sharp-nosed animal, about the size of a cat, of a glossy black color, with a white stripe down each side of its back and waving a long, fluffy, handsome tail, chanced to be nosing along the fence in search of mice, beetles, or grasshoppers. His sharp eyes detected the richly laden procession of the ants just as the head of the column reached the fence.

The skunk was not particularly partial to full-grown ants as an article of diet, because the formic acid in their poison sacks was rather pungent for his taste. But their young, whether in the form of larvae or of pupae, he regarded as a delicacy.

Standing astride the procession, he began hastily licking up as many as he could, munching and gulping down captives and captors together with huge satisfaction. Formica, with her burden, just evaded this horrid fate. Alert and observant as always, she slipped under the edge of a pebble as the long red tongue of the skunk was descending upon her. But the hot breath of the devouring monster filled her with wholesome fear. Still clinging to her precious burden, she crept aside from the crippled column, taking a path of her own, and rejoined it only under the shelter of the fence.

When the remnants of the rear guard had escaped him the skunk climbed through the fence, hoping to find the procession again on the other side. In this, however, though he searched diligently, he was disappointed, for the line of march lay for several yards along beneath the bottom rail before emerging again into the open. The skunk, stumbling upon a mouse nest in the grass, forgot all about the ants. And the expedition, diminished by fully a third of its number, made its way back to the citadel without further misadventure, the survivors still clinging doggedly to their booty.

As Formica was one of the wisest, most efficient and most courageous citizens of the community, she was usually hunting and foraging farther afield than most of her comrades.

Sometimes, she being inveterately hostile to all other ants except those of her own tribe, she got into savage duels, from which she always came off victorious, though frequently not without scars. Once in a while, moreover, she was rash enough to tackle a quarry too powerful and pugnacious for her—a nimble hunting spider or a savage little bronze scavenger beetle with jaws as destructive as her own. When she made a mistake of this sort she was driven to using the pungent venom at the tip of her abdomen in order to confuse the foe and enable her to escape.

Being thus endowed beyond her fellows with wisdom and quick perception to direct her courage, Formica would probably have lived to follow the fortunes of her tribe through several eventful summers had it not been for her restless and intrepid curiosity. She was of the stuff of which explorers are made. One day, adventuring through a patch of blueberry scrub many yards upon the forest side of the fence, she came upon a strange plant, quite unlike any she had ever seen before. There was no main stalk; but a cluster of stout stems, arising from the crown of the root, bore each one leaf, some three or four inches in length, shaped like a broad-lipped water jug. The leaves were of a lucent, tender green, veined and striped with vivid crimson, and gave forth a subtle odor, perceptible to none but the most delicate senses, which seemed to suggest honeydew. What reasonable ant could resist the lure of honeydew? Formica could not.

But if she had known that this was the terrible carnivorous pitcher plant, the relentless devourer of insects, she would have fled in horror.

Instead of fleeing, however, she eagerly ran up the nearest stem, and up the cool, translucent, red-veined globe of the lower leaf, delighted to find that the firm hairs which covered stem and leaf alike all pointed upwards instead of downwards, and so offered no obstacle to her progress. Gaining the rim of the pitcher, she peered inside, looking for the source of that honeydew fragrance. Beneath her she saw a fairylike interior, filled with cool green light, and about half full of water. In the water, to be sure, there floated the drowned bodies of a wasp, a spider, and several small flies. But this fact conveyed no warning to Formica. Rather it suggested to her the hope of easy prey after she should have found the honeydew which she was seeking.

The broad lip of the pitcher offered her an easy path; and she was gratified to find that those fine hairs, which on the outside all slanted upwards, were now, most conveniently, all slanting downwards. The slope grew steeper and steeper, till presently, when she saw the water just beneath, she found the hair so slippery that she had great difficulty in keeping her foothold. At this point she became apprehensive. Deciding to seek a safer path, she turned to retrace her steps. But now those treacherous hairs, which had so sweetly aided her progress, turned hostile. They became an array of sharp needle points, leveled in her face. She tried to thrust them aside, to penetrate them; but in vain. In a sudden panic she forced herself against them desperately. For an instant they yielded; and then, with savage recoil, they hurled her, kicking and sprawling, into the watery abyss.

A few hours later a young girl, a summer visitor at the farmhouse on the hillside, chanced to be wandering along the edge of the woods, looking for wild flowers. Overjoyed to find a specimen of the Sarracenia, she dug it up carefully by the roots to take it hone. But first, of course, she emptied the lovely, pale-green, ruby-veined pitchers, pouring forth upon the moss, among other victims, the bodies of a wasp, a spider, several small flies—and Formica.

Background and Contexts

Charles G.D. Roberts, Lady Joan Roberts fonds (MGL27c) University of New Brunswick, Archives & Special Collections. Harriet Irving Library. Reprinted with permission.

Terry Whalen
Charles G.D. Roberts – The Call of the Wild and the Call of the Work*

Charles G.D. Roberts was regarded as an august literary figure in his own time, but in the past two decades both his personal and literary reputation have been reassessed by critics with a more hesitant attitude to the giving of praise. Looked at from the outside, Roberts' life appears to have a selfish side to its bearing—yet, in a time when men, too, are being seen as victims of the stereotypical social roles that are handed to them, it might well be argued that the circumstances of Roberts' life were far from ideal and that he should be granted at least a bit of sociological room for his flaws. Biography should include a will to generosity, just as literature, as W.B. Yeats would have it, is often about the forgiveness of sins.

* This biographical essay is a modified and updated version of a biographical commentary first published as part of Terry Whalen's "Charles G.D. Roberts" in *Canadian Writers and Their Works*, Ed. Robert Lecker, Jack David, and Ellen Quigley. Fiction Series, Vol. II. Toronto: ECW, 1989, pp. 159-64. The previously-published portions are reprinted here with the permission of ECW.

Many have handed to them roles that they have difficulty surviving, and they are handed such roles by social traditions and conventions that care very little for their individual desires and their needs. Roberts lived a life in which his inclinations as a writer were in conflict with, sometimes creative conflict with, his role and responsibilities as a conventional family patriarch. His days were replete with tensions caused by the competition within him between conservative and wandering values. He was both defiant of and awkwardly obedient to the social conventions of his time, but he was also a man gifted with an enormous amount of natural human energy and a capacity for hard work—gifts that would assure the worth of a number of his literary achievements, not the least of which was his co-founding of the modern 'realistic' animal story.

Two relatively contemporary biographical texts, John Coldwell Adams' *Sir Charles God Damn: The Life of Sir Charles G.D. Roberts* (1986) and Laurel Boone's edition of *The Collected Letters of Charles G. D. Roberts* (1989), are detailed and valuable book-length studies related to Roberts' life, and they should be read along with Elsie Pomeroy's much earlier, *Sir Charles G.D. Roberts: A Biography* (1943). Adams' and Boone's works imply a largely accurate image of Roberts as a man of contrasts and/or contradictions. While a patriarchal, establishment figure in many ways, Roberts was also a philandering adventurer. A genteel, very social man in one aspect, he also loved the call of the wild and the solitude of nature. He was a good friend to many, and a thoughtful lover to some, but he was unsteady in his first marriage, and the details of his dalliances suggest that he sometimes had a very manipulative attitude to women. He appears to have loved his children deeply, even if it appears that he sometimes neglected their needs in the name of his freedom and his career. He was often equivocal in his attitudes to those around him and lived a life that included many contradictory impulses.

Pomeroy's biography misses some of the contradictions in Roberts' life, partly because she worked so close to Roberts as his friend and secretary for twenty-four years. She viewed (and even knew that she viewed) Roberts with an awe that was constant and uncritical: "When I was a child at public school, I was thrilled by the patriotic poem, 'O Child of Nations, giant-limbed,' Charles G.D. Roberts became the subject of my hero-worship" ("Final Chapter" 6). Nevertheless, while Adams and Boone give us an arguably more candid and informed view of Roberts' life, Pomeroy's older (and yet younger) work remains valuable for other, mostly historical reasons. Roberts was in some ways quite secretive about his life, and Adams has remarked that there "are many instances in Roberts' life where available information does not justify any definite conclusions" ("Post Biography" 77). If readers keep this caveat in mind, all three of these books (by Adams, Boone, and Pomeroy) are useful in their indirect illumination of Roberts' works. Roberts was an immensely complicated writer, so it is unsurprising that his person was very complicated as well.

Roberts was born in Douglas, near Fredericton, New Brunswick, on 10 January 1860. He was the child of Reverend George Goodridge Roberts and Emma (Bliss) Roberts. Cousin to Bliss Carman on his mother's side of the family, he was a distant relative of Ralph Waldo Emerson. His background was an Anglican and a United Empire Loyalist one, and, again like Carman, he would later move to the United States and earn for himself a reputation as a popular writer, one who would produce nearly six dozen titles of prose and poetry during his eighty-four years of what Desmond Pacey, in *Ten Canadian Poets* (1958), termed a life of spiritual "restlessness" (57). This quality of restlessness shows up in given of the animals in his stories—see particularly, "The Homesickness of Kehonka," "A Stranger to the Wild," for instance, and it is a quality which appears as both a virtue and a burden.

Adams suggests that Roberts' restlessness is a quality he inherited from his mother, for, while his father was reputedly a steady and conservative figure, his mother, "on the other hand, was given to moods as unpredictable and 'ever changing' as the tides of the Tantramar. There are various rumours about her unconventional behaviour—all of them reflecting unfavourably upon a clergyman's wife in the Victorian era—including one story that she smoked a corncob pipe" (Post Biography 78). Further, " . . . the serious side of Roberts' nature, conscious of propriety and sharing the high ideals of his father, was forever in conflict with the earthy and rebellious genes of his mother"

(Post Biography 78). Whatever its source, his was a restlessness that would ultimately have an upending effect on his domestic life, just as it was arguably also the fountain source of his prodigious literary intensity.

The Roberts family moved to Westcock, N.B., in August 1861, and for the first fourteen years of his life, Roberts was tutored by his father and also implicitly by the woods, waters, and animals visible to him around the Tantramar River district of New Brunswick. His landscape shaped him as surely as did his parents. The Tantramar is one of the two rivers which some commentators see as highly formative of Roberts' imaginative life. The other river he grew to know intimately was the Saint John, after the Roberts family moved to Fredericton in 1874 when his father was appointed rector of St. Ann's Church and canon of Christ Church Cathedral. Charles was enrolled in Fredericton Collegiate School and was taught an appreciation of classical, Romantic, and Victorian poetry by the school's energetic headmaster, George Parkin, a man who was part of what Roberts later named a "strange aesthetic ferment" ("Bliss Carman" 416) in the New Brunswick capital during Carman's and Roberts' undergraduate years. Roberts was an athletic, intelligent, and accomplished youth, and he composed his first verses ("Sonnet: On the Dying Year" and "Spring") during 1874-75, items which were later published in the *Canadian Illustrated News* (30 March 1878) when he was eighteen years of age. He graduated with highest honours in 1876 and enrolled in the University of New Brunswick in the fall of that year.

Roberts graduated from university in 1879 with honours in philosophy and political economy, scholarships in Latin and Greek, and a medal in Latin prose competition. In September of that year, he was appointed headmaster at the Chatham Grammar and High School in Chatham, N.B. In December 1879 Roberts became engaged to Mary (May) Isobel Fenety, daughter of the King's Printer, and they married in December of 1880. With the help of his father-in-law, he published his first book, *Orion and Other Poems* (1880). So at the age of twenty, he was the author of an acclaimed book, one which helped earn for him the title "Father of Canadian Poetry" (Stringer 61), a title suggesting a magnificent plumage that would set him up for future deflation by a number of his more recent critical commentators. In his own time, it spoke to the high calibre of his abilities and to the emerging esteem in which he became held by the Canadian literary establishment of his day. Such precociousness marks and disturbs much of Roberts' life, and it is obvious that his intense talent had already begun, by the 1880s, to interfere with his peace of mind and with the stability of his domestic life.

An uncomfortable quality of haste and confusion can be detected in Roberts' life after his marriage to May Fenety. They seemed unsuited at the outset, as she was uninterested in the goings on of the tumultuous literati and disappointed by the lowering of her socio-economic status that came as a consequence of having married a teacher and aspiring writer. The period from 1881 to 1885 provides us with a short version of the choices Roberts had to make in the midst of his busy, but highly creative, day-to-day existence: He received a master's degree from U.N.B. in 1881, while still teaching as a means of making a living. He resigned from the Chatham School in January 1882 to be appointed headmaster of York Street School in Fredericton, only to resign from that post in the summer of 1883 to take up an appointment as editor of Goldwin Smith's *The Week* in Toronto in November of the same year. Because of his disagreements with Smith's political views—Smith was an annexationist, Roberts a nationalist (he was later an imperialist)—he resigned the editorship in February 1884, in a gesture of moral authenticity. He spent just over a year in Fredericton, trying to survive on freelance work, and he travelled to New York for a brief visit to forage for more work. His restlessness always included a capacity for hard work, and there was more of it yet to come.

By the time of Roberts' appointment as a professor of English and French at King's College, Windsor, Nova Scotia, in September 1885, he was the father of two sons, Athelstan (b.1882) and Lloyd (b.1884). Edith Roberts was born in 1886, and Douglas Roberts was born in 1888. At the age of twenty-eight, Roberts now had what, in "Sir Charles G.D. Roberts and His Time," Pelham Edgar terms a "bevy of young children" (122) and had begun a ten-year term at King's College, where he was very popular as a teacher and was active in the community. In this period he managed to author three books of poetry (*In Divers Tones* [1886], *Autochthon* [1889], *and Songs of the Common Day*, and *Ave: An Ode for the Shelley Centenary* [1893]); two guidebooks (*The Canadian Guide-Book* [1891] and *The Land of Evangeline and the Gateways Thither* [1895]; and three novelettes (*The Raid from Beausejour, and How the Carter Boys Lifted the Mortgage: Two Stories of Acadie* [1894] and *Reube Dare's Shad Boat: A Tale of the Tide Country* [1895]. He also translated Phillipe Aubert de Gaspe's *Les Anciens Canadiens* (1863) as *Canadians of Old* (1890), and largely completed his *A History of Canada* (1897), in which he demonstrated his political bias as a Canadian imperialist.

If there was a "strange aesthetic ferment" in Fredericton during the last two decades of the nineteenth century, the presence of Roberts in Windsor from 1885 to 1895 also made possible a miniature, somewhat mixed bohemian and civilized life of letters at King's College. As his son, Lloyd Roberts, reports in his *The Book of Roberts* (1923), the Roberts household was at the centre of an aesthetic ferment of its own. During these years, Carman would often visit Roberts with his friend the American Vagabondia poet Richard Hovey in tow. Roberts had many other literary visitors as well. The most significant literary event during the Windsor decade, for our purposes, is the publication of Roberts' first animal story, "Do Seek their Meat from God," in 1892. The 'realism' of that story suggests the emerging hallmark of Roberts' best animal story style. It is also a story resonant with metaphorical suggestions about life as Roberts was experiencing it himself, as it is an animal story about the struggle for basic survival and the struggle to find the most rudimentary of family provisions. In a letter to Sir George Parkin on 6 June 1895, Roberts complains about the pressure of what he calls "this dead drive for the bread-and-butter," which, he says "has made me a vile correspondent" (qtd. in Boone 203). "Do Seek their Meat from God" is also a story about the tensions of love and responsibility. "When Twilight Falls on the Stump Lots" and "The Nest of the Mallard," among others, are additional stories relevant to Roberts' struggles in this relation. Roberts was often to say that it was necessary to see animals as beings in themselves, yet it is clear that he also drew them with a close sympathy that came from his own identification with their struggle for life's basic provisions.

Roberts felt the strain of being the head of a growing family. He had the patriarchal example of his father to fall back on, but he eventually came to resent the confines of conventional married life, and his domestic responsibilities conflicted with his preference for the more gregarious lifestyles of his literary friends. As well, he became increasingly interested in other women, and began to view May more as a legal domestic partner than the encompassing love of his life. Boone tells us that in Windsor he also "took up with at least two women," one of whom was a young woman who "joined the Roberts household as the children's governess" (53). It was as though life in Windsor demonstrated to him, in an untimely way, that everything that he valued he could not enjoy conventionally. He resigned his professorship at King's College in 1895 and once again tried to survive on freelance work in Fredericton until February of 1897. He was ready for a move as early as 1891 and by 1892 he felt thoroughly trapped at King's. "In 1892 his restlessness is more marked, and letters to Carman show how strongly the urgency for wider horizons seized his imagination" (Edgar 122). In one of these letters he remarks, "Get away we must. Have change we must. Readjust the focus of life we must. We must soar out of our present fetters. . . . I hunger and thirst fiercely for escape" (qtd. in Edgar 122).

The move to Fredericton felt like the escape that would energize him once again, and his first historical romance novel, *The Forge in the Forest*, and his first collection of nature stories, *Earth's Enigmas*, were published in 1896. He was also having some continued success with his nonfiction prose. Roberts always viewed himself as primarily a writer called to poetry, but the success he was having with his novels and short stories persuaded him that he could best provide for himself and his family on his earnings from the pragmatic call of his fiction. The vogue for romance fiction, and the sudden new market for animal stories provoked by the sales success of Ernest Thompson Seton's *Wild Animals I Have Known* (1898), were eventually to convince Roberts that he had better live for poetry, but make a living by prose—that even though his heart was primarily in his verse, he had better be sensible about where his imaginative energies should flow. His stay in Fredericton was not long-lived, only transitional, and he was soon pursuing a better income closer to his professional connections in the United States.

In February 1897 Roberts departed on his own to seek work in New York, where he took up a position as an assistant editor for *The Illustrated American*. From this point onward he entered a state of permanent separation from May, even though he was continually to visit his family in Fredericton after this point, and promise that they would eventually settle with him in New York. In October 1897 Roberts' son Athelstan came down with typhoid fever, followed by meningitis. May was slow to inform Roberts, and Athelstan died on 16 October, only three days after Roberts arrived back from New York. There has been speculation that Athelstan's death was caused indirectly by the reduced and unwholesome circumstances Roberts left his family in when he went to New York, so Athelstan's death was a compounded tragedy for the family. Roberts was devastated by the blow and decided at this point to commit himself to a genteel bohemian life of freelance work, making his intellectual life amidst the literati, travelling, and writing less poetry and more fiction—the romance and wilderness fiction which would earn for him a literary reputation on both sides of the Atlantic. His children visited him often, sometimes travelled with him, and he continued to provide for his family's material well being as best he could. His son Douglas would much later move in with him, but the promise that his whole family would eventually come to settle in New York became a family myth offered primarily to make respectable the stress of an evaporating marriage.

Roberts resigned his position at *The Illustrated American* in January 1898, and made his way involved with other literary, mostly writing activities. He was a success in New York, for all of his initial unease as a writer from the northern wilds, and he later considered these years to have been among the best of his literary life. He was elected a member of the Author's Club of America in 1897 and was elected as the only non-American charter member of the National Institute of Arts and Letters in 1898. The close to ten years he lived in New York were punctuated with trips to England, France, Holland,

and Cuba—where he twice visited the poet Francis Sherman, a Fredericton native, who often made return visits to Roberts in New York. Roberts published eight books of fiction during his time in New York, including the novels *The Heart of the Ancient Wood* (1900), *Barbara Ladd* (1902), *The Mademoiselle* (1904), and *The Heart That Knows* (1906). The major collection of animal stories he published in this period was *The Kindred of the Wild* (1902). He also published in this period *The Watchers of the Trails* (1904), his highly successful novel, *Red Fox* (1905), and, in 1907, *The Haunters of the Silences*, another collection of stories.

Personally, however, Roberts became again very restless to leave New York, and he moved to Europe in November of 1907; during the next seven years he lived in Italy, France, Germany, and England, and his son Douglas travelled with him for the first fifteen months of this period. He published more collections of stories, including *The House in the Water* (1908) *Kings in Exile* (1909), *Neighbours Unknown* (1910), *More Kindred of the Wild* (1911), *Babes of the Wild* (1912), *The Feet of the Furtive* (1912) and *Hoof and Claw* (1913). In spite of being fifty-four years of age at the outbreak of World War I in 1914, he enlisted in the British army. He was promoted to captain in late 1915, was transferred to the Canadian War Records Office in London in 1916 with a promotion to major, and was sent to France in December of the same year as a press correspondent, where he remained until the spring of 1918. He was demobilized from the army in 1919 and resided in London until February 1925. During this time he made visits to North Africa, Switzerland, and Italy and published several collections of stories, including *Wisdom of the Wilderness* (1922) and *More Animal Stories* (1922). His novel about prehistoric life, *In the Morning of Time*, appeared in 1919. When he returned to Canada in 1925 he was immediately greeted with honours and with a great deal of new work.

Roberts resided in Toronto from 1925 until his death on 26 November 1943. He crossed the country on a reading tour in 1925 and again the following year. In 1926 he was awarded the Lorne Pierce Gold Medal of the Royal Society of Canada and accepted the presidency of the Toronto branch of the Canadian Authors Association. Bliss Carman died in June 1929, and

Roberts' wife, May, died in May 1930. She had lived with the thought that there might at some point be a reconciliation with her estranged husband, but it never happened, and Roberts felt quite cruel in the way he avoided her and avoided dealing forthrightly with the issue of their relationship. He did not arrive at her bedside in time, and when she died he was full of remorse. He and May had been technically married for fifty years, but, as we know, their relationship was difficult, distant and unresolved during most of that time. Roberts was a very successful writer but a misfit as a husband, and he seems to have known that with a sense of chagrin much of the time.

During the 1930s Roberts acted on the editorial boards of the *Standard Dictionary of Canadian Biography* and the *Canadian Who's Who*. He was knighted in 1935, and a year later his *Selected Poems* appeared as evidence of his continuous interest in writing poetry. During the last three years of his life he continued to receive honours. He had received an honorary LL.D. from the University of New Brunswick in 1906, and Mount Allison University, Sackville, N.B., presented him with a Litt.D. in 1942. After ten years of companionship, he married Joan Montgomery in October 1943. In his later years he encouraged and scrutinized Pomeroy's *Sir Charles G.D. Roberts: A Biography*. In addition to his other works, he published during his lifetime nine novels and romances, five volumes of stories for young adults, nineteen volumes of original short stories, and five selections of stories. His restlessness was a highly creative one, to say the least.

Roberts had copious success as a fiction writer, in both market and critical terms. *Barbara Ladd*, to cite but one sales example, sold over eighty thousand copies in the United States alone, and, according to Pomeroy, *The Heart of the Ancient Wood*, in addition to seeing many editions in the United States and England, was "translated into French, German, Dutch, Czecho-Slovakian, Danish and Swedish" and "sold well in all these countries" ("The Novels" 3). He had written stories for *Harper's Monthly*, *Cosmopolitan*, *Lippincott's Monthly Magazine*, *The New York Times*, *The Atlantic Monthly*, *Saturday Evening Post*, *The Metropolitan*, and *The Fortnightly Review*, to mention only a few of many. He had earned the encouragement of Mathew Arnold, Oliver Wendell Holmes,

Hamlin Garland, and George Meredith—among others—and by the time of his death in 1943, he had an international reputation as poet, novelist and co-founder of the modern 'realistic' animal story. The call of the work had been intense.

Works Cited

Adams, John Coldwell. *Sir Charles God Damn: The Life of Sir Charles G.D. Roberts*. Toronto: U of Toronto Press, 1986.

———. "Sir Charles G.D. Roberts: Post Biography." *Canadian Poetry: Studies/Documents/Reviews*, 21 (Fall/Winter 1987), 77-80.

Boone, Laurel. ed. *The Collected Letters of Charles G.D. Roberts*. Fredericton: Goose Lane, 1989.

Edgar, Pelham. "Sir Charles G.D. Roberts and His Time." *Rev. of Sir Charles G.D. Roberts: A Biography*, by Elsie M. Pomeroy. *University of Toronto Quarterly*, 13 (Oct. 1943), 117-26.

Pacey, Desmond. *Ten Canadian Poets: A Group of Biographical and Critical Essays*. 1958. Toronto: Ryerson, 1969.

Pomeroy, Elsie.M. *Sir Charles G.D. Roberts: A Biography*. Toronto: Ryerson, 1943.

———. "Sir Charles G.D. Roberts: Final Chapter." *The Canadian Author and Bookman*, 20. No.20 (June 1944), 5-6.

———. "The Novels of Charles G.D. Roberts." *The Maritime Advocate*, April 1950. Rpt. privately in pamphlet form.

Roberts, Charles G.D. "Bliss Carman." *The Dalhousie Review*, 9 (Jan. 1930), 409-17.

Roberts, Lloyd. *The Book of Roberts*. Toronto: Ryerson, 1923.

Stringer, Arthur. "Eminent Canadians in New York, II: The Father of Canadian Poetry." *The National Monthly of Canada*, Feb. 1904, pp. 61-64.

Documentary

Charles G.D. Roberts
The Animal Story*

Alike in matter and in method, the animal story, as we have it to-day, may be regarded as a culmination. The animal story, of course, in one form or another, is as old as the beginnings of literature. Perhaps the most engrossing part in the life-drama of primitive man was that played by the beasts which he hunted, and by those which hunted him. They pressed incessantly upon his perceptions. They furnished both material and impulse for his first gropings toward pictorial art. When he acquired the kindred art of telling a story, they supplied his earliest themes; and they suggested the hieroglyphs by means of which, on carved bone or painted rock, he first gave his narrative a form to outlast the spoken breath. We may not unreasonably infer that the first animal story—the remote but authentic ancestor of "Mowgli" and "Lobo" and "Krag"—was a story of some successful hunt, when success meant life to the starving family; or of some desperate escape, when the truth of the narrative was attested, to the hearers squatted trembling about their fire, by the sniffings of the baffled bear or tiger at the rock-barred mouth of the cave. Such first animal stories had at least one merit of prime literary importance. They were convincing. The first critic, however supercilious, would be little likely to cavil at their verisimilitude.

Somewhat later, when men had begun to harass their souls, and their neighbours, with problems of life and conduct, then these same animals, hourly and in every aspect thrust beneath the eyes of their observation, served to point the moral of their tales. The beasts, not being in a position to resent the ignoble office thrust upon them, were compelled to do duty as concrete types of those obvious virtues and vices of which alone the unsophisticated ethical sense was ready to take cognisance. In this way, as soon as composition became a *métier*,

* Introductory to *The Kindred of the Wild* (Boston: L.C. Page, 1902), pp.15-29.

was born the fable; and in this way the ingenuity of the first author enabled him to avoid a perilous unpopularity among those whose weaknesses and defects his art held up to the scorn of all the caves.

These earliest observers of animal life were compelled by the necessities of the case to observe truly, if not deeply. Pitting their wits against those of their four-foot rivals, they had to know their antagonists, and respect them, in order to overcome them. But it was only the most salient characteristics of each species that concerned the practical observer. It was simple to remember that the tiger was cruel, the fox cunning, the wolf rapacious. And so, as advancing civilisation drew an ever widening line between man and the animals, and men became more and more engrossed in the interests of their own kind, the personalities of the wild creatures which they had once known so well became obscured to them, and the creatures themselves came to be regarded, for the purposes of literature, as types or symbols merely,—except in those cases, equally obstructive to exact observation, where they were revered as temporary tenements of the spirits of departed kinsfolk. The characters in that great beast-epic of the middle ages, "Reynard the Fox," though far more elaborately limned than those which play their succinct rôles in the fables of Aesop, are at the same time in their elaboration far more alien to the truths of wild nature. Reynard, Isegrim, Bruin, and Greybeard have little resemblance to the fox, the wolf, the bear, and the badger, as patience, sympathy, and the camera reveal them to us to-day.

The advent of Christianity, strange as it may seem at first glance, did not make for a closer understanding between man the lower animals. While it was militant, fighting for its life against the forces of paganism, its effort was to set man at odds with the natural world, and fill his eyes with the wonders of the spiritual. Man was the only thing of consequence on earth, and of man, not his body, but his soul. Nature was the ally of the enemy. The way of nature was the way of death. In man alone was the seed of the divine. Of what concern could be the joy or pain of creatures of no soul, to-morrow returning to the dust? To strenuous spirits, their eyes fixed upon the fear of hell for themselves, and the certainty of it for their neighbours, it smacked of sin to take thought of the feelings of such evanescent products of corruption. Hence it came that, in spite of the gentle understanding of such sweet saints as Francis of Assisi, Anthony of Padua, and Colomb of the Bees, the inarticulate kindred for a long time reaped small comfort from the Dispensation of Love.

With the spread of freedom and the broadening out of all intellectual interests which characterise these modern days, the lower kindreds began to regain their old place in the concern of man. The revival of interest in the animals found literary expression (to classify roughly) in two forms, which necessarily overlap each other now and then, viz., the story of adventure and the anecdote of observation. Hunting as a recreation, pursued with zest from pole to tropics by restless seekers after the new, supplied a species of narrative singularly akin to what the first animal stories must have been,—narratives of desperate encounter, strange peril, and hairbreadth escape. Such hunters' stories and travellers' tales are rarely conspicuous for the exactitude of their observation; but that was not the quality at first demanded of them by fireside readers. The attention of the writer was focussed, not upon the peculiarities or the emotions of the beast protagonist in each fierce, brief drama, but upon the thrill of the action, the final triumph of the human actor. The inevitable tendency of these stories of adventure with beasts was to awaken interest in animals, and to excite a desire for exact knowledge of their traits and habits. The interest and the desire evoked the natural historian, the inheritor of the half-forgotten mantle of Pliny. Precise and patient scientists made the animals their care, observing with microscope and measure, comparing bones, assorting families, subdividing subdivisions, till at length all the beasts of significance to man were ticketed neatly, and laid bare, as far as the inmost fibre of their material substance was concerned, to the eye of popular information.

Altogether admirable and necessary as was this development at large, another, of richer or at least more spiritual significance, was going on at home. Folk who loved their animal comrades—their dogs, horses, cats, parrots, elephants—were observing, with the wonder and interest of discoverers, the astonishing fashion in which the mere instincts of these so-called irrational creatures were able to simulate the operations of reason. The results of this observation were written down, till "anecdotes of animals" came to form a not inconsiderable body of literature. The drift of all these data was overwhelmingly toward one conclusion. The mental processes of the animals observed were seen to be far more complex than the observers had supposed. Where instinct was called in to account for the elaborate ingenuity with which a dog would plan and accomplish the outwitting of a rival, or the nice judgment with which an elephant, with no nest-building ancestors behind him to instruct his brain, would choose and adjust the teak-logs which he was set to pile, it began to seem as if that faithful faculty was being overworked. To explain yet other cases, which no accepted theory seemed to fit, coincidence was invoked, till that rare and elusive phenomenon threatened to become as customary as buttercups. But when instinct and coincidence had done all that could be asked of them, there remained a great unaccounted-for body of facts; and men were forced at last to accept the proposition that, within their varying limitations, animals can and do reason. As far, as least, as the mental intelligence is concerned, the gulf dividing the lowest of the human species from the highest of the animals has in these latter days been reduced to a very narrow psychological fissure.

Whether avowedly or not, it is with the psychology of animal life that the representative animal stories of to-day are first of all concerned. Looking deep into the eyes of certain of the four-footed kindred, we have been startled to see therein a something, before unrecognised, that answered to our inner and intellectual, if not spiritual selves. We have suddenly attained a new and clearer vision. We have come face to face with personality, where we were blindly wont to predicate mere instinct and automatism. It is as if one should step carelessly out of one's back door, and marvel to see unrolling before his new-awakened eyes the peaks and seas and misty valleys of an unknown world. Our chief writers of animal stories at the present day may be regarded as explorers of this unknown world, absorbed in charting its topography. They work, indeed, upon a substantial foundation of known facts. They are minutely scrupulous as to their natural history, and assiduous contributors to that science. But above all are they diligent in their search for the motive beneath the action. Their care is to catch the varying, elusive personalities which dwell back of the luminous brain windows of the dog, the horse, the deer, or wrap themselves in reserve behind the inscrutable eyes of all the cats, or sit aloof in the gaze of the hawk and the eagle. The animal story at its highest point of development is a psychological romance constructed on a framework of natural science.

The real psychology of the animals, so far as we are able to grope our way toward it by deduction and induction combined, is a very different thing from the psychology of certain stories of animals which paved the way for the present vogue. Of these, such books as "Beautiful Joe" and "Black Beauty" are deservedly conspicuous examples. It is no detraction from the merit of these books, which have done great service in awakening a sympathetic understanding of the animals and sharpening our sense of kinship with all that breathes, to say that their psychology is human. Their animal characters think and feel as human beings would think and feel under like conditions. This marks the stage which these works occupy in the development of the animal story.

The next stage must be regarded as, in literature, a climax indeed, but not the climax in this genre. I refer to the "Mowgli" stories of Mr. Kipling. In these tales the animals are frankly humanised. Their individualisation is distinctly human, as are also their mental and emotional processes, and their highly elaborate powers of expression. Their notions are complex; whereas the motives of real animals, so far as we have hitherto been able to judge them, seem to be essentially simple, in the sense that the motive dominant at a given moment quite obliterates, for the time, all secondary motives. Their reasoning powers and their constructive imagination are far beyond anything which present knowledge justifies us in ascribing to the inarticulate kindreds. To say this is in no way to depreciate such work, but merely to classify it. There are stories being written now which, for interest and artistic value, are not to be mentioned in the same breath with the "Mowgli" tales, but which nevertheless occupy a more advanced stage in the evolution of this genre.

It seems to me fairly safe to say that this evolution is not likely to go beyond the point to which it has been carried to-day. In such a story, for instance, as that of "Krag, the Kootenay Ram," by Mr. Ernest Seton, the interest centres about the personality, individuality, mentality, of an animal, as well as its purely physical characteristics. The field of animal psychology so admirably opened is an inexhaustible world of wonder. Sympathetic exploration may advance its boundaries to a degree of which we hardly dare to dream; but such expansion cannot be called evolution. There would seem to be no further evolution possible, unless based upon a hypothesis that animals have souls. As souls are apt to elude exact observation, to forecast any such development would seem to be at best merely fanciful.

The animal story, as we now have it, is a potent emancipator. It frees us for a little from the world of shop-worn utilities, and from the mean tenement of self of which we do well to grow weary. It helps us to return to nature, without requiring that we at the same time return to barbarism. It leads us back to the old kinship of earth, without asking us to relinquish by way of toll any part of the wisdom of the ages, any fine essential of the "large result of time." The clear and candid life to which it reinitiates us, far behind though it lies in the long upward march of being, holds for us this quality. It has ever the more significance, it has ever the richer gift of refreshment and renewal, the more humane the heart and spiritual the understanding which we bring to the intimacy of it.

Charles G.D. Roberts
Prefatory Note to *The Watchers of the Trails**

In the preface to a former volume[1] I have endeavoured to trace the development of the modern animal story and have indicated what appeared to me to be its tendency and scope. It seems unnecessary to add anything here but a few words of more personal application.

The stories of which this volume is made up are avowedly fiction. They are, at the same time, true, in that the material of which they are moulded consists of facts,—facts as precise as painstaking observation and anxious regard for truth can make them. Certain of the stories, of course, are true literally. Literal truth may be attained by stories which treat of a single incident, or of action so restricted as to lie within the scope of a single observation. When, on the other hand, a story follows the career of a wild creature of the wood or air or water through wide intervals of time and space, it is obvious that the truth of that story must be of a different kind. The complete picture which such a story presents is built up from observation necessarily detached and scattered; so that the utmost it can achieve as a whole is consistency with truth. If a writer has, by temperament, any sympathetic understanding of the wild kindreds; if he has any intimate knowledge of their habits, with any sensitiveness to the infinite variation of their personalities; and if he has chanced to live much among them during the impressionable periods of his life, and so become saturated in their atmosphere and their environment;—then he may hope to make his most elaborate piece of animal biography not less true to nature than his transcript of an isolated fact. The present writer, having spent most of his boyhood on the fringes of the forest, with few interests save those which the forest afforded, may claim to have had the intimacies of the wilderness as it were thrust upon him. The earliest enthusiasms which he can recollect are connected with some of the furred

* From *The Watchers of the Trails* (Boston: L.C. Page, 1904), vii-ix.

or feathered kindred; and the first thrills strong enough to leave a lasting mark on his memory are those with which he used to follow—furtive, apprehensive, expectant, breathlessly watchful—the lure of an unknown trail.

There is one more point which may seem to claim a word. A very distinguished author [JohnBurroughs]—to whom all contemporary writers on nature are indebted, and from whom it is only with the utmost diffidence that I venture to dissent at all—has gently called me to account on the charge of ascribing to my animals human motives and the mental process of man. The fact is, however, that this fault is one which I have been at particular pains to guard against. The psychological processes of the animals are so simple, so obvious, in comparison with those of man, their actions flow so directly from their springs of impulse, that it is, as a rule, an easy matter to infer the motives which are at any one moment impelling them. In my desire to avoid alike the melodramatic, the visionary, and the sentimental, I have studied to keep well within the limits of safe inference. Where I may have seemed to state too confidently the motives underlying the special action of this or that animal, it will usually be found that the action itself is very fully presented; and it will, I think, be further found that the motive which I have here assumed affords the most reasonable, if not the only reasonable, explanation of that action.

C.G.D.R., NEW YORK, *April, 1904*.

Endnote

1 Roberts notes this as "The Kindred of the Wild."

Charles G.D. Roberts
Prefatory Note to *Red Fox**

In the following story I have tried to trace the career of a fox of the backwoods districts of Eastern Canada. The hero of the story, Red Fox, may be taken as fairly typical, both in his characteristics and in the experiences that befall him, in spite of the fact that he is stronger and cleverer than the average run of foxes. This fact does not detract from his authenticity as a type of his kind. He simply represents the best, in physical and mental development, of which the tribe of the foxes has shown itself capable. In a litter of young foxes there is usually one that is larger and stronger, and of more finely coloured fur, than his fellows. There is not infrequently, also, one that proves to be much more sagacious and adaptable than his fellows. Once in awhile such exceptional strength and such exceptional intelligence may be combined in one individual. This combination is apt to result in just such a fox as I have made the hero of my story.

The incidents in the career of this particular fox are not only consistent with the known characteristics and capacities of the fox family, but there is authentic record of them all in the accounts of careful observers. Every one of these experiences has befallen some red fox in the past, and may befall other red foxes in the future. There is no instance of intelligence, adaptability, or foresight given here that is not abundantly attested by the observations of persons who know how to observe accurately. In regard to such points, I have been careful to keep well within the boundaries of fact. As for any emotions which Red Fox may once in a great while seem to display, these may safely be accepted by the most cautious as fox emotions, not as human emotions. In so far as man is himself an animal, he is subject to and impelled by many emotions which he must share with not a few other members of the animal kingdom. Any full presentation of an individual animal of one of the more highly developed species must depict certain emotions not altogether unlike those which a human being might expe-

* From *Red Fox* (Boston, L.C. Page, 1905), pp. vii-ix.

rience under like conditions. To do this is not by any means, as some hasty critics would have it, to ascribe human emotions to the lower animals.

C. G. D. R.
FREDERICTON, N.B., *August, 1905.*

Interview: Defends Nature Stories*

While Charles George Douglas Roberts resents being put in President Roosevelt's list of "nature fakirs," he said last night on his arrival on the White Star liner *Adriatic* that he did not want to get into any controversy. He declared that he had much admiration for Mr. Roosevelt, but he thought the President was mistaken in criticizing some of his stories of animal habits and deeds in the article which appeared in the June *Everybody's*. The Author of *The Kindred of the Wild*, *The Return to the Trails*, and *Red Fox* said that he had read the article which brought out Mr. Long's challenge to the President while in Naples. He declared that he intended to write a defense.

"I am of the opinion," said Prof. Roberts, "that the whole question is not one of veracity but of judgment. The President undoubtedly when he referred to my story, 'On the Night Trail,' had in mind a different kind of lynx. In the story, I told of a fight in which a lynx was pitted against eight wolves. The lynx which the President has in mind is the *Felis rafa*, or the Rocky Mountain lynx, which is really the bobcat of the Rockies. The lynx of which I have written is a different kind. I wrote about the *Felis canadensis*, and he frequently weighs 50 or 60 pounds.

"In another respect the President probably labors under a mistake. I told of the wolves, and he in his criticism probably had in mind the big timber wolves of the West. I was not writing about them. The species I referred to was the Eastern wolf or the cloudy wolf of Canada, which is only about half the size of the Western wolf.

"The animals of which I write and those the President had in mind are entirely different, and I must assume that the President, whose experience in the backwoods was limited to the Western part of the United States, is not familiar with the wild animals of other localities. A New Brunswick lumberman would laugh at the assertion of Mr. Roosevelt that the lynx could not take care of itself.

"I am going to send out a general and emphatic defense of the school of nature writers. I will go into the subject, but what

* From *The New York Times* (June 14, 1907), p. 6.

I do will be entirely my affair, and I will assume no responsibility for the writings of Mr. Long, Ernest Seton Thompson and others."

Explaining further, he said:

"There are two classes of nature writers. One is headed practically by John Burroughs, who believes that the actions of animals are governed by instinct. The opposite school is concerned in animal psychology—and this is the view taken by backwoodsmen, trainers, and trappers. They have given the subject as much careful study as have the others. Mr. Hornaday is one of this last class. Animals are actuated in varying degrees by a process akin to reason. They do think and compare."

"What do you think of the President's opinions?" he was asked.

Prof. Roberts answered that he would in a friendly way try to correct some of Mr. Roosevelt's views, but that he wanted it understood that he had the greatest admiration for the President, and that he did not want to get into any altercation with him. He said:

"I have made slips that even John Burroughs and Mr. Roosevelt have not discovered. No, I am not going to say what they are, but I will correct them later."

Charles G.D. Roberts
Prefatory Note to *The Haunters of the Silences**

The present collection of stories dealing with creatures of the wilderness differs from its companion volumes, "The Kindred of the Wild" and "The Watchers of the Trails," in one important particular. It contains certain studies and depictions of a sphere of wild life which presents peculiar difficulties to the observer, viz.: the life of the dwellers in the deep sea. Our investigation of these remote kindreds is at best spasmodic, and conducted always at the extreme of disadvantage; and the knowledge which we may gain from such investigation must always remain in a measure fragmentary. It is not easy for any observer to be intimate with a sawfish; and the most ardent naturalist's acquaintance with an *orca*, or "killer" whale, must be essentially a distant one, if he would hope to put his observations upon record. Needless to say, my own knowledge of the orca, the shark, the narwhal, or the colossal cuttlefish of the ocean depths, is not of the same kind as my knowledge of the bear, the moose, the eagle, and others of the furtive folk of our New Brunswick wilderness. When I write of these latter I build my stories upon a foundation of personal, intimate, sympathetic observation, the result of a boyhood passed in the backwoods, and of almost yearly visits, ever since my boyhood, to the wild forest regions of my native province. But when I write of the kindreds of the deep sea, I am relying upon the collated results of the observations of others. I have spared no pains to make these stories accord, as far as the facts of natural history are concerned, with the latest scientific information. But I have made no vain attempt at interpretation of the lives of creatures so remote from my personal knowledge; and for such tales as "A Duel in the Deep," "The Terror of the Sea Caves," or "The Prowlers," my utmost hope is that they may prove entertaining, without being open to any charge of misrepresenting facts. On the other hand, in certain of the

* From *The Haunters of the Silences* (Boston, L.C. Page, 1907). pp. v-vii.

stories dealing with the results of my own observation and experience, I have dared to hope that I might be contributing something of value to the final disputed question of animal psychology. For such stories, which offer in the form of fiction what my observations have compelled me to regard as fact, I have presented my case already, in the prefaces to "The Watchers of the Trails" and "Red Fox." To those prefaces I would add nothing here; and from the conclusions therein stated I have nothing to retract. I would merely take this occasion to reaffirm with confidence the belief, which I find shared by practically all observers whose lives are passed in the closest relationship with animals,—by such vitally interested observers, for instance, as keepers, trainers, hunters, and trappers,—that the actions of animals are governed not only by instinct, but also, in varying degree, by processes essentially akin to those of human reason.

C. G. D. R.

Charles G.D. Roberts
Introductory to *Eyes of the Wilderness**

In the make-up of most normal human beings there is something always ready to respond to the call of the wilderness. Civilization, with all those characteristics which are a product of it, is but a veneer which has been slowly and laboriously applied upon the foundations of the primitive. Where the foundations are sound, it is good for soul and body alike to be kept mindful of them, to get back to them from time to time and be reassured as to their substance and their truth.

When we are overwrought by the strains and stresses of to-day's high-pressure life, the call of the wilderness come to us with compelling insistence. The call is sounded on many notes, and carries a persuasion varied to invite as many divergent tastes and temperaments. For some it is an invitation to the old, fierce thrills of the chase, of the hunting and slaying of our furred and feathered kindred,—an invitation of persistent urgency, reminding us that we are still close to the days when we had to hunt and kill for our daily food. The healthy and virile, if somewhat savage, instincts which leap to the urge are still potent in our blood. For others the invitation sings of rod and reel, of the gay fly dropped expertly in the tail of the rapid or beside the whirling foam-cluster on the amber pool, of the swirl and the strike, of the breathless, uncertain contest of deft wrist and delicate tackle against the swift rushes of the flashing quarry. To yet others the call is to unspoiled solitudes of sea or plain, forest or mountain, of unnamed, lonely lakes, of wild rivers flooding away to the unknown. And to many, many others, less adventurous in their dreams, the voice whispers chiefly of escape to green spaces and quiet waters and woodland-scented airs. Their craving is

> 'Mid task and toil a space
> To dream on Nature's face.

and they remember longingly that

> Leisure in the sun and air
> Makes the spirit strong and fair.

---

* From *The Eyes of the Wilderness* (Toronto: Macmillan, 1933), pp. 1-6.

But whatever form the invitation may take for him whose heart is open to it, the call is always, in essence, the same. It is the summons to us to turn back a little while, for soul and body's health, to the primitive, the simple, the unpretentious, the unbetraying.

North, south, east or west, I doubt if there be any corner of the kind old mothering earth where Nature calls us back to her with such varied persuasions, or so abundantly fulfils for all the promise of her lures, as in the vast half-continent of Canada. Here swarm the wild kindreds of fur, feather and fin. Here are spacious solitudes awaiting all who crave them. Here are yet nameless lakes and streams to be explored. Here is every kind of sublimity, every kind of beauty (save that of the tropics), that untamed Nature can offer to the eyes of her lovers. Here is adventure to satisfy the most avidly restless spirit; and here all the refreshment and renewal that the most intimately lovely of landscapes, the most tonic of breezes, the most blossomy of meadows and clearly sparkling of skies can offer for the healing of tired nerves.

For my own part,—and I feel that I need make no apology for introducing the personal note,—being a child of the woodland country and the little, homely farms, I have always been keenly alive to the lure of the wild, and to all its various invitations I have responded ardently. Of them all there is but one which has lost its attraction for me. Hunting to kill has for me no longer any zest. To trail, to outwit, to ambush the wary dwellers of the wilderness,—to match my woodcraft against theirs and expose their furtive tactics,—yes, that will never lose its thrill. But, that done, the killing becomes so easy,—and so unneighbourly! And alive they are so much more beautiful, so infinitely more interesting! And the look in the eyes of a mortally wounded deer may sometimes damp one's triumph. To my mind the field-glass or the camera is a more exciting weapon than the rifle or the shotgun, and may yield results of a more lasting value. Let me confess, however, that my attitude of sympathy and fellowship towards the wild creatures has its limitations. With unabashed inconsistency I remain an enthusiastic fisherman. When a fresh-run salmon or a lusty trout has taken my "Silver Doctor" or my "Parmachene Belle," I have no difficulty in forgetting that the joy of the sport is all on one side. The warm-blooded folk of hide and fur and feather I acknowledge as my kin. But it is hard to feel comradely towards a fish.

Always, these Canadian wilds of mine, whose spirit is native to my blood,—whether in their softest and most enchanting beauty or in their bleakest austerity, whether in their storm and turbulence or in their most withdrawn and mystic quietudes,—always, their call to me comes clear and compelling. Naturally, my response to the call takes many forms; but of them all the one which gives me the most deep and lasting satisfaction consists in the sympathetic study of the life that peoples the wilderness.

To me it seems not enough to approach this fascinating study with merely the curious eyes of the naturalist. To really know the wild creatures something more is necessary than to note their forms and colours, their seasons and their habits, their food, their tracks, their dwellings and their matings. All these points, of course, are the first essentials. They are the fundamental facts on which further study must be based; and lack of exact, painstaking observation may vitiate all one's conclusions. But having got one's facts right,—and enough of them to generalize from safely,—the exciting adventure lies in the effort "get under the skins," so to speak, of these shy and elusive beings, to discern their motives, to uncover and chart their simple mental processes, to learn to differentiate between those of their actions which are the results of blind, inherited instinct, and those which spring from something definitely akin to reason; for I am absolutely convinced that, within their widely varied yet strictly set limitations, the more advanced of the furred and feathered folk do reason. In other words, there is a psychology of the creatures lower in the scale of creation than ourselves. It is so profoundly different from human psychology, however, that to forget the difference is to go hopelessly astray in one's deductions. To investigate that psychology, and to interpret it, is one of the most fascinating of enterprises for the Nature lover. To be successful in it demands a sensitive understanding and an unwearying patience, but the reward is worth all the effort. Moreover even if, through lack of skill or special aptitude in the beginning, the measurable results should seem but small, it should be remembered that the effort itself is its own ample reward. In schooling ourselves to the attitude of our humbler kindred, so as to look at the perilous adventures of life through their eyes,—which is the only way we can come really to know them,—we cannot but enlarge our capacity for the understanding of our fellow men, and grow in a gentleness which will add grace and serenity to our days.

Reviews

Review of *Earth's Enigmas**

In the silent Canadian forests and sea-born Tantramar marshes, one might hope, if anywhere, to be rid of 'Earth's Enigmas,' but it is just in these lonely, lovely places that Mr. Roberts has found riddles plentiful and profound: why unconsidered trifles are mile stones of destiny; why gratified ambition turns out Dead Sea fruit; why the happiness of young love is smitten in an instant by tragedy; why superstitions are often justified by facts, and why no man can always believe his own eyes or any evidence of his senses. Fortunately Mr. Roberts has not attempted to analyze the inscrutable or to explain the inexplicable. His tales are objective, tales of moral and physical courage, of accident from floods and high tides, of fights for life with wild beasts, and of terror, of supernatural omens and portents. His questions are matters of inference, and it is possible to read the tales without suspecting any far-reaching speculation. The incidents are scenes fit each other admirably, and the characterization is strong, clear, and interesting. Sometimes the beauties and wonders of nature are overwrought, but the defect is excused when we remember that a poet of nature is struggling with the limitations of a plain prose tale. Much more surprising than decorative excursions are the vivid presentation of rough and primitive people, and a vigorous directness at critical moments which we are accustomed to find only in very accomplished writers of prose fiction.

Earth's Enigmas. By C.G.D. Roberts. Lamson, Wolffe & Co.

---

* From *Nation*, 62 (May 21 1896), 399

"The Relation of Man and Beast" Review of *Kindred of the Wild* *

In the introduction to "The Kindred of the Wild" Mr. Roberts gives a brief sketch of the animal story from its origin in the engrossing part played in the life-drama of primitive man by the beasts which he hunted and those which hunted him through its development in the comradeship between man and his various animal pets, to its literary climax in Mr. Kipling's "Mowgli" stories, and its psychological culmination in Mr. Ernest Seton's story of "Krag, the Kootenay Ram."

The title embodies the close relation between man and beast which every page of the book shows to be the author's conviction and epitomizes the distinction he makes between the literature that frankly humanizes animals—of which he considers Mr. Kipling the great master—and the literature whose interest centres in the "personality, individuality, and mentality" of the animal from the purely animal point of consideration. In this field of animal psychology he believes Mr. Ernest Seton to have reached limits to which the only further evolution possible must be that based upon the hypothesis that animals have souls.

These character sketches—for Mr. Roberts's delightful book is neither more nor less than a collection of delicate and penetrating studies of the minds and hearts of our kindred of the wild—are based upon the objective psychology of Mr. Seton, rather than upon what the author defines as Mr. Kipling's brilliant subjectivity. Interest is claimed for the animal shorn of man's humanity, but instinct with the latent potentialities that make for kinship, sympathy, rivalry, and enmity.

It is out of this inherent kinship and enmity that Mr. Roberts draws the compensations which he makes his reader feel are coexistent with the unalterable law of "survival of the fittest." If one's heart aches over the love and death of the moose mother, the she-wolf, famishing and agonizing in the

* From *New York Times*, July 12, 1902.

darkest corner of the cave, licking in grim silence the raw stump from which she has gnawed off her own paw as the price of freedom, is a tragic and commanding figure, and her gray mate's quest for food as admirable as it is cruel. That all three should be sacrificed to the well-being of the young mother and child is the natural and ascending step of the scale of a creation which has civilized as well as peopled. The weasel is the only member of the animal family for which Mr. Roberts has no sympathy, because it is the only that kills merely for the pleasure of killing.

"The Kindred of the Wild" is written with the finish and delicacy that make the author's style distinctive and evinces an insight and a gift for picturesque presentation which will hold captive the young as well as the older reader. It is a book that for its education value should be in the hands of every boy and girl who cares nothing for animal life and is ignorant of woodsman craft and within the reach of those happier boys and girls who are alert for more knowledge upon a subject they already know and love.

THE KINDRED OF THE WILD, A BOOK OF ANIMAL LIFE, Charles G.D. Roberts. With illustrations by Charles Livingston Bull. Pp. 375. 8vo. Cloth. 1902. Boston: L.C. Page & Co. $2.

Review of *The Watchers of the Trails* *

The Watchers of the Trails. By Charles G.D. Roberts. Illustrated by Charles Livingstone [sic] Bull. Cloth. Pp. 361. Price, $2.00. Boston: L.C. Page & Company.

ALL LOVERS of nature and the wild creatures of forest and field cannot fail to be delighted with this new volume of nature stories. Mr. Roberts does not belong to that class of authors who endow animals and birds with absolutely human powers of reasoning; neither does he belong to that other but smaller class who seem to regard them as devoid of all reasoning faculty. The author spent much of his early youth on the outskirts of a great forest, where he learned to know and love the

* From *Arena*, 32 (Sept. 1904), 340-41.

denizens of the wood; to understand their habits and mental processes. Animals have personalities differing as widely as do those of human beings, and he who lives much among them will come to recognize these differences of temperament and understand the motives which underlie their various actions. And in these tales, many of which are vouched for as absolutely true in detail, while all are true in essence, Mr. Roberts has endeavored to make clear these motives and mental processes of the "kindred of the wild." With respect to his attempt in this direction Mr. Roberts says:

"The psychological processes of the animals are so simple, so obvious, in comparison with those of man, their actions flow so directly from their springs of impulse, that it is, as a rule, an easy matter to infer the motives which are at any one moment impelling them. In my desire to avoid alike the melodramatic, the visionary and the sentimental, I have studied to keep well within the limits of safe inference. Where I may have seemed to state too confidently the motives underlying the special action of this or that animal, it will usually be found that the action itself is very fully presented; and it will, I think, be further found that the motive which I have here assumed affords the most reasonable, if not the only reasonable, explanation of that action."

The volume contains twenty-two stories, of which perhaps the best are *The Alien of the Wild*, *The Freedom of the Black-Faced Ram*, and *The Kill*. The book is beautifully and profusely illustrated by Charles Livingstone [sic] Bull.

Review of *Neighbours Unknown**

Neighbours Unknown. By Charles G.D. Roberts. With 13 full-page Plates. 6s. (Ward, Lock)

This volume belongs probably to the class which Mr. Roosevelt attacked as attempts to "fake" nature. But Mr. Roberts manages to interest his readers in the wild creatures without any illegitimate methods, unless it is illegitimate to explain their actions by means of the natural emotions of fear,

* From *The Bookman*, 39 (Jan. 1911), 205.

love, hatred, and hunger. It is a book especially for young people, and, although the majority of the heroes and heroines are Transatlantic, British readers will appreciate their stories, with a sense of gratitude that lynxes and wolves are not their personal neighbours and also that they are better known, at least in print, after the author's graphic descriptions. "The Isle of Birds" should be read first. Like many authors, Mr. Roberts forgets to begin with his best work. The sketches entitled "The Sentry of the Sedge Flats" and "A torpedo in Feathers" are much superior to "Grey Lynx's Last Hunting." All over, however, these thirteen sketches keep up a good level, and it was quite worth while to rescue them from the passing vogue of a magazine.

Review of *Babes of the Wild* and *The Feet of the Furtive* *

BABES OF THE WILD.

By Charles G.D. Roberts. With 33 illustrations by Warwick Reynolds. 6s. (Cassell.)

THE FEET OF THE FURTIVE.

By G. D. Roberts, With 8 illustrations by Paul Bransom. 6s. (Ward, Lock.)

Although we have bracketed together these two volumes by Mr. Charles G.D. Roberts, we have no intention of comparing them or of criticising one against the other. Indeed, so even is the level of all Mr. Roberts' best work, that such a course would be almost impossible. In literary merit, and even in the general style of the author's treatment, we doubt whether there is anything whatever to choose between the two books. As regards the manner of them both, we imagine that the general public is already sufficiently familiar with Mr. Roberts' work to know that he invariably writes short dramatic stories which tend to bring out certain definite characteristics in the animals with which he deals. Both "Babes of the Wild" and "The Feet of the Furtive" are the same in this. The first has the advantage of two characters which occur in all the stories—a small boy

* From *The Bookman*, 43 (Dec. 1912), 65.

and his uncle, who is represented as the narrator—and thus serve to give the book a certain measure of continuity. On the other hand, it is a trifle unfortunate that the boy should degenerate into a juvenile Dr. Watson, which is what has happened before you have reached the end of the book. We have no preferences for any one story in either of the two collections. It is possible that the fish tales—of which there are representatives in both books—strike rather a fresher note than those which deal with the better-known animals, and this is a branch of nature-study which Mr. Roberts clearly recognizes that it would be well to develop. In conclusion, we would thank the author for the ease and the restraint of his writing. Always he is polished, unforced, natural, and above all he is interesting. Both Mr. Warwick Reynolds and Mr. Paul Bransom are efficient artists, and the drawings with which they have illustrated these volumes are mostly worthy of high praise.

"The New Roberts Animal Book" Review of Eight Volume set by The Macmillan Company*

It was just about the beginning of the present century, when Charles G. D. Roberts, having devoted himself mainly to poetry for twenty years, and having just issued the "Collected Poems" which still stands as his most certain claim to immortality, discovered a new literary device which proved to be extraordinarily successful in attracting the attention and admiration of the larger public. The year 1900 is the date, not only of the "Collected Poems" but also of "The Heart of the Ancient Wood," the first of the volumes in which the dramatis personae consist largely of animals instead of human beings; and by 1902 the new method was in full operation in "The Kindred of the Wild". There may be some question of priority in this new adventure between Dr. Roberts and Ernest Thompson Seton (both, singularly enough, were born in the same year, viz., 1860, but Dr. Roberts had nearly twenty years the start in literature), for the latter's "Trail of the Sand-Hill Stag" was

* From *Canadian Bookman*, 4,2 (Jan. 1922), 53.

published in 1899. There can be little dispute as to the artistic superiority. Seton was an animal painter and a scientist, and his earlier efforts to dramatise the life of the woods were intended for the consumption of children, for whom he would doubtless have continued to write if their elders had not elbowed the youngsters out of the audience. Roberts was a matured literary artist when he entered the field of zoological fiction.

The recipe for zoological fiction is extremely simple, but the very simplicity of the device and of the subject matter increases the necessity for high technical perfection in the treatment. The modern reader has shown unmistakable signs of an acute interest in physical conflict, probably because there is, comparatively speaking, so little of it in our ordered present-day life. Now the life of the wild animals resembles that of more primitive man in being one continuous series of conflicts of the most murderous character. If, therefore, the individual creatures engaged in these conflicts can be so depicted as to enlist the reader's sympathy and belief, the result is an unlimited supply of fights-to-the-death, each with a strong sporting interest, and carried on in surroundings which make a strong appeal to man's imagination simply because man is totally absent from them.

All such efforts at dramatising animals involve, of course, a certain amount of pathetic fallacy. It is necessary to attribute to the combatant animals various mental states and processes of whose very existence in their minds we cannot be certain, and of whose nature we can know nothing. We conjecture the mental processes of our fellow human beings, not merely by observing the behaviour of many thousands of them in varying circumstances, but by judging every item of that behaviour in the light of what goes on in our own private and personal minds, which we assume to be similar in general characteristics to those of all the other human beings. The animals we can judge only by their behaviour; we have no internal knowledge of their mental processes. That animals feel pain and pleasure (within a much more limited range than ours) we cannot doubt; but pain and pleasure can be purely physical sensations. That they feel fear seems equally certain, but it must be a very different thing from the absorbing emotion which passes by that name among human beings. The writer has seen a rabbit in a state of the most intense alarm at one minute, and placidly eating grass within thirty seconds after the cause of its alarm had been removed. Indeed the prospect of a violent death is, to a rabbit, so omnipresent and perpetual that it seems as if nature must have accommodated the poor animal to his circumstances by giving him a reasonably philosophical attitude towards it—Ralph Hodgson to the contrary notwithstanding.

Dr. Roberts has indulged less in this pathetic fallacy than any other of the writers of his school. His animals do no talking, and not much more thinking than can reasonably be attributed to them in view of their behaviour. Dr. Roberts' knowledge of the economic processes at work in the woods and the waters is vast and authentic, and is thus the source of the apparently inexhaustible supply of plausible plots for animal-conflict stories upon which he has been drawing for twenty years. No one can read these stories without greatly enlarging his knowledge of natural history—not that old-fashioned natural history which consists in a catalogue of bones and muscles, but the modern science which concerns itself with the habits, disposition and economic situation of the creature. And since increased knowledge of any of God's creatures means increased love for them, we suspect that the Roberts nature stories have done much to advance that far-off millennium when man will no longer inflict any unnecessary pain upon the least of his fellow-creatures upon the planet that has been given to him.

The entire list of short nature stories from the pen of this famous Canadian, over one hundred in number, has now been brought together in a single uniform edition by the Macmillan Company. They are in eight volumes, handsomely illustrated by Paul Bransom and others, and sold in Canada at the very moderate price of $1.10, separately or complete. The Macmillan Company are to be heartily congratulated upon getting out so important a collection by one of the greatest of Canadian writers at the very moment when the Canadian Book Week is drawing the attention of Canadians to the scope and excellence of their own national literature.

Criticism

W.J. Keith
Roberts' Animal Stories*

Many of Roberts' animal-stories depend for their effect on the remorseless presentation of the life in nature. In "The Isle of Birds," for example, although it is at first suggested that the setting represents "a very paradise of the nesting sea-birds" (*Neighbours* 35), we soon learn that they exist in a world of fear, hostility and sudden death. Puffins, skuas and saddle-back gulls all inhabit the island, and Roberts demonstrates how each species has mapped out its own territory and how the strengths and weaknesses of each are perilously balanced. The story itself involves a skua that has just robbed a puffin of its rightful prey. On returning to its nest, it encounters three saddle-backs who are plundering the unhatched eggs; it attacks them and dies in the struggle. But the saddle-backs themselves are marauding because their own nests have previously been destroyed in their absence by hostile skuas. It is a sombre story of theft and violence, and since no attempt is made to individualize any of the participants, the focus is upon the island as a paradigm of nature itself. Similarly, "Mothers of the North" (in *Neighbours*), despite the sentimental suggestions of its title, presents a bleakly effective incident in which a mother polar bear kills a baby walrus for the good of her own cub. The loss of the walrus, the gain of the bear, the sacrifice of one creature that another may live—these are the unavoidable facts of wild life which the story presents with all the detached inevitability of a historic chronicle.

The endings of Roberts' stories are especially important in this respect. Whether the subject dies or escapes, Roberts is too much of a realist to underplay the constant danger of life in the wild, and we are generally left with an impression that is both

---

* This commentary is excerpted from a longer one, "Stories of the Wild," which first appeared as Chapter IV of W.J. Keith's *Charles G.D. Roberts* (1969), 85-121. It is reprinted here with the permission of its author.

sobering and uncomfortable. Take, for example, the end of "The Black Fisherman":

> The dead cormorant, supported by her feathers and her hollow bones, lay floating, belly upward, with sprawled wings, on the surface. Her mate, alighting beside her, swam around her several times, eyeing her with an intense gaze. Then, realizing that she was dead, he slowly swam away to take up the double duties now thrust upon him. After all, as there were now but two mouths left in the nest to feed, there was no doubt that he would be equal to the task. (*Wisdom* 43-44)

This is intensely moving because Roberts has here avoided the anthropomorphic danger. There is no attempt to imagine the inner reaction of the male cormorant; moreover, no emotion is forced upon the reader. We are uncertain whether to lament the death of the cormorant or rejoice that the young stand a good chance of surviving. The possible reactions thus cancel out, and we are left with the bald facts. Absence of emotion is an essential part of Roberts' effect; Nature, he is saying with a brutal simplicity, is like that. The same is true of many of the stories in which man intrudes upon the life of the wild. "When Twilight Falls on the Stump Lots" concerns a strayed cow that valiantly defends her calf against a black bear. But her success in this venture is severely qualified by Roberts' final paragraph which he writes in the role of detached and neutral commentator:

> As for the red calf, its fortune was ordinary. Its mother, for all her wounds, was able to nurse and cherish it through the night; and with morning came a searcher from the farm and took it, with the bleeding mother, safely back to the settlement. There it was tended and fattened, and within a few weeks found its way to the cool marble slabs of a city market. (*Kindred* 284)

Out of context, this might he interpreted as an attack upon man's treatment of the lower animals, but a fuller experience of Roberts' art will convince us that he is deliberately demonstrating the fact of man's connection with, and reliance upon, the world of nature. Just as the baby walrus must die so that the bear cub may live, so the life of the calf is sacrificed to the life of man. Once again, Nature is like that.

In his prose Roberts never pontificated; he made no attempt to impose his view of the world upon his readers. None the less we have been able to extract from the short stories a coherent position which may without undue pretentiousness be called a vision of nature. In his article, "The Precious Speck of Life," Joseph Gold describes it as "an affirmative vision in which the conditions of a wilderness struggle for survival are accepted and confirmed." Roberts created, he argues, a genuine Canadian mythology: "The principal feature of this myth is that, while individual creatures constantly lose the struggle for survival, life itself persists."(25). This, of course, is neither an original nor a profound position; moreover, as we have already noted, it differs in many important respects from the world-view presented in his poetry. Where the latter reflects the religious orthodoxy of Westcock parsonage, Robert's home in his youthful days, the prose mirrors the a-moral, a-religious "Nature red in tooth and claw" of the backwoods. I have already indicated my own preference for the prose, but this is a position that may well be challenged. Why, it might be argued, should not the two views be resolved? Man, after all, possesses both a soul and a body; if Roberts chooses to present the life of the body in his animal-stories and the life of the soul in the higher mode of poetry, is not this reasonable and decorous? Is not a preference for "the normal savagery of Nature" merely a modish, twentieth-century cynicism, and an example of what Robert Frost sardonically called "downward comparisons"? I think not, because I see the difference as literary rather than philosophic. I prefer the prose because I believe it to attain a noticeably higher degree of artistic success than the poetry. The rest of this commentary will attempt to defend this view by examining the formal and verbal devices in Roberts' prose.

Roberts was well aware of the formal problems that confronted him. By a deft selection of material and incident, he tried, without sacrificing his claim to realistic accuracy, to suggest—at least for artistic purposes—an ordered pattern beneath the apparent anarchy of the natural world. In other words, he attempted to create the illusion of form in what is seemingly formless, to maintain a balance between the demands of his subject-matter and the requirements of art. As we have already seen, Roberts liked to build his fiction upon the foundation of a strong plot, but in the animal-story even the possibility of plot may be legitimately questioned. Here it is worthwhile recalling E. M. Forster's distinction of terms in *Aspects of the Novel*: 'We have defined a story as a narrative of events arranged in their time-sequence. A plot is also a narrative of events, the emphasis falling on causality. 'The king died and then the queen died,' is a story. 'The king died, and then the queen died of grief' is a plot"(93). But since causality is an essentially human concept, a plot is unlikely to arise out of a natural incident; instead, it will be imposed by the writer who explains by motives and causes what may in fact be merely fortuitous juxtapositions of events.

Whether Roberts consciously "thought through" these distinctions may be doubted, but his practical response to the problem can be traced in the kinds of animal-story which he wrote. He distinguished two kinds in his own work, "the story of adventure and the anecdote of observation" (*Kindred* 21). We may add a third which I shall call the representative chronicle. These three kinds necessarily overlap to some extent, but the distinctions are none the less useful, and it may be helpful to separate their characteristic features.

The story of adventure is at once the most familiar and the least "natural." It has, in the traditional sense, a beginning, a middle and an end. "The Isle of Birds," already discussed at the outset, is an example. We are aware that Roberts has deliberately shaped the material, tied the loose ends together, and produced a convincing and satisfying story. At the same time we realize that the natural world rarely if ever provides so neat a plot. The danger with the story of adventure is that the overall pattern may become little more than an empty formula. Since Roberts published well over two hundred animal-stories, and since the majority of them fall into this category, it is scarcely surprising that certain basic situations recur again and again. A distraught mother avenges the death of her young; an animal is killed at the moment of its triumph over another; a human hunter spares his victim at the last moment when the creature distinguishes itself in its efforts to evade capture. One cannot read for long in Roberts without encountering one or other of these basic stories, and I have no wish to underestimate the artistic dangers involved. At the same time, we should not be disturbed unduly, since in most instances Roberts is merely being true to his subject-matter in underlining the repetitive patterns of Nature. Thus if any wild animal has a hostile encounter with a skunk or a porcupine, the varieties of outcome are essentially limited. Moreover, it is a fact of nature that, ninety-nine times out of a hundred, the individual creature will respond to a standard situation in a standard way. "In the wilderness world," writes Roberts, "as in the world of men, history has a trick of repeating itself" (*Kindred* 341). He is well aware that there is always the hundredth case so welcome to any story-teller. It is "the exceptions rather than the rules," he says, "which make the life of the wilderness exciting" (*Wisdom* 13)—and his insistence upon this almost becomes a formula in itself. But we cannot criticize him on the one hand for anthropomorphizing his animals and on the other for failing to provide variety and originality within the monotonous routine of the natural world. His strength, indeed, is that he is usually able to maintain an acceptable balance between the two.

The representative chronicle, in contrast, finds a unity in subject rather than in plot. Here we follow the fortunes of a single creature over an extended period of time and so witness a collection of individual adventures which accumulate to become representative of the species. Seton specialized in this kind of animal-story which he called the animal-biography; it is a kind that was to be perfected in England by Henry Williamson in *Tarka the Otter* and *Salar the Salmon*. Roberts used it less frequently but with undoubted success. *Red Fox* is his most extended and ambitious attempt. Others include "The King of the Mamozekel" (*Kindred*), which traces the growth of a moose calf from birth to maturity, "The Last Barrier" (*Haunters*), the story of a salmon that has been brilliantly analyzed by Joseph Gold in his article, "The Precious Speck of Life," and "Queen Bomba of the Honey Pots" (*They Who Walk*), the story of a beehive. Roberts tended to employ this kind more often as he grew older. It avoids many of the dangers of the more tightly-constructed tale of adventure. The story is shaped by the natural exigencies of time and place, and there is less pressure to fall back on a stock formula to provide a climax; moreover, emphasis on the typical rather than the individual life neatly sidesteps some of the objections of the traditional naturalists.

The anecdote of observation is a sketch rather than a story and attempts no more than a straightforward presentation of a simple natural occurrence. It differs from the other kinds in that it is almost always "true literally" (*Watchers* vii) while the story of adventure and the representative chronicle can only partake of a more general, eclectic truth. The distinction is of some importance. The most that Roberts can claim of *Red Fox*, for example, is that "every one of these experiences has befallen some red fox in the past" (*Red Fox* viii). In this respect he is, of course, claiming no more than every novelist and short-story writer is free to assume within a realistic convention; but the distinction none the less affects our response to his stories. In the anecdote of observation (and, to some extent, in the representative chronicle) the intrusion of the author into the story is less noticeable. He is inevitably a selector of incident, but he is not necessarily a manipulator, and when literal truth is at a premium, an exciting climax to a thrilling tale of adventure may be less acceptable than a "slice of (wild) life" which includes nothing unusual or unexpected. In Forster's terms, the anecdotes of observation are stories but not plots, and although there is often no climax and no resolution, these can rank among Roberts' most impressive and satisfying creations. "The Keepers of the Nest" (*Feet*), for example, is merely an account of how on two occasions a pair of swans guard their nest—once from a fisher, once from a lynx. There is no thematic connection between the two incidents, and therefore no plot in the precise sense, but as a vignette of wild life the anecdote is both credible and successful.

We have seen, then, that Roberts distinguished and used a number of forms of the animal-story. In addition, he employed various formal devices to hold his anecdotes and chronicles together. These are for the most part the standard patterns that are always available to literature—the traditional elements of earth, air and water, the daily cycle from dawn to sunset, the seasonal cycle from spring to winter. Other patterns, more limited but particularly appropriate to Roberts' subject-matter, include those provided by animal hibernation and the continual process of mating and separation. Such devices have been analyzed in some detail by Joseph Gold (23, 25). It is interesting to note, however, that similar patterns are to be found in Roberts' diction. These verbal effects have received considerably less attention.

Even a casual reading of Roberts will reveal an unusual number of repeated words and phrases. "The wild kindred," "the furtive folk," "the Fate of the wilderness," "the savage and implacable sternness of the wild"—these and others occur so frequently as to recall the repeated patterns of oral formulaic that are now recognized as a characteristic feature of primitive poetry. This effect in Roberts has sometimes been attributed to lack of originality or the carelessness of haste, but it is clearly deliberate and carries considerable literary significance. Just as the Anglo-Saxon poets, members of small human communities surrounded by the vast unknowns of nature, evolved a poetry that reflected a world in which Law and Rule were omnipotent though often mysterious, so here Roberts has made use of related rhetorical devices that appropriately embody the rules of the wilderness itself. They continually remind us of continuity behind the ever-changing face of nature, the impersonality that endures and is eternal. Individuals die but "life itself persists"; the single life is expendable, but the type remains. Through reiterated words and phrases, these natural patterns and rhythms are made manifest.

Moreover, the effect is not confined to diction; it extends to image and metaphor. In the Introduction to *King of Beasts and Other Stories*, Joseph Gold has quoted with approval a passage from "The Aigrette" (*Secret Trails*) where the birds "looked like bits of Japanese screen brought to life" and has shown how the image suggests "a civilized pattern in the midst of wilderness."(xviii). But this image is repeated on several occasions by Roberts in almost identical words (see, for example, *Haunters*, 197; *Wisdom*, 58; *Watchers*, 145). In this way he emphasizes the motif, inviting us to go further and see the "civilized pattern" as itself the reflection of a larger natural one. The stillness of the screen is representative of the stillness of nature; it suggests not so much an artistic stasis as what Roberts calls "the stillness of vast, untraversed solitude" (*The House* 11). The pattern which the Japanese painter transforms into art is, like that which Roberts portrays in words, a distillation of the recurrent, instinctive actions constantly repeated in the wild.

Once we become aware of the presence and effect of these formal and technical devices, we are in a better position to appreciate the unquestioned but curiously elusive merits of Roberts' prose style. Perhaps its most remarkable quality is a consistent competence that enables him to describe any scene, express any idea, evoke any response with accuracy, vividness and economy. He is not a "stylist"; that is to say, he does not use words as either ornament or veneer. He is in command of words without being self-consciously aware of his power over them. We never feel that he is deliberately striving for an effect. As a consequence, it is difficult to illustrate the qualities of Roberts' prose in the present inevitably brief discussion. No particular passages demand attention; moreover, since its effect lies in a cumulative excellence rather than in scattered set-pieces, a specific passage may not seem in any way remarkable when separated from the context to which it belongs. One can, however, quote one or two passages that illustrate the variety of effect that Roberts can achieve. Here, for instance, is a straightforward descriptive passage from *Red Fox*. It concerns a farmyard that is about to be attacked by foxes, a "scene of secure peace" soon to be changed into a place of violent slaughter:

> All was peace about the little farmyard. The golden lilac light made wonderful the chip-strewn yard, and the rough, weather-beaten roofs of cabin and barn and shed. The ducks were quacking and bobbing in the wet mud about the water-trough, where some grain had been spilled. The sleepy chickens were gathering in the open front of the shed, craning their necks with little murmurings of content, and one by one hopping up to their roosts among the rafters. From the sloping

> pasture above the farmyard came a clatter of bars let down, and a soft tunk-a-tonk of cowbells as the cows were turned out from milking. (*Red Fox* 64-65)

The scene is etched in smoothly and effortlessly. The range of detail is remarkable, but even this is surpassed by the variety of sense-impressions through which our response is extended and deepened. Thus the visual light-effect is followed by images of sound and movement with the ducks "quacking and bobbing;" the senses of touch and texture are evoked by "the rough, weatherbeaten roofs" and "the wet mud about the water-trough;" and the tone of the whole farmyard is expressed by the "sleepy chickens" with their "little murmurings of content." Detail follows detail until the essence of a Maritime farmyard has been communicated.

Roberts is skilled at evoking scenes of peace, but he is no less adept at presenting action. The following passage represents the climax of an early story, "The Young Ravens that Call upon Him":

> The lamb seemed afraid to take so many steps. It shook its ears and bleated piteously. The mother returned to its side, caressed it anew, pushed it with her nose, and again moved away a few feet, urging it to go with her. Again the feeble little creature refused, bleating loudly. At this moment there came a terrible hissing rush out of the sky, and a great form fell upon the lamb. The ewe wheeled and charged madly; but at the same instant the eagle, with two mighty buffetings of his wings, rose beyond her reach and soared away toward the mountain. The lamb hung limp from his talons; and with piteous cries the ewe ran beneath, gazing upward, and stumbling over the hillocks and juniper bushes. (*Earth's Enigmas* 65)

This is in a sense a controversial example since the likelihood of an eagle carrying off a young lamb has been strongly challenged by naturalists. Roberts convinces us, however, by the sheer authority of his prose. Each action is described in short staccato phrases. The emphasis is appropriately on the verbs—

"bleated," "caressed," pushed," "wheeled," "charged." By a bold stroke on Roberts' part, the climactic action is not shown. The eagle's descent is so sudden, so fast, that it is only after he has soared away that we learn how "the lamb hung limply from his talons." At the same time, Roberts gives us a number of enhancing but inessential details: the eagle gives *two* mighty buffetings of its wings; the ewe stumbles over hillocks and *juniper* bushes. The specific references heighten the vividness of the scene and at the same time detach us from it. The description is paradoxically both involved and neutral. Characteristically, there is nothing ostentatious about this prose. The diction is simple, the rhythms conventional. Its prime virtue lies in its transparent naturalness; it never intrudes between reader and subject-matter.

Perhaps the most effective way of stressing the quiet authority of Roberts' prose is to juxtapose a passage with a comparable extract from his verse. The following descriptions are similar in subject, and may be accepted, I think, as fair examples. Both reveal his characteristic strengths; neither is obviously outstanding. The verse passage is one of the sonnets from *Songs of the Common Day*, "The Flight of the Geese":

> I hear the low wind wash the softening snow,
>   The low tide loiter down the shore. The night,
>   Full filled with April forecast, hath no light.
> The salt wave on the sedge-flat pulses slow.
> Through the hid furrows lisp in murmurous flow
>   The thaw's shy ministers; and hark! The height
>   Of heaven grows weird and loud with unseen flight
> Of strong hosts prophesying as they go!
>
> High through the drenched and hollow night their wings
>   Beat northward hard on Winter's trail. The sound
> Of their confused and solemn voices, borne
> Athwart the dark to their long Arctic morn,
>   Comes with a sanction and an awe profound,
> A boding of unknown, foreshadowed things.

(*Selected* 97)

The same experience which formed the basis for this sonnet was obviously revived a few years later when Roberts came to write the opening paragraphs of his short story, "The Homesickness of Kehonka":

> The April night, softly chill and full of the sense of thaw, was closing down over the wide salt marshes. Near at hand the waters of the Tantramar, resting at full tide, glimmered through the dusk and lapped faintly among the winter-ruined remnants of the sedge. Far off—infinitely far off it seemed in that illusive atmosphere, which was clear, yet full of the ghosts of rain—the last of daylight lay in a thin streak, pale and sharp, along a vast arc of the horizon....
>
> Presently, from far along the dark heights of the sky, came voices, hollow, musical, confused. Swiftly they journeyed nearer; they grew louder. The sound—not vibrant, yet strangely far-carrying—was a clamorous monotony of honk-a-honk, honk-a-honk, honka, honka, honk, honk. It hinted of wide distance voyaged over on tireless wings, of a tropic winter passed in feeding amid remote, high-watered meadows of Mexico and Texas, of long flights yet to go, toward the rocky tarns of Labrador and the reed beds of Ungava. As the sound passed straight overhead the listener on the marsh below imagined, though he could not see, the strongly beating wings, the outstretched necks and heads, the round, unswerving eyes of the wild goose flock in its V-shaped array, winnowing steadily northward through the night. (*Kindred* 117-118).

While the sonnet is competent and workmanlike, there can be little doubt that the prose is more effective. The verse is marred by the dull, predictable rhymes, the conventional poeticisms ("in murmurous flow," "an awe profound") and the vague ending in which we are expected to share in the poet's emotion but are given no clues as to what that emotion is. By contrast, the prose is light and varied. "The April night, softly chill and full of the sense of thaw" compares favourably with the rather pompous, "poetic" phrases "Full filled with April forecast" and "The thaw's shy ministers" (a rather feeble echo, incidentally, from Coleridge's "Frost at Midnight"). "The salt wave on the sedge-flat pulses slow" is flat and uninspired compared with the prose equivalent where the Tantramar waters "lapped faintly among the winter-ruined remnants of the sedge." Where in the prose the voices of the geese are "hollow, musical, confused," each adjective contributing to the overall effect, in the poem they are "confused and solemn," the last word being weak to the point of cliché, and the word "hollow" is transferred, with less felicity, to the night. In view of Roberts' acknowledged preference, it is curious how conventional his poetic diction is by comparison with that of his prose. It seems as if he is so concerned with the problems of metre and rhyme that he fails to bring to his poetry that acute and observing intelligence that is so rewarding a feature of his prose. In short, we learn so much more in the second passage; the details are more vivid, the rhythms more natural and assured. It is no defence to retort that the sonnet is confined by its fourteen-line limit—no one required Roberts to express himself in this particular form. It is more to the purpose to point out that he was noticeably more relaxed in prose, while a self-conscious stiffness is too common a characteristic of his verse. Indeed, it may well be just because he took his prose less seriously, was less concerned to achieve the elevated dignity which he so unfortunately connected with the art of poetry, that the most individual and admirable qualities of his prose—precision, smoothness, variety, directness—were released and made manifest.

Roberts' chief claim to our attention would seem to lie, indeed, in his mastery of the animal-story. If both critics and serious readers have hitherto been reluctant to admit this, the reasons are not far to seek. It must be granted that the animal-story is not generally considered an important—or even a dignified—form. We think of *Black Beauty* or *Bambi*, assume that sentimentality or cuteness are necessary ingredients, and refuse to recognize it as an "adult" or sophisticated taste. Such a verdict cannot be defended, however, upon rational grounds.

When the debate is argued in general terms, few (one assumes) would be prepared to assert that some subjects are automatically beyond the pale of art. In principle, then, there is no reason why, if modern poets are free to write about such conventionally unpoetic objects as trains and aeroplanes, Roberts should not be at liberty to take the animal world as his province. Ironically, this is a traditionally-sanctioned subject, and it might well be argued that Roberts' fresh and challenging approach is especially deserving of literary praise. For the artist must ultimately be judged, not on his choice of subject-matter, but on what he has created out of it. If we are to dismiss Roberts' animal-stories as in some way inferior, we should remember that we are also condemning the subject-matter of D. H. Lawrence's poem-sequence, *Birds, Beasts, and Flowers*, where another attempt is made to "get under the skins" of non-human life.

It is true that some subjects may seem less immediately appealing than others. A story concerning schoolboys on an uninhabited island sounds unpromising for a work of substance, yet in *Lord of the Flies* William Golding was able to make it the basis for an original and probing criticism of life. Similarly Roberts, in his animal-stories, has confined himself to a limited area which, when, viewed as a microcosm, is seen to expand in application and become relevant to the whole world of man. He takes as his major theme the age-old problem of man's relation to the earth upon which he lives, but the questions he raises are as challenging as ever and are phrased in a new way. Where Tennyson looked forward (however tentatively) to a time when future generations would read Nature "like an open book," when inheritances from the jungle would be outgrown and man no more be classified as "half-akin to brute," the post-Darwinian Roberts is more doubtful. For him, the book of nature communicates a different message. It questions the possibility of "working out the beast" in terms, not of ape and tiger, but of wolf and lynx. Man, he tells us, may well emerge triumphant, but his triumph will be that of the hunter. In Roberts' animal-stories, man is always seen *within* the context of an all-embracing struggle for existence. To quote Joseph Gold, he attains his humanity "only by his supremacy as an animal."(20). This may not constitute Roberts' firm "philosophy of life." He was not, after all, a philosopher, and his poems present a far more optimistic picture. But it is a meaningful possibility, and Roberts presents it dramatically and acutely. We may freely grant that he wrote too much, that his weakness for both the sensational and the exotic is a blemish. In his prose, as in his verse, a winnowing process is required. But whereas we are left in his poetry with a number of skillful, satisfying but unallied poems, in his animal-stories we find a distinct body of work that can ultimately stand as representative of the "world" of Charles G. D. Roberts. This is a generally unrecognized but none the less substantial achievement that deserves to be accepted as a permanent contribution to a specifically Canadian literature.

Works Cited

Forster, E.M. *Aspects of the Novel.* 1927. Harmondsworth: Penguin, 1968.

Gold, Joseph. "The Precious Speck of Life." *Canadian Literature* 26 (Autumn 1965): 22-32.

———. Intro. to *King of the Beasts and Other Stories.* By Charles G.D. Roberts. Toronto: Ryerson, 1967.

Roberts, Charles G.D. *Earth's Enigmas.* 1896. Boston: L.C. Page, 1903.

———. *The Kindred of the Wild.* Toronto: Copp Clark, 1902.

———. *The Watchers of the Trails.* Toronto: Copp Clark, 1904.

———. *Red Fox.* 1905. Boston: L.C. Page, 1913.

———. *The Haunters of the Silences.* Boston: L.C. Page, 1907.

———. *The House in the Water.* London: Ward, Lock, 1908.

———. *Neighbours Unknown.* 1910. New York: Macmillan, 1921.

———. *The Feet of the Furtive.* 1912. New York: Macmillan, 1921.

———. *The Secret Trails.* 1916. New York: Macmillan, 1921.

———. *Wisdom of the Wilderness.* 1922. New York: Macmillan, 1928.

———. *They Who Walk the Wild.* 1924. New York: Macmillan, 1925.

———. *Eyes of the Wilderness.* Toronto: Macmillan, 1933.

———. *Selected Poems.* Toronto: Ryerson, 1936.

Joseph Gold
The Ambivalent Beast*

It is not difficult I think to make the case that the animal stories are the most entertaining, ambitious and lasting production from Sir Charles G. D. Roberts' pen. What led to the neglect of these stories for a considerable time is the change of, or the disappearance of, their audience. How this happened is worthy of some discussion and speculation. Roberts' poetry is frequently pious and depersonalized. The influence of English romanticism, itself thoroughly characterized by natural piety, as well as romanticized classicism, has been well noted. Professor W. J. Keith among others has done much to familiarize us again with these poems and their place in the canon. Suffice it to say here that Roberts writes poetry in the light of a clearly identifiable tradition and influence. Similarly, the novels are part of a romantic tradition immensely popular in North America, aimed in my view at a largely female audience and characterized by a highly stylized language, a faintly erotic tone, slightly Gothic events, and a neo-historical chivalry. The main progenitor is clearly Scott. There is much splendid writing in these novels, but they do not have, as far as I can see, the energy and power of the troubled vision of the deep and authentic Roberts, the sense of the artist straining after his own truth, that we get in the animal fiction.

Here Roberts can be more original, free and daring. What I want to do here is to suggest briefly some of the possible reasons for their continuing, intriguing power. This involves, I believe, their place in cultural history and the nature of their audience's anxieties and concerns. These stories are designed to be convincing. The writer's imagination takes them over, less constrained by the bounds of religious, social, and literary convention. By turning to a world that can never be contained in English drawing rooms, Roberts can take off his tie, light up his pipe, and be himself. But this is not to say that he can leave

---

* This article first appeared in *The Proceedings of the Sir Charles G.D. Roberts Symposium* (1984), 77-86. It is reprinted here with the permission of the author and the Centre for Canadian Studies, Mount Allison University.

aside his deepest concerns. On the contrary, it is because he has found a medium for the expression of his creative energy that he can include his troubled perceptions of man. What we find in this fiction is man characterized by duality and ambivalence, part animal, part god, part pagan, part civilized, the subscriber to Olympian deities with all their whimsies and intrigues, and the product and follower of Yahweh, carrying inside himself the power to choose and the moral imperatives of right and wrong. Man loves and hates nature—either of which is a detached and alien response and he is part of nature at the same time. These conflicts and these warring elements are present in the fiction, are present in the human participants in the animal fiction, even though they are not explicit.

Put another way, the animal stories provided Roberts the means to be speculative and subversive. If the stories are weakened or less perfect because they permit the inclusion of human beings who are imperfect, confused and confusing, they are also strengthened by the range of problems embodied in that inclusion. Much of Roberts is Victorian and perhaps this is another way of approaching what we find here. These stories made possible the expression of a great many feelings and ideas otherwise to be repressed. One could argue that the vogue of animal fiction is part of the history of middle-class mental liberation and part of a post-Darwinian and post-Freudian encounter with human nastiness and brutality that give the lie to the conspiracy of the genteel. The bestial in man, himself black, white, or red in tooth and claw, could be presented directly or indirectly in animal stories. This is the antithesis of Beatrix Potter and Walt Disney, both reversions to the repression implicit in Victorian sentiment. Bestial, immoral, amoral, savage man is part of the ambivalent man found in the animal fiction. What is innocence in animals is brutality in human beings. This is the intriguing paradox that informs this writing. It is a matter of curiosity and revelation that Roberts can at one time be writing poetry like

> I have sought God beyond His furthest star —
> But here I find Him, in your quickening dust;[1]

writing scenes of Victorian melodrama like this:

> Now, it was my honest intention at that instant to do just her bidding and no more; but when I touched her fingers reason and judgment flowed from me. I bowed my head over them to the edge of the hammock, and with both my hands crushed them to my lips. She sank back upon her cushion, with a little catching of her breath.
>
> After a few moments I raised my head—but with no speech and with no set purpose—and looked at her face. It was very grave, and curiously troubled, but I detected no reproach in the great eyes that met mine. A fierce impulse seized me to gather her in my arms—but I durst not, and my eyes dropped as I thought of it. By chance they rested upon her feet—upon the tiny, quill-worked, beaded white moccasins, demurely crossed, the one over the other. Her skirt was so closely gathered about her ankles that just an inch or two of one arched instep was visible over the edge of the low-cut moccasin. Before I myself could realize what I was about to do, or half the boldness of the act, in a passion that was all worship I threw myself down beside her feet and kissed them.
>
> It was for an instant only that my daring so prevailed. Then she suddenly slipped away. In a breathless confusion I sprang to my feet, and found her standing erect at the other side of the hammock. Her eyes blazed upon me; but one small hand was at her throat, as if she found it hard to speak.
>
> "How could you dare?" she panted. "What right did I give you? What right did I ever give you?"
>
> I leaned against the pillar that supported one end of the hammock.
>
> "Forgive me! I could not help it. I have loved, worshipped you, so long!" I said in a very low voice.
>
> "How dare you speak so?" she cried. "You forget that"—
>
> "No, I remember!" I interrupted doggedly. "I forget nothing. You do not love him. You are mine."

> "Oh!" she gasped, lifting both hands sharply to her face and dropping them at once. "I shall never trust you again."
>
> And in a moment she had flashed past me, with a sob, and disappeared into the house.[2]

At the same time Roberts is telling his audience stories about animals tearing each other to pieces, dripping with blood, driven to frenzy by hunger or oestrus, and describing nightmare worlds of the sea where huge fishes become masses of entrails to feed the crabs in oceans turning red with blood; he describes a man eaten alive by wolves and a man keeping himself alive in the snow by sitting next to an exhausted caribou and drinking the blood pouring from the knife wounds he has just made. This would all have been underground literature in Victorian England. In Victorian Canada, where the ghost of the queen still haunts the land, it can only be read as part of frontier realism, distasteful but understandable in a land as savage as this. But admitted or not, these stories enable readers to get in touch with parts of themselves forbidden by polite and civilized society. They were never stories for children. They were consumed by the best-behaved, middle-aged adults. They lost their appeal and went out of fashion and print through the aftermath of the first Great War, in the twenties, and in the Depression of the thirties, though some were reprinted in the late forties after a long interval and the last two decades have seen the beginning of a revival. They had become simply outmoded. The audience changed from post-Victorians looking for adventure in print to survivors of the hideous experience of war and depression and more war. The violence of our own era, the newsreels of Belsen, Dachau, and Buchenwald make the savagery of the wilderness less shocking and less intriguing on the one hand, but more familiar on the other. The dichotomy of man is less odd to us. The savage is nearer to us than we had thought and repression and sublimation have come to seem irrelevant and inappropriate.

All of our pressures today include the demand for honesty, openness, authenticity, and a part of that necessity to consult our feelings will be an admission of confusion, insecurity, and doubt, and a confession of a range of desires and emotions within us which were forbidden to Victorian middle-class consciousness. Within the limits of his time, place and talent Roberts came daringly close to exposing some of these human impulses by using the device of animal behaviour. In the process he raises the question whether human beings are animals like other animals. By and large the answer is a "qualified yes". Stories like "Mothers of the North," "When Twilight Falls on the Stump Lots," and "How a Cat Played Robinson Crusoe" are not designed to show us what animals are like, but what we are like. This is where we came from and how to a large extent we still are. But in the process of evolving into Humanity we became different, socialized, compassionate, reflective and creative. This left us the same and quite different. Not since medieval speculation had the place of man in creation been in the centre of literature and not before, with isolated exceptions, had fiction used a naturalistic animal world to explain the nature of human behaviour. These were fables with a wilderness setting drawn from life, and without moral conclusions. Along with Zola and Dreiser, Roberts finds his own way to present atavistic-civilized man.

Let us look at some of the ways in which this original fiction conveys the human alien. Roberts' animal tales can hardly be credited with engrossing us by anything complicated enough to be called a plot, and yet we are seduced by his language into the vivid experience of imagined sensory perception. We hear the bull moose thrashing in the brush, we see the "loon far out on the silver sheen of the lake" and hear the "peal of his startling and demoniacal laughter". We believe in the mating passion, humanized for us by Roberts—"All the yearning of all the mating ardour that has triumphed over insatiable death and kept the wilderness peopled from the first was in that deceitful voice." The use of the term "peopled" suggests Roberts' inclination to brush out the line between animal and human. Almost all the stories are skillful, fascinating, intriguing, but what deepens some of them, what sets them resonating, is the confusion and complication of human presence. The wonderful, deceitful voice that lures the splendid bull moose to its death belongs to a human hunter, one who could "slay the cunning kindred of the wild by a craft finer than their own". The man who can be a cow moose one moment, reverts to his human separateness the next.

> With a sudden outburst of voices, the two hunters sprang up, broke from their ambush, and ran to view the prize. They were no longer of the secretive kindred of the wilderness, but pleased children. The old woodsman eyed shrewdly the inimitable spread of the prostrate antlers. As for the boy, he stared at his victim, breathless, his eyes a-glitter with the fierce elemental pride of the hunter triumphant.[3]

In *The Heart of the Ancient Wood*, Roberts' most earnest attempt to bring together the human and the animal world, Miranda quickly rejects her innocent kinship with the prelapsarian world of the wilderness and kills her bear to save her man. The nice ambiguity of this mating sacrifice is left with us as the fulfilment of the story. In *The House in the Water* the ubiquitous boy, of whom I shall say more in a moment, steps out of his god-like detachment and becomes the superior animal who kills him from a distance. Jabe Smith, his equally ubiquitous adult friend, objects to the boy's hypocrisy, "But I thought as how ye wouldn't kill anything." The answer is, "Had to. That was self-defense. Those beavers are my beavers and I've always wanted a real good excuse for getting a good lynx skin anyway."

This Jabe Smith, who can then say, "I don't blame ya a mite for standin' by them beaver", is the same Jabe Smith who traps the furry critters, crushing their little feet and legs in heavy steel traps, and drowning them quite cheerfully. Jabe Smith and the boy are really parts of the same person and present us with the clearest and crudest allegory of ambivalent response to the wilderness. For all of the awkwardness and self-consciousness of their portrayal, they appeal to conflicts in ourselves and here I speak particularly as a male reader. There is not, as far as I know, a single female hunter in Roberts. In fact both the naturalist-observer and the hunter are male embodiments like Jacob and Esau. The boy, with his much more educated accent and his studious habits, characteristics totally unaccounted for, is very much a part of Roberts the man; but Roberts' fascination with the rough, big hearted, tough and resilient male trappers and lumbermen is everywhere in evidence. Can both exist in amicable balance? The answer is clearly "no". They are always in conflict, never free from each other, and the tension between them provides some of the interest we experience in this fiction. Sometimes the boy and the man change roles, the man becoming the enthusiastic boy in the beaver-watching episodes of *The House in the Water* and the boy becoming trophy hunter as he confesses above. In *Red Fox* the boy is closely allied to the fox itself and studies its habits and becomes in ways like it, at one point carrying it over his shoulder while it plays dead. The boy tries to be a creature of the wilds and fails. He also observes Jabe's futile attempts to outwit the fox as a kind of curiosity of nature. The paradox that the more natural, less educated man is more like the hunter-animal kindred of the wild, while the educated, detached observer conservationist is more civilized and human is an irony well known to professors who live in the country and to bird-watching academics.

The ambivalence of the human animal placed in an animal world and being not wholly of it, attracted to and repelled by his own links to this world, is far more complex than the boy-Jabe Smith conflict suggests. Man, as we are told in *King of Beasts*, is "the master animal", able in addition to his other skills to fashion weapons to assist him in his killing. Johns in that story can swim, climb trees, and extend his reach greatly by sharpening an ashwood spear with which to kill a tiger. Put a real macho man, almost certainly a Canadian, back into an island jungle Eden and he will revert to all his primitive prowess and dominate all the other animals. But men kill or refrain from killing for every imaginable reason and this, too, makes them quite unlike their fellow creatures. Some men kill out of prejudice. The woodsman in *Mustela*, who "did not like hawks", shoots one. (I can't resist noting that this story appears no later than 1920 and Bridges' edition of Hopkins, containing of course, "The Windhover", appeared in 1918.) Having shot the hawk, the woodsman then refrains from shooting the sable out of an "unexpected attack of sentiment". Jim Atkinson shoots a tame puma at the conclusion of the story called "Mishi" out of ignorance and self-defense. A tame lion is a freak of nature and it was a man who civilized and so corrupted the animal. The trophy hunter in "Antlers of the Caribou", becomes so fascinated by the moonlight meeting of two bull caribou that he simply forgets to shoot and thus brings about two unnecessary animal deaths. These two great caribou bulls actually lock horns so that they are doomed to a slow and lingering death without the intervention of some outside force, in the first instance the arrival of a bear, and in the second instance the arrival of the hunter. There is a slightly Shakespearean quality to the ending of this story, that is worth quoting:

> Straightening himself up, he stared for a few moments at the three great lifeless carcasses on the sand. Then he let his glance sweep out over the glassy waters and level, desolate shores. How strange was the sudden silence, the still white peace of the moonlight, after all that madness and tumult and rage which had just been so abruptly stilled! A curious revulsion of feeling all at once blotted out his triumph, and there came over him a sense of repugnance to the bulk of so much death. Stepping around it, he sat down with his back to it all, on a stranded log, and proceeded to fill his pipe.[4]

This ability to turn one's back, to philosophize, to light one's pipe, to opt out is uniquely human and shows us how strange this in-it-but-not-of-it quality fascinates and even dominates the animal fiction. Even some of the titles of the collections reveal this human closeness/distance riddle: *Neighbours Unknown*, *Wisdom of the Wilderness*, *Kings in Exile,* and *Watchers of the Trails*, *Children of the Wild*—and even *Hoof and Claw* which sounds like a medieval Satan, are apt illustrations. No matter how much free choice man has or appears to have, once he enters the animal world he is subject to unpredictable events and uncontrollable forces that determine strange outcomes. The "Fisher in the Chutes" is a story with a deliberately ambiguous title, the fisher being both a merganser duck and the fisherman whose salmon flies tangle up a falcon to the dismay of bird and man, and in the consequence, save the other fisher's life. Roberts delights in twisting together such strands of irony and complexities of fate. The strongest, the purest stories are probably those without a human presence in which the forces of survival can be isolated, captured, and presented in a world uncomplicated by morality or philosophy or human psychology. The stories free of human interference are the most aesthetically pleasing. But the most interesting stories, even when they are not so neat or uncomplicated, are those where human intervention violates the clarity of natural law. If human beings could be represented as superior animals untroubled by religion or post-Victorian dilemmas of faith and philosophy, one might have a smoothly integrated story containing both animals and people. This is what is attempted in *In the Morning of Time*, where Roberts comes closest to achieving a synthesis which is so clearly and troublingly elusive elsewhere: man as an animal that thinks, feels, reasons, talks, plans ahead and yet fully participates and is part of the animal world. Yet this strangely contemporary novel evades the very issues that most trouble and challenge Roberts and his own contemporaries and therefore is in some ways less satisfying because more self-limiting and less ambitious. To show "man the superior animal" is neatly to beg the question: is man different only in degree or in kind, or does the one become the other? With language, tools and fire, man is quickly set apart and on a different route. The animals know this and man is often represented as a god to them, as their fate, but for man himself, his animal instincts are far too frequently much less than divine.

The animal stories are elegant proof of a theoretical and metaphorical world. In it, human actors love and hate their kinship with the wild and the bestial, but they cannot ignore it. Now like archaeologists of psychic history we are sifting through layers of reluctant confessions, the shards and fragments of broken disguises. We are looking to our recent yet strangely remote ancestry to assist us in the essential task of recapturing some of our lost awe, some of our faith in the rightness of things. We see in these stories that the ambivalence of man the hunter and of man the outsider cannot be rationalized away. Perhaps we are less sure now than we were in the sixties that we can get it all together. Roberts' rejection of Victorian delicacy involved an acceptance of confusion, complexity, and conflict in the makeup of human beings. Roberts' people are ambivalent because Roberts could not be false in order to be pleasing. He could not leave the human out, but he could not get it to act naturally after he had dragged it onstage. Being human hardly seems to be natural at all. It is mostly a mysterious state. And that seems to be just about where we are even now, standing here, awkward and slightly embarrassed to be saying anything, not totally comfortable with our language that sets us apart from the animals; not knowing quite what to do with our hands, getting our lines wrong and fidgeting in front of a backdrop of the Canadian wilderness. Sir Charles may have been more right about us than we have been willing to admit.

Notes

[1] Sir Charles G.D. Roberts, "O Earth, Sufficing All Our Needs," in *Selected Poetry and Critical Prose*, ed., intro. and notes W.J. Keith (Toronto and Buffalo: University of Toronto Press, 1974), p. 187.

2 Roberts, *A Sister to Evangeline* (1898; rpt. Boston: L.C. Page, 1900), pp. 56-57.

3 Roberts, "A Treason of Nature," in *"King of Beasts" and Other Stories*, ed. and intro. Joseph Gold (Toronto: Ryerson, 1967), p. 75.

4 Roberts, "The Antlers of the Caribou, " in *Neighbours Unknown* (Toronto: Macmillan, 1924), p. 65.

Terry Whalen
Roberts and the Tradition of American Naturalism*

In his semi-autobiographical novel *Martin Eden* (1909), Jack London speaks of his early intention as a writer to achieve a balance between two competing traditions of American fiction, the school of romance and the school of naturalism. Of the writer Martin Eden, he says,

> [Martin] had discovered, in the course of his reading, two schools of fiction. One treated man as god, ignoring his earthly origin; the other treated man as clod, ignoring his heaven-sent dreams and divine possibilities. Both the god and clod schools erred, in Martin's estimation, and erred through too great a singleness of sight and purpose. There was a compromise that approximated the truth, though it flattered not the school of god, while it challenged the brute-savageness of the school of clod.[1]

On one level, London's fiction embodies the American realist's struggle to sustain a sense of the mystery and integrity of Creation while at the same time absorbing the Charles Darwin—and Emile Zola—inspired tradition of fiction which was moving away from what Malcolm Cowley (after Frank Norris) calls "teacup tragedies,"[2] the novel of genteel manners and drawing room settings. The work of such American adherents to the new realism as Hamlin Garland, Stephen Crane, Frank Norris, Theodore Dreiser, and London invited the reader into the relatively more raw settings of the slum, the rural frontier, and the wilderness. Theirs is a fiction which sought to observe life in a directly experiential way, and to view it with the lens of recent developments in scientific thought.

---

* This article first appeared in *The Sir Charles G.D. Roberts Symposium* (1984), 127-42. It is reprinted here with the permission of the author.

To different degrees, and using various unconventional settings, their works participate in the tradition of American naturalism, a tradition alert to discoveries about the 'laws of nature' and concerned with the consequences of such laws as they relate to the human condition. Theirs is a tradition attentive to the findings of biology, chemistry, geology and psychology; and it struggles—and very often fails—to reassert the dignity of the human being and the credibility of God in spite of its severe qualms about the power of deterministic forces and especially the power of chance or accident to sweep through nature, making waste of animal and human life as it proceeds. In its darkest moods and thoughts it is a fiction which views the human being as a victim and it concludes that God is dead. Existential despair and a sense of the futility of human action is therefore not uncommon in its vision.

Hence Jack London's fiction is centrally about the forces, both natural and social, which shape the lives of human beings. More particular to our concerns with Charles G. D. Roberts, London's wilderness fiction deals specifically with such American naturalism-inspired concerns as: the atavistic or instinctual origins of human consciousness; laws of survival in the state of nature; the importance of accident or chance in the shaping of creature destiny; suspicions about the identity of God next to the circle of fear and death visible in nature; and the modification of our views on beauty, given the fact of violence in nature and its daily enactment of individual creature tragedies. Like Roberts, London is a writer of both idea and witness, one who is wise to the dark consequences of the Darwinian-nature set and anxious, at the same time, to sustain a confidence in the purpose and wholeness of Creation in spite of what he witnesses at first hand in the midst of his quest for meanings in the physical wilderness.

Tighter local affinities between London and Roberts are not very hard to find. E. M. Pomeroy, in her biography of Roberts, reminds us that Roberts considered his animal stories more like London's than strictly empirical naturalists', more interested in animal psychology and less literal than the work of writers like John Burroughs. President Roosevelt is helpful to us here in that he once referred to London and Roberts in the same breath, dismissing them both as "nature fakirs,"[3] writers who often severely warped the facts of empirical nature. As well, Roberts and London read and contributed to many of the same American magazines during the two decades that stand on either side of the turn of the century;[4] and we know that London at least allows that he read Roberts in 1900, a year in which he wrote to Sinclair Lewis that "I read or tried to read a volume of short stories by some Canadian writer the other day, and think the man was Roberts."[5] I too have a hunch that the man was Roberts, and the volume was possibly *Earth's Enigmas* (1895), a book containing such stories as "The Butt of the Camp," one which conceivably influences London's fiction about the social codes of the north in stories like those in his *The Son of the Wolf* (1900). *Earth's Enigmas* also contains Roberts' "Do Seek their Meat From God," the story about the death-ridden and violent aspects of the laws of survival in nature as made emphatic by the ironies of the food cycle, its fierce and grim logic wherein the life of one creature of necessity means the death of others. On the evidence of London's many stories about this 'law of life,' and specifically on the basis of three chapters in his 1905 novel, *White Fang* (entitled "The Trail of Meat," "The Hunger Cry," and "The Law of Meat"), there is sufficient consonance to suggest that the spirit of Roberts sometimes strolls behind similar settings, plots, and characters in London's wilderness world.

The affinity works to Roberts' advantage as well; it also moves in the other direction. W. J. Keith has noticed that Roberts' novel *In the Morning of Time* (1919), a quasi-scientific re-enactment of the struggles of emerging prehistoric man, shares with London's novel about the atavistic ground of human consciousness, *Before Adam* (1906), a shape and thematic concerns which hint at a marginal influence.[6] Roberts' novel is somewhat more corny, melodramatic, and thrilling—it is designed more with an adolescent audience in mind—than London's, but it shares with London a close imaginative grappling with the double nature of emerging man as both surviving beast and brooding angel, both "clod" and "god," if you like. In both novels the growth of human consciousness is dramatized as an intuitive awareness which becomes more upright as rudimentary forms of curiosity, wonder, and idealism. Simultaneously, the growth of mind also fails to free the man-beasts from atavistic fears, the racial memory of wounds, and tragedies of the species, commonly referred to in more recent lingo as the primal fears of the sub-conscious.

But it is in the animal stories especially that a comparison of the two writers implies affinities and differences worthy of more detailed notice. In his concise historical overview of the animal story, written as an introduction to *The Kindred of the Wild* (1903), Roberts refers to the three sub-species of the genre: (1) the animal adventure story, (2) the anecdote of observation, and (3) the animal biography or psychological chronicle. The latter species is the most recent one, he explains, and also the most interesting. Nevertheless, there are aspects of all three of the structures variously blended in Roberts' individual stories, just as they are also variously blended in London's work.

The matter of difference is more illuminating, and it is chartable as an issue of reality versus metaphor. In the main, Roberts tends to be a more mimetic writer than London, more empirical than metaphorical, even though many of his stories are laden with allegory and thick, on occasion, with a moral earnestness. While Roberts maintained that "As far, at least, as the mental intelligence is concerned, the gulf dividing the lowest of human species from the highest of the animals has been these days reduced to a very narrow psychological fissure," he felt that Rudyard Kipling's animal stories, for instance, were limited by a narrative intrusiveness in their excess of metaphor, their humanization of creatures to the level of narrow symbolism. "In these tales the animals are frankly humanised," he says. "Their individualisation is distinctly human, as are their mental and emotional processes, and their highly elaborate powers of expression."[7] Relatedly, London was profoundly influenced by Kipling's stories, and this other affinity accounts for the difference that, relative to the more mimetic graces of Roberts' animal fiction at its best, London writes in closer kinship with the anthropomorphic mode of Kipling. There are occasions in London's stories when his creatures do most things humans would do, short of read newspapers and write letters home about the weather and their social lives. Relatively speaking (only), Roberts' animals are more real.

Roberts' evocative and empirical gifts as a writer surpass those of London's partly as a corollary of his quite conscious view of the animal story as being a medium through which both the writer and the reader might be re-united with the experiential wisdom of the natural world, with reality as a vital presence, as something outside the self and something wondrous in its spiritual purport. Significantly, Roberts valued the animal story as a "potent emancipator" primarily because it had the potential for returning us to a "clear and candid life to which it reinitiates us, far behind though it lies in the long upward march of being."[8] Because of his interest in this recovery of nature, it is obvious that he also writes in the wider tradition of mimetic, observing nature writers of the twentieth century, a tradition that includes such latter-day animal story writers as England's Ted Hughes, a poet who has remarked that if one is to write about animals with any degree of success one must overcome the pathetic fallacy to the extent that the work is an act of sympathy and re-creation at once, an intimate empirical capturing of the vitality, mystery, and presence of the creature, its otherness.[9]

There is, in other words, a beholding dimension which is epistemologically central to Roberts' animal fiction and it is strong in his canon in spite of the congruent presence in his work of a couple of philosophical bears and a complicated lynx or two, not to mention a particular weasel which has all of the mythic cunning of a snake (notice the metaphors).[10] In short, London is more abstractly concerned with the metaphors for human behaviour he finds in (or intrudes upon) the animal world than is Roberts, more concerned with the suggestive way in which instinctive will and animal behaviour looks, for instance, like a metaphor for the dark, ambiguous, and untapped energies of our own minds. Comparatively, Roberts is the more precisely observant writer and he is also more confident that the flash of animal instinct is but part, and a lesser part, of the human reality after all. Roberts is compelled but not absorbed by the nature he observes.

This very basic difference in perspectives on reality weighs into the different craft of both writers in an interesting way critically. Roberts is the more polished stylist, on the whole, more poised in the quality of his vision of the human and animal worlds. His writerly achievement, viewed next to London's, is chartable, I think, as a grace of mind and style; he manages an artistic triumph over the contradiction between matter and spirit, nature and man, reality and mind, "clod" and "god," which contrarily defeated London as time went on. London is certainly the more exciting 'social' novelist of the two, but it is in Roberts that we find a more complex purchase on the tension caused, next to reality, by the findings of the American school of naturalism.

At the same time, the stimulating way in which London's works appear to have influenced Roberts in the perfection of his concerns is interesting in a focusing way. Each writer seems to have provided suggestive frameworks that the other decided to pursue. Roberts' novel *Red Fox* (1905) is an informative case in point. It exists, I am convinced, as a more poised and refined rewriting of London's 1903 novel, *The Call of the Wild.* Both novels are about creatures (a dog in the London text, the fox in Roberts' case) which live through a series of adventures in both the human and animal worlds. The creatures learn as they proceed about the dangers within these worlds and learn how to survive in them both. These are popular novels, and both sold very well—London's *The Call of the Wild* was his first best-seller and it liberated him from poverty and marked the beginning of his more fortunate professional years. Both novels include aspects of all three of the animal-story structures which Roberts speaks of in his introduction to *The Kindred of the Wild.* Most centrally, however, they share a formal affinity in their identities as primarily animal biographies.

These are the bare bones, but the flesh of the novels, their vision of life, is contained in the narrative performances of each writer, similarly in some ways, and tellingly different in others. London uses the medium of the animal biography to plot a course which leads the mongrel dog, Buck, after long service as a sled dog, away from civilization and into the wilderness, back to the atavistic ground of his wilder brethren, the wolves. He learns how to survive and learns suspicion of the human and animal worlds at once, what London terms the "law of club and fang";[11] and he learns how to kill for his own defence and for food. He is a bit of a 'macho' dog, a fact which shows up in his very much humanized desire to dominate situations and be a 'leader of the pack,' for example, when in service as a sled dog. There is a deep and solid extent, that is, to which Buck is a study in human will as much as a creature with his own biography. London is writing metaphorically throughout. Here and elsewhere in London's fiction, a fascination with power and a desire to escape from the burdens of awareness sometimes take a worrisome turn toward a worship of the savage god, toward an arguably naive primitivism which is not uncommon in the American tradition of naturalism.

Two of the more positive dimensions of London's regard for the primitive ground of being are also available in *The Call of the Wild* as, firstly, a joyful celebration of the sheer élan of life as figured in the freedom of the creature once it recovers its more basic instincts; and, secondly, as London's evocation of that primordial wonder which he found most readily available in the landscape of the wilderness where the immensities of the sky charge the spirit with an elemental sense of ambiguous mystery. Hence, on the first point, *The Call of the Wild* imaginatively participates in the enacted "joy of living" which intermittently comes to Buck throughout the novel, and which reaches an especially ecstatic pitch in a scene where he chases after a rabbit. The scene moves London toward the following abstraction:

> There is an ecstasy that marks the summit of life, and beyond which life cannot rise. And such is the paradox of living, this ecstasy comes when one is most alive, and it comes as a complete forgetfulness that one is alive. This ecstasy, this forgetfulness of living, comes to the artist, caught up and out of himself in a sheet of flame; it comes to the soldier, war-mad on a stricken field and refusing quarter; and it came to Buck, leading the pack, sounding the old wolf cry, straining after the food that was alive and that fled swiftly before him through the moonlight. He was sounding the deeps of his nature, and of the parts of his nature that were deeper than he, going back into the womb of Time. He was mastered by the sheer surging life, the tidal wave of being, the perfect joy of each separate muscle, joint, and sinew in that it was

> everything that was not death, that it was aglow and rampant, expressing itself in movement, flying exultingly under the stars and over the face of dead matter that did not move. (CTW, p. 130).

More quietly and in a more controlled, less spiritually dangerous embrace, Roberts also, in *Red Fox* and in many of his shorter animal stories, appreciates the primitive surge of life, its beauty as a form of instinctual motion, though he is not as narratively noisy as London is in the passage above.

London's second achievement as a novelist fascinated with the primitive ground of being—his capacity for a primordial wonder—is also present as an ambiguous reality in *The Call of the Wild.* His wilderness settings are usually suspenseful and solitary and are poetically present in the novel as an index of his religious dimension as a writer who seeks to unmask the face of the god behind the physical world he observes. There is an edginess in London's mystical concerns as a thinker, and that quality of agitated awe is present in typical passages like the following:

> The months came and went, and back and forth they twisted through the uncharted vastness, where no men were and yet where men had been if the Lost Cabin were true. They went across divides in summer blizzards, shivered under midnight sun on naked mountains between the timber line and the eternal snows, dropped into summer valleys amid swarming gnats and flies, and in the shadows of glaciers picked strawberries and flowers as ripe and fair as any the Southland could boast. In the fall of the year they penetrated a weird lake country, sad and silent, where fowl had been, but where there was no life nor sign of life—only the blowing of the chill winds, the forming of ice in sheltered places, and the melancholy rippling of waves and lonely beaches. (CTW, p. 170).

In London's fiction the north is both beautiful and desolate; it is inspiring and dreadful at the same time. The ambiguity of wonder felt in its presence often leads the novelist to the anxiety born of an equivocal perspective on existence, a confusion of spirit that echoes the appearance of equivocation in the natural world itself.

A more finely written example of that equivocal spiritual and natural world is available in "The White Silence," a story from London's 1900 collection, *The Son of the Wolf.* It states an experience of awe and dread with the degree of immediacy which has led at least one commentator to associate London's religious depth with Blaise Pascal, and associate it with Pascal because of the imaginative thunder of the novelist's experience of humility next to the 'incredible spaces' which surround the stage called the world:

> The afternoon wore on, and with the awe, born of the White Silence, the voiceless travellers bent to their work. Nature has many tricks wherewith she convinces man of his finity—the ceaseless flow of the tides, the fury of the storm, the shock of the earthquake, the long roll of heaven's artillery—but the most tremendous, the most stupefying of all, is the passive phase of the White Silence. All movement ceases, the sky clears, the heavens are as brass; the slightest whisper seems sacrilege, and man becomes timid, affrighted at the sound of his own voice. Sole speck of life journeying across the ghostly wastes of a dead world, he trembles at his audacity, realizes that this is a maggot's life, nothing more. Strange thoughts arise unsummoned, and the mystery of all things strives for utterance. And the fear of death, of God, of the universe comes over him,—the hope of the Resurrection and the Life, the yearning for immortality, the vain striving of the imprisoned essence,—it is then, if ever, man walks alone with God.[12]

Accomplished passages of highly poetic prose such as the above have encouraged critics to speak of London as a mystical writer. The sense of place and the kind of mind which is nourished and formed by that reality are critically prized in his work continually. It is the absence of just such an imaginative awareness in the main character in "To Build a Fire" which leads to his ironic fate, his death as an unfortunate and mentally limited man who expires in the indifferent "white silence."

Roberts and London share a basic recognition of the value of imaginative receptivity of mind, a receptivity which is tutored by a sense of the smallness and pathos of creatures who live amidst an immense and startling Creation. Those who are ignorant of its thunder are more quickly destroyed in the state of nature, or are, as in Roberts' *The Heart of the Ancient Wood* (1900), confined to the narrow world of society and social gossip alone. In the work of both novelists, those who live unalert to the mysterious presence of the physical world are viewed as limited, narrow and morally dangerous.

Nevertheless, wonder is often threatened by a closely related experience of existential perplexity and moral nausea, in both Roberts and London. They know by experience and by reading that the natural world is strewn with the carnage of nature's 'law of meat,' and both writers, therefore, entertained the possibility that the face behind nature is the sickly face of a grinning and malevolent God. Like other writers in the tradition of American naturalism, Roberts and London notice that all creatures, including the human, are subject to what Roberts in "The Tantramar Revisited" calls the "Hands of chance and change," hands which have "marred or moulded, / or broken / Busy with spirit or flesh, all I most have adored."[13] They share a compelling, sometimes obsessive perception of the centrality of chance or accident as a shaping force in destiny. They recognize that survival is not only the result of being fit, but also a matter of being lucky. Such a notion is organic to the plots of their stories and novels, which often turn in the direction of catastrophes precipitated by chance, or avert tragedy quite simply by virtue of sheer accidental events.[14] This strong recognition of the power of chance, combined with their detailed knowledge of violence in nature, threatens the stability of the experience of wonder in their canons.

Obviously, London's appreciation of the mystery of Creation is at best problematic. His figuration of man in the silent northern spaces as given to dread amidst an epiphany, stated as "this is a maggot's life, nothing more," demonstrates the extent to which his religious sense is related to an honest sensation of existential terror, one that is blank, frightened, and close to despair. At least one critic, James I. McClintock, argues that what London ultimately finds in the northern wilderness is a Conradian 'heart of darkness,' a horror and emptiness at the heart of the northern wood, the centre of reality. It is a horror which London refers to as the "White Logic," a primary truth visible in the desolate landscape, "the argent messenger of truth beyond truth, the antithesis of life, cruel and bleak as interstellar space, pulseless and frozen as absolute zero, dazzling with the frost of irrefragable logic and unforgettable fact . . . ."[15] To employ more of Joseph Conrad's diction, implacable forces brood over inscrutable intentions quite often in London's wilderness, and such a view of reality leads him to a sense of the universe as cold and indifferent, potentially imbecilic, and provocative of spiritual alienation and despair.

Roberts is, I think, on easier terms with his particular battle over the tensions created by the effects of the school of naturalism, the tradition which worries that this is "a maggot's life, nothing more," but he is so because he is a deliberately poised writer, not because he is evasive or soft on the issue. He certainly *considers* the possibility that the violence, chance reality, and intractable quiet of the wilderness are metaphors for the futility of life, disturbing significations of the ephemerality of the mind and the self. Interestingly, when Dave Titus, in *The Heart of the Ancient Wood*, instructs the all-too-innocent Miranda with his own disposition next to nature and reality, he remarks to her that while he thinks ". . . this life *might* be somethin' finer than the finest kind of dream," he also prefaces that hope with the sad statement that "Oftentimes it's seemed to me all life was jest like a few butterflies flitterin' over a graveyard."[16] Still, the 'heart of the ancient wood,' for all of that recognition, is not seen as the heart of darkness, it does not lead to 'the horror, the horror'; it is evoked, rather, as the candid and complex centre of reality where all thoughts and feelings are tested for their real integrity.

As critics such as Joseph Gold, Robin Mathews, and Patricia Morley have variously noted,[17] "the heart of the ancient wood' is a place where love and fear, birth and death, heroism and savagery, violence and beauty, calm and storm, spirit and matter all eventually circle one another. It is a complex reality which is most intimately understood when it is witnessed in the process of 're-initiation' which perhaps only essentially mimetic art can relate with any degree of conviction or sense of living wisdom. In Roberts' wilderness fiction, 'the heart of the ancient wood' is a locus of candour where a sanity of thought becomes possible, a sanity which is not inseparable from the frank recognition of both the beauty and the violence of reality, its paradoxical texture. It is a locus where a balanced perspective on reality is encouraged, one which is neither uncritical in its sensation of mystery, nor despairing in its attention to the ironies of fate and the carnage created by ostensibly wasteful natural laws. His is an art which attempts to accommodate the mind to reality, adjust the spirit to natural existence and its ambiguities.

And that ambitious aim of Roberts' best wilderness fiction is in large measure made more compelling by the genius of his writerly gifts. I have previously referred to London's passage where he speaks of the 'ecstasy' that "comes to the artist, caught up and out of himself in a sheet of flame." London, that is to suggest, is a writer less detached than Roberts, less formed by the classical and restrained virtues of mind and style visible in Roberts' calmer and more poised talent for transparent observation and for what Keith lists as the "precision, smoothness, variety, and directness"[18] of his paragraphs. Very like his aptly named character in *The Iron Heel* (1908), "Ernest Everhard," who Earle Labor notices is London's "exact physical replica,"[19] London often expresses himself with a narrative energy inspired by the fire of his essentially romantic temperament. His achievement is of a different order than Roberts'. His vigorous temperament as a writer often moves about in his style as an inability to find poise and balance, a falling short of the stable equanimity which is more familiar in Roberts' contrasting narrative gifts.

No doubt, the Classical background of Roberts' reading has a great deal to do with the quality of detachment or restraint in his style, but it is also buttressed, I believe, by a very real stoicism and somewhat opaque intentionality in the wilderness settings he observes. There is an energy and enthusiasm in Roberts' writing, plenty of it, and he was to say in "The Outlook for Literature" that "Our climate with its swift extremes is eager and waking, and we should expect a sort of dry sparkle in our page, with a transparent and tonic quality in our thought. If environment is anything, our work can hardly be proven tame."[20] But it is the simultaneous quality of candour in his writing which I am attempting to appreciate, and it is precisely that quality which makes *Red Fox* so radically different and more interesting than London's *The Call of the Wild.* In his wilderness fiction, Roberts is quintessentially the narrator as involved and detached observer in the same stroke, the impersonal and calm narrator who returns all of his thoughts and sensations to the poise of a sanely balanced purchase on reality.[21]

Red Fox is framed as an animal biography and an adventure story. It is also thick with anecdotes of observation about the fox's exceptional cunning and ability to circumvent its foes, both human and animal. It is a brilliant novel purely on the level of its careful portrayal of the otherness of the creature and that complex reality I have referred to previously—using Roberts' compact locution—'the heart of the ancient wood.' Significantly, while London's novel is enthusiastic about the paradoxical degeneration of the mongrel dog (Buck) back to the level of the wolf, Roberts' novel is struck by the ascending movement of the chain of being upward through the very intelligent fox and in the direction of kinship with, or quiet bond with, a sensitive adolescent named "the Boy" by the fox. The boy is in some ways a young brother spiritually to the narrator, and the narrator embodies a great deal of the wisdom of Dave Titus of *The Heart of the Ancient Wood.* The intelligence, the dignity, and the beauty of the fox is appreciated in the novel. Simultaneously, a violent aspect of its nature, its participation in the 'law of meat' and its ferocity when confronted with its enemies are candidly reported without shock or anxiety—even as that bloody dimension of its instincts for survival take it straight through the flesh of other living creatures. The energy of nature as it moves through its intractable, ultimate purposes and through its more immediate needs are celebrated without either being envied or motioned toward as a complete metaphor for human reality.

As is the case in a number of Roberts' best animal stories, it is the observing and appreciating imagination, the spiritual 're-initiation,' that the author seems intent on nourishing in the reader. *Red Fox* resists anything like an invitation back to the energetic primitivism of the fox, a primitivism London was to associate with the animal, the soldier, and the exuberant artist all in one breath; Roberts is not attracted to the primitive as a source of new or retrieved power for the aristocrats of the human will. Malcolm Cowley has written that the American school of naturalism deals, in a series of ways, with the "minification of persons,"[22] and it is true that this is a tradition which is fascinated, appalled, and sometimes thrilled by the animal aspects of the human being. In the fiction of Frank Norris, for instance, and especially in *McTeague* (1899), a Zola-inspired interest in the savage dimension of the human takes on a quite unconsciously humorous dimension when characters, like McTeague himself, are portrayed as hyperbolic in their animal traits, are figured as somewhat furry types of people who exist for long spaces of action on the level of the brute.[23] American naturalism is given to hyperbole.

Roberts adjusts such considerations more carefully. In *Red Fox*, for instance, he places a group of distinctly unimaginative fox hunters (hounds, horses, and all) far below the level of the fox in the chain of being quietly implicit in the novel. The "scarlet hunters"[24] are the final obstacles the fox overcomes before he returns to the wilderness after his captivity late in the action. Their immoral bloodlust and unimaginative intelligence are satirically and nicely-whimsically placed; next to the amoral integrity and surviving genius of the fox they are found wanting, stupid and sub-civilized in a doubly ironic way. The instinctual savvy of the creature—a quality which is always close to the intuitive gifts of imaginative human beings in Roberts' anatomy of the mind—triumphs over the thick-headedness of the hunters. But the hunters do not represent humanity in the main. Roberts never loses sight, as many critics have asserted, of the spiritual ascendency of the human being. "Clod" reaches upward toward "god" in his scale of being, and he does not romanticize the primitive ground of being nor envy its energy to an exaggerated extent. As he moves from mimesis to abstract meaning, what he finds in his creatures is a dignity, a call for respect that is required by the "clear and candid life" they quite naturally represent.

The division in reality between beauty and violence does not create a corresponding anxiety (or fascination) in the tonal dimension of Roberts' narration. He is remarkably cool, Olympian at times, in his witness to the fact of violence. Very often, that equanimity in his style is most controlled in scenes where his graphic portrayal of terror and death are most *potentially* disturbing. *Red Fox* opens with hunters in pursuit of the protagonist's father, and the first chapter, "The Price of His Life," ends with the death of the father at the jaws of a pack of hounds:

> Together they flung themselves upon him, to get lightning slashes almost simultaneously, on neck and jaw. Both yelped angrily, and bit wildly, but found it impossible to hold down their twisting foe, who fought in silence and seemed to have the strength and irrepressibility of steel springs in his slender body. Presently his teeth met through the joint of the hound's fore paw, and the hound, with a shrill *ki yi*, jumped backward from the fight. But the black and white mongrel was of better grit. Though one eye was filled with blood, and one ear slit to the base, he had no thought of shirking the punishment. Just as the yelping hound withdrew from the mix-up, his long, powerful jaws secured a fair grip on the fox's throat, just back of the jawbone. There was a moment of breathless, muffled, savage growling, of vehement and vindictive shaking. Then the valorous red body straightened itself out at the foot of the rock, and made no more resistance as the victors mauled and tore it. At a price, the little family in the burrow had been saved. (TFX, pp. 10-11).

Roberts is sometimes strained in the tonal pathos of those animal stories he has designed for consumption by an adolescent audience. Some of his stories are allegories of family life and deal melodramatically with courage, loyalty, and self-sacrifice. But in his best instances in the animal fiction he manages a mimetic equilibrium, one which saves the above passage from didactic earnestness. This somewhat typical portrayal of violence in nature is handled with a mimetic grip and clarity that is tonally controlled in the degree of its pathos. And it is balanced in its unsentimental confrontation with terror. There are countless scenes such as this in Roberts' animal fiction, scenes wherein death is candidly dramatized without an excess of pathos.[25]

And if Roberts is building an emerging metaphor here it is not one as pale as the cliché that life is nasty and brutish and short, but a metaphor which complexly manifests the courage of the creature next to the many jaws of death—and notices in the first place the creature's instinct to lead the pack of hounds away from the burrow where its children live in their helpless state. As in many other instances in his animal fiction, there is a pathos here but there is a realism, a frankness or honesty, which sustains the mind, keeps it above anxiety, and subdues any thoughts of despairful metaphors. The meaning is in the control. In a manner which misses callousness by a hair-breadth, and which sometimes implies an indictment of the Creator of nature, Roberts portrays the felt reality of terror and violence in nature with a matter-of-factness that is a measure of his realism as a writer who is aware of the "brute-savage-ness of the school of clod," yet free from its habit of emotional hyperbole. He accommodates the mind to fact.

Roberts' sense of mystery survives in *Red Fox* and is visible in the many passages of sober natural beauty evoked in its pages. It is there in the settings and atmosphere of the work, and in the beholding reverence expressed for the otherness and the dignity of the fox.[26] In *Red Fox*, and the shorter animal stories as a whole, the perception of violence and the recurrent recognition of "chance and change" do not destroy, even if they qualify, Roberts' expressiveness as an evolutionary idealist who is informed by the artistic gift of negative capability. There are doubts and tensions in Roberts' work but they serve only to mature his sense of mystery toward realism, and render him discriminating about the limitations of, for instance, the inarticulate mysticism he expresses suspicion of in such poems as "To a Certain Mystic."

Roberts keeps the spiritual concerns of the "school of god" alive in his fiction even if, like any sane post-Darwinian artist, he has his moments of irony and doubt, moments in which he casts a moral glance at the skies in the name of suffering creatures and humanity. His sense of mystery is subdued and made more serious by the violence and terror that he also observes in the heart of the ancient wood. There are grounds for an existential anxiety in his canon, but—like many of his Canadian contemporaries—he doubts the adequacy of an ultimate pessimism. He recognizes the need to accommodate the mind to the complexity of reality as it is, not as it is filtered through the screen of a narrow joy, or a narrow pessimism.

The sense of mystery evoked in his settings is typically nervous, suspenseful, in that the sometimes eerie stillness witnessed veils a background of truth and sorrow which gradually moves into the light as poignant epiphanies of the law of survival or the law of meat, or emerges as those tragedies of destiny which are likely always to make the unillusioned artist suspicious that the surface effect of beauty is not entirely trustworthy, that beauty isn't necessarily truth after all, just a significant part of it. Roberts is not spiritually defeated even if he is sobered by his witness to an ambiguity in nature and in reality. It is part of his achievement as a writer, I think, that he manages to encompass the beauty and the terror of nature at once, and accommodate it to his art. It was Oscar Wilde who said that ". . . he who can look on the loveliness of the world and share in its sorrow, and realise something of the wonder of both, is in immediate contact with divine things, and has got as near to God's secret as anyone can get."[27] The poise of such a purchase on reality, its comprehensiveness and ability with ambiguity, is strong in Roberts' canon and to say so is a way of praising the capacity of his imagination.

I have found the diction of the tradition of American naturalism valuable in my attempt to underline aspects of Roberts' achievement as a writer of wilderness fiction. I think it is one of the measures of his vigour, as both a Canadian and cosmopolitan artist, that he participated in that tradition in a quietly contributory, not a derivative, manner. Certainly, to say that he participated in that tradition is not at all to detract from his many other achievements, which this volume [of conference papers] is reassessing and celebrating. It is simply to find additional reasons for praise.

There has already been some discussion in other [conference] papers of Roberts' ambiguous, if not equivocal, writing personality, his writing from two impulses or 'rivers' of concern. So it is perhaps the more appropriate that I conclude my remarks with a comment about "two rivers of thought" made by George C. Walcutt in his *American Literary Naturalism, A Divided Stream* (1956):

> American transcendentalism asserts the unity of Spirit and Nature and affirms that intuition (by which mind discovers its affiliation with Spirit) and scientific investigation (by which it masters Nature, the symbol of Spirit) are equally valid approaches to reality. When this mainstream of transcendentalism divides, as it does toward the end of the nineteenth century, it produces two rivers of thought. One, the approach to Spirit through intuition nourishes idealism, progressivism, and social radicalism. The other, the approach to Nature through science, plunges into the dark canyon of materialistic determinism. The one is rebellious, the other pessimistic; the one ardent, the other fatal; the one acknowledges will, the other denies it. Thus "naturalism," flowing in both streams, is partly defying Nature and partly submitting to it. . . .[28]

Roberts writes out of an awareness of the tensions created by these two rivers as well. And as one who sustained his qualified idealism in the face of the dark canyon of determinism and pessimism, he makes a valuable contribution to the American tradition of naturalism. He recognized that it is only through a 're-initiation' into reality, a careful imaginative grasp of its complexity, that we might begin slowly to retrieve the tragic imbalance between 'Spirit and Nature' which characterizes a great deal of modern art and thought.

Endnotes

1 Jack London, *Martin Eden*. 1909; rpt. ed. Sam S. Baskett (New York: Rinehart, 1956), p. 212.

2 Malcolm Cowley, "Naturalism: No Teacup Tragedies," in *The Literary Situation* (1947, rpt. New York: The Viking Press, 1966), pp. 74-95.

3 See E.M. Pomeroy, *Sir Charles G.D. Roberts: A Biography*, introd. Lorne Pierce (Toronto: The Ryerson Press, 1943), pp. 178-79. Pomeroy includes excerpts from Roberts' reply to Roosevelt's criticism of his work in *Everybody's Magazine* (June 1907) wherein he was called a nature fakir. Roberts says: "The statement made by the President and similar statements made by John Burroughs, the naturalist, mark the establishment of two separate and distinct schools of nature students in this country. The school headed by President Roosevelt and Mr. Burroughs maintains that the action of animals is governed by instinct. The school in which Jack London, Mr. Lang and myself are classed believe that animals are actuated by something distinctly akin to reason. . ." (p. 179).

4 For a relevant and interesting discussion of Canadian writers' awareness of and contribution to American periodical publications during this period, see James Doyle's "Duncan Campbell Scott and American Literature," in *The Duncan Campbell Scott Symposium*, ed. and introd. K.P. Stich (Ottawa: University of Ottawa Press, 1979), pp. 101-109. For an extensive treatment of London's awareness of periodical publications of the day, see James I. McClintock's *White Logic: Jack London's Short Stories* (Cedar Springs, Michigan: Wolf House Books, 1976), pp. 1-33.

5 Jack London, Letter to Sinclair Lewis, March 10, 1900, in King Hendricks and Irving Shepard (eds.), *Letters from Jack London, Containing an Unpublished Correspondence Between London and Sinclair Lewis* (London: MacGibbon and Kee, 1966), p. 100.

6 For Keith's analysis of *In the Morning of Time*, see his *Charles G. D. Roberts, Studies in Canadian Literature*, Gen. eds. Hugo McPherson and Gary Geddes (Toronto: Copp Clark, 1969), pp. 80-84. London claimed that his own source of inspiration for *Before Adam* was Stanley Waterloo's *The Story of Ab*, but Andrew Sinclair shows that the more likely source was H.G. Wells' "A Story of the Stone Age." See Sinclair's *Jack: A Biography of Jack London* (London: Weidenfield and Nicholson, 1978), p. 131. I am indebted to Jack Adams for this last reference. He kindly sent the details on to me after the conference proceedings.

7 Charles G.D. Roberts, "The Animal Story," Introduction to *The Kindred of the Wild: A Book of Animal Life* (London: Ward, Lock, 1902), p. 23, p.27 respectively.

8 Ibid, p.29.

9 In his *Poetry in the Making* (London: Faber & Faber, 1967), Hughes has written a chapter entitled "Capturing Animals" which deals at length with the respect needed to write about "things which have a vivid life of their own" (p. 15).

10 The issue is complicated in Roberts' canon. For example, he quite consciously creates animals in *The Heart of the Ancient Wood* which are humanized, made Kiplingesque as a way of demonstrating Miranda's *mistaken* view of the animal species as being more friendly than not, and more human than animal. The weasel, by the way, is housed in "In Panoply of Spears," in *The Kindred of the Wild*, pp. 371-74. He is referred to as "the universal enemy" (p. 374).

11 Jack London, *The Call of the Wild*, 1903: rpt. ed. and introd. Arthur Calder-Marshall, *The Bodley Head Jack London*, vol. 1 (London: Bodley Head, 1963), p. 111. Future references to this work (CTW) are in the text.

12 Jack London, "The White Silence," in *The Son of the Wolf* (Boston: Houghton Mifflin, 1900), pp. 6-7. The "one critic" I refer to is Earle Labor. See his *Jack London*, Twayne United States Authors Series, no. 230. Gen. ed. Sylvia E. Bowman (New York: Twayne Publishers, 1974), p. 62.

13 Charles G.D. Roberts, "The Tantramar Revisited," 1886; rpt. ed. and intro. W.J. Keith, *Selected Poetry and Critical Prose: Charles G.D. Roberts*, Literature of Canada: Poetry and Prose in Reprint series, Gen.ed. Douglas Lochhead (Toronto and Buffalo: University of Toronto Press, 1974), p. 51.

14 *The Heart That Knows* (1906) is, of course, the novel containing the thickest series of chance occurrences. As Alec Lucas has remarked, Roberts shares an affinity with Thomas Hardy, at least to the extent that the protagonists of his stories about people are sometimes like "Hardy's peasants in the wilderness." See his introduction to *The Last Barrier and Other Stories*, New Canadian Library No. 7, Gen. ed. Malcolm Ross (Toronto and Montreal: McClelland and Stewart, 1970), p. x. It is possible that Roberts absorbed a strong sense of the power of chance from Hardy's fiction as well, even though the American tradition of naturalism is almost obsessed with the notion and Roberts was aware of that tradition's concerns.

15 Jack London, *John Barleycorn* (New York: Century, 1913), p. 308. For McClintock's view of London's arrival at pessimism, see his *White Logic: Jack London's Short Stories*, especially pp. 79-119.

16 Charles G.D. Roberts, *The Heart of the Ancient Wood*, 1900; rpt. intro. Joseph Gold, New Canadian Library No. 110, Gen. ed. Malcolm Ross (Toronto: McClelland and Stewart, 1974), pp. 243-44.

17 See Joseph Gold's introduction to *The Heart of the Ancient Wood*; Robin Mathews' *Canadian Literature: Surrender or Revolution*, ed. Gail Dexter (Toronto: Steel Rail Educational Publishing, 1978), pp. 45-62; and Patricia Morley's "We and the

Beasts are Kin: Attitudes Towards Nature in Nineteenth and Early Twentieth-century Canadian Literature," in *World Literature Written in English*, 16, no. 2 (November 1977), 345-58.

18 Keith, *Charles G.D. Roberts*, p. 119.

19 Labor, p. 102. See note 12 for full reference.

20 Charles G.D. Roberts, "The Outlook for Literature," 1866; rpt. in *Selected Poetry and Critical Prose*, p. 261.

21 For a discussion of Roberts' detachment as a poet, see Tom Marshall's *Harsh and Lovely Land* (Vancouver: University of British Columbia Press, 1979), pp. 9-16.

22 Cowley, p. 76.

23 In Norris's *McTeague*, McTeague is described as "a young giant, carrying his huge shock of blond hair six feet three inches from the ground: moving his immense limbs, heavy with ropes of muscle, slowly, ponderously. His hands were enormous, red, and covered with a fell of stiff, yellow hair; they were hard as wooden mallets, strong as vises, the hands of the old-time car boy. . . . His head was square-cut, angular; the jaw salient, like that of the carnivora." See *McTeague*, 1899; rpt. with afterword, Kenneth Rexroth (New York: New American Library, 1964), p. 7. McTeague is a bear and a Frankenstein at once. As a version of the beast-man he is somewhat of an archetype in the fiction of naturalism.

24 Charles G.D. Roberts, *Red Fox*, 1905; rpt. intro. David McCord, illus. John Schoenerr (Boston: Houghton Mifflin, 1972), p. 187. Future reference to this work (TFX) is in the text.

25 For a cluster of such scenes, see *The Last Barrier and Other Stories*, pp. 38-39, 77-78, 99-100, 106. For other scenes in *Red Fox*, see pp. 71, 110-11.

26 For prominent examples, see *Red Fox*, pp. 5, 85-89, 165, 187.

27 Oscar Wilde, *De Profundis*, 1905; rpt. ed. Richard Aldington, in *The Portable Oscar Wilde* (New York: The Viking Press, 1971), p. 554.

28 Charles C. Walcutt, *American Literary Naturalism: A Divided Stream* (Minneapolis: University of Minnesota Press, 1956), pp. vii-viii.

T.D. MacLulich
The Animal Story and the "Nature Faker" Controversy*

Many Canadian critics have taken a special interest in the animal story. Indeed, the animal story has surely received more critical attention than any other branch of wilderness writing. Much of this attention is motivated by literary nationalism, for the animal story is the only literary genre for which a specifically Canadian origin has been claimed. As early as 1926, in one of the first full-length studies of Canadian writing, Lionel Stevenson claimed the animal story as "a wholly new 'genre' which Canadian authors have contributed to the world's literature."[1] The majority of critical writing on the animal story, however, has appeared as part of the upsurge of interest in Canadian writing that took place during the 1960s and 1970s. During this period several articles and chapter-length discussions—and even one small book—have sought to define the special qualities of the Canadian animal story.[2] In particular, the work of Ernest Thompson Seton and Charles G. D. Roberts, both of whom once enjoyed wide international popularity, has provided an attractive rallying point for those seeking to establish the distinctiveness of Canadian literary culture.

The most sweeping claims for the importance of the animal story are made by Margaret Atwood, who devotes an entire chapter of *Survival* to her discussion of the form. Atwood uses the animal story to support her overall thesis that Canadian literature is pervasively marked by Canada's political subservience, first as a colony of Britain, and then as an economic appendage of the United States. In effect, Atwood interprets Canadian animal stories as political allegories. She argues that Canadian writers and readers project their sense of political impotence onto the doomed protagonists of animal stories. It seems probable, she contends, "that Canadians them-

---

* This article first appeared in *Essays on Canadian Writing*, 33 (Fall 1986), 112-24. It is reprinted here with the permission of *Essays on Canadian Writing*.

selves feel threatened and nearly extinct as a nation, and suffer also from life-denying experience as individuals—the culture threatens the 'animal' within them—and that their identification with animals is the expression of a deep-seated cultural fear." As a result, or so Atwood insists, the animal story is "a *genre* which provides a key to an important facet of the Canadian psyche."[3]

Atwood contends that the animal stories of Canadian writers have two traits in common. First, they are told from the animal's viewpoint; and second, they have a tragic outcome. But there are several difficulties in the way of accepting her account. Most obviously, the stories are more varied in outcome and tone than Atwood allows; they simply do not all feel like stories of doomed animals. At some deep psychological level, there may be a kernel of truth in Atwood's claims. But before her sweeping hypothesis is accepted, it seems wise to investigate a simpler possibility.

Whatever else the animal story may have become, it began as a literary genre that sought to spread a particular scientific view of the natural world to an audience of non-scientific readers. Moreover, most writers of animal stories vigorously insist that their stories dramatize bits of accurately observed natural history. It may be necessary to forgo the excitement of identifying the animal story as a symbolic mirror of the national psyche, and instead take the authors at their word. The best way to understand the animal story, at least in its early years, is as a literary form that sought to present turn-of-the-century readers with a scientifically informed view of the natural world.

Specifically, the animal story became involved in a quarrel over the proper interpretation of animal behaviour, a quarrel that was a version of the long-standing nature versus nurture dispute. In the years around the turn of the century, the science of ethology was struggling to be born.[4] Some pioneering ethologists suggested that the sources of animal behaviour might lie not in instinct, as was traditionally thought, but in animal psychology. Many animal stories speculate upon the mental processes that accompany particular episodes of animal behaviour, and thus offer examples of the sort of inferences that early ethologists were making. Animal stories often show that animals can, within limits, think rationally about the situations they encounter, and can even learn from experience. When these stories are based on accurate observations made in the field, they provide strong evidence against the position that animal behaviour is motivated almost exclusively by instinct.

One way to highlight the scientific dimension of the animal story is to examine a journalistic debate that was conducted in the American press shortly after the turn of the century. At that time Seton and Roberts, along with several other writers of animal stories, were embroiled in a debate that became known as the "nature faker" controversy. Neither Seton nor Roberts suffered permanent damage to their reputations during this debate, which soon turned into an attack on the questionable natural history purveyed by one writer, William J. Long. Nonetheless, the occurrence of the controversy illustrates the high public visibility of the animal story during this era, and the involvement of Seton and Roberts confirms their position as important nature writers; moreover, the terms in which the debate was conducted help to clarify the scientific issues that underlie the emergence of this genre as a popular literary form.

The controversy opened in 1903 when the respected nature writer John Burroughs published an argumentative essay in *The Atlantic Monthly* titled "Real and Sham Natural History." Burroughs singled out four books for special attention: Roberts' *The Kindred of the Wild*, William Davenport Hulbert's *Forest Neighbours*, Seton's *Wild Animals I Have Known*, and William J. Long's *School of the Woods*. In contrast to authors whose books were "real contributions" to natural history, Burroughs complained, many recent authors seem to seek to profit by the popular love for the sensational and the improbable."[5] In the books of Seton and Long, Burroughs wrote, "I am bound to say that the line between fact and fiction is repeatedly crossed, and that a deliberate attempt is made to induce the reader to cross, too, and to work such a spell upon him that he shall not know that he has crossed and is in the land of make-believe" (p.300).

Burroughs' essay is a plea for scrupulous accuracy in reporting one's observations of the natural world, and for caution in interpreting the meaning of those observations. Near the beginning of his essay he warns naturalists—himself included—against "the danger of making too much of what we see and describe,—of putting in too much sentiment, too much literature,—in short, of valuing these things more for the literary effects we can get out of them than for themselves" (p.299). In other words, Burroughs prefers to maintain a clear-cut distinction between literary and scientific writing; he objects to animal stories because they collapse this distinction.

When he examines specific cases, Burroughs assigns varying degrees of culpability to different writers. Hulbert is exonerated completely, and Roberts escapes with only mild chastisement. Burroughs concedes that *The Kindred of the Wild* "is in many ways the most brilliant collection of animal stories that has appeared," and he admits that Roberts' stories usually "follow closely the facts of natural history." He does question a few of Roberts' details, but his most significant point is a general one. He complains that in Roberts' stories "the animals whose lives are portrayed—the bear, the panther, the lynx, the hare, the moose, and others—are simply human beings disguised as animals; they think, feel, plan, suffer, as we do; in fact, exhibit almost the entire human psychology." That is, Burroughs feels that Roberts has projected human emotions into the minds of the animals he portrays. Burroughs warns that "it is mainly guesswork how far our psychology applies to the lower animals" (p.299).

Seton does not escape as lightly as Roberts does. Burroughs accuses Seton of manipulating the facts of natural history without warning readers that liberties are being taken. For example, he argues—with some justice—that no fox was ever as clever as Seton's Springfield Fox. He says of many of Seton's stories: "True as romance, true in their artistic effects, true in their power to entertain the young reader, they certainly are; but true as natural history they as certainly are not" (p.300). He also quarrels with some of Seton's detailed observations, such as the account of the behaviour of crows given in "Silverspot, the Story of a Crow." Burroughs insists that crows do not have recognized flock leaders, and he doubts that crows have the distinctive calls with clearly defined meanings that Seton describes. In this quarrel, contemporary ornithology would probably support Seton, though with some reservations about his more extreme claims.

Burroughs' greatest scorn, however, is reserved for William J. Long, whom he describes as Seton's "awkward imitator" (p.300). Long was a clergyman with literary and outdoors interests, who wrote several books of purported natural history. He particularly offended Burroughs by claiming, in the preface to *School of the Woods*, that instinct plays a smaller part in animal behaviour, and experience a larger part, than was supposed in Darwinian theory. Burroughs is quite dogmatic in interpreting virtually all animal behaviour as instinctive rather than learned by experience. In rebuttal of Long, he writes firmly, "The young of all the wild creatures do instinctively what their parents do and did" (p. 305). Burroughs rightly makes fun of Long's more fanciful scenes, such as an account of a partridge that could count to eleven, a tale of a great blue heron that chummed its fishing waters with fragments of a frog it had previously caught, and a description of a porcupine that deliberately rolled itself down a hillside, gathering leaves on its quills as it went, in order to make itself look large and fearsome (pp. 306-07). Burroughs is fully justified in ridiculing Long's more extravagant claims; but he seems greatly to overstate the scope of animal instinct when he asserts that a fox "knows a trap from the jump" by virtue of inherited knowledge (p. 304).

As the chief target of Burroughs' attack, Long felt particularly aggrieved. He quickly published a defense of the accuracy of his natural history, but in his replies indignation often outweighs good judgement. In his first response to Burroughs, Long makes the sound point that he is writing personal nature essays, not scientific reports. From the nature writer the reader requires "not simply eyes and ears and a notebook; but insight, imagination, and, above all, an intense human sympathy, by which alone the inner life of an animal becomes luminous, and without which the living creatures are little better than stuffed specimens." This is a sensible enough position, and is in exact agreement with the practice of Seton and Roberts. But Long goes on to undermine his authority as a naturalist when he makes several remarks that clearly convict him of gullibility. His willingness to believe virtually any story about animal behaviour, however farfetched, is indicated when he writes that "no animal story told me as fact by an honest man will leave me incredulous."[6] Long continued to be at the centre of the ensuing controversy, but since his stories have not lasted either as literature or as natural history, he need concern us no further.

Burroughs' charges are based on a strict view of scientific morality. The liberties Seton and Roberts would justify on artistic grounds, Burroughs considers simply as falsehoods. "No pleasure to the reader," he insists, "no moral inculcated, can justify the dissemination of false notions of nature" (p.305). Burroughs' strict standards seem justified when he uses them against Long's incredible yarns. But the limitations of his outlook become apparent when he also criticizes writers such as Seton and Roberts, whose artistic manipulations give their stories greater interest, and so help to convey the overall view of nature that these authors wish to express.

Burroughs was particularly bothered by the apparent anthropomorphism of Seton's and Roberts' stories. Clearly, as Burroughs argued, it is bad natural history to portray animals as miniature human beings. Yet some degree of anthropomorphism is probably inevitable in the animal story, for we can only understand the unfamiliar by means of the familiar; we can only understand the experiences of other beings by extrapolating from our own experience. Seton and Roberts are trying to present an animal's experiences—which are non-verbal—by means of human language. The use of language to convey an animal's awareness necessarily transposes the animal's private consciousness—whatever that might be like—into the terms that humans use to describe conscious thought. But Seton and Roberts, for the most part, perform this transposition in a responsible and temperate manner.

Seton and Roberts insisted that the natural history contained in their stories was basically truthful, and that they did not go beyond the bounds of probability in attributing ideas and emotions to their animal characters. They undoubtedly found it galling to be associated, however loosely, with an unreliable naturalist such as Long. The nature faker controversy centred on Long's works, but Seton and Roberts may have feared that their sales and their reputations might also suffer. Therefore, although Seton and Roberts were careful to treat their main opponent with respect, they defended themselves against charges of nature fakery in the prefaces to the books they published during the period of the controversy.

In the preface to *The Watchers of the Trails*, Roberts specifically responds to Burroughs. He carefully points out that his stories are "avowedly fiction." But he adds: "They are, at the same time, true, in that the material of which they are moulded consists of facts,—facts as precise as painstaking observation and anxious regard for truth can make them."[7] He politely but firmly disputes the justice of Burroughs' attack, as it pertains to his stories:

> A very distinguished author—to whom all contemporary writers on nature are indebted, and from whom it is only with the utmost diffidence that I venture to dissent at all—has gently called me to account on the charge of ascribing to my animals human motives and the mental processes of man. The fact is, however, that this fault is one which I have been at particular pains to guard against. (p. ix)

Roberts insists that he has only made the most careful and straightforward inferences about the motives of the animals he describes. He asserts: "The psychological processes of the animals are so simple, so obvious, in comparison with those of man, their actions flow so directly from their springs of impulse, that it is, as a rule, an easy matter to infer the motives which are at any one moment impelling them" (p. ix).

In some of his stories dating from the period of the controversy, Roberts also makes comments that refer directly to the quarrel with Burroughs. One of the clearest examples occurs in the title story of *The House in the Water*. As in many of Roberts' stories, the protagonist is known simply as "the Boy." By careful observation of a family of beavers, the Boy learns much about their habits, and comes to sympathize deeply with the animals. He saves the beavers from the efforts of two malicious trappers, and he particularly likes to watch them at work on their dam. Roberts says of the Boy: "The more he studied the structure, the more his admiration grew, and his appreciation of the reasoning intelligence of its builders; and he smiled to himself a little controversial smile, as he thought how inadequate what men call instinct would be to such a piece of work as this."[8]

Seton felt Burroughs' criticism even more strongly than Roberts did. Seton, after all, was trying to establish himself as a professional naturalist, whereas Roberts was only a literary figure who dabbled in natural history. Yet Seton did not publicly refer to Burroughs' accusations. Instead, he bided his time until the opportunity arose to challenge Burroughs privately. At a dinner party held by the industrialist Andrew Carnegie, Seton met Burroughs and put the older naturalist through the following catechism:

> "Mr. Burroughs, did you ever make a special study of wolves?"
> "No"
> "Did you ever hunt wolves?"
> "No."
> "Did you ever photograph or draw wolves in a zoo?"
> "No."
> "Did you ever skin or dissect a wolf?"
> "Did you ever live in wolf country?"
> "No."
> "Did you ever see a wild wolf?"
> "No."
> "Then by what rule of logic are you equipped to judge me, who have done all of these things hundreds of times."

According to Seton, Burroughs soon made a "public apology" for his attack on Seton's stories.[9] Actually, Seton's memory of the affair is selective. Burroughs did write, in a subsequent article, that Seton "as an artist and *raconteur*, ranks by far the highest in this field." But he immediately added a rider that Seton chose not to remember. "To those who can separate the fact from the fiction in his animal stories," Burroughs mischievously warns, "he [Seton] is truly delightful."[10]

Seton's real rebuttal to Burroughs, however, came about in another way. Partly prompted by Burroughs' attack on his abilities as an observer of animal life, Seton worked intensively over the next few years on the book that was meant to establish once and for all his credentials as an expert field naturalist. This project became *Life Histories of Northern Animals*, a work published in two volumes in 1909. It is ironically appropriate that an enlarged later edition of this book, *Lives of Game Animals* (1925-28), was awarded the Burroughs Medal in 1927, a prize named after the venerable naturalist who had once impugned Seton's veracity.

The quarrel between Burroughs and Long had more or less died out, when in 1907 it was revived by none other than President Theodore Roosevelt. Roosevelt is best-known as a jingoistic rough-rider, a deadly hunter of big game, and the man who spoke softly but carried a big stick. He was also a lifelong student of the outdoors, and he acquired a considerable reputation as an amateur naturalist. Even in the White House, Roosevelt found time to read the work of other naturalists and popular nature writers. Like Burroughs, he was particularly annoyed by the stories of Long, whose nature books were widely read and were taken as fact, especially by young readers. In Roosevelt's view, Long was little better than a credulous simpleton. He had apparently believed every tall tale that any mischievous guide or backwoods farmer ever told him. In conversations and letters Roosevelt often denounced Long and other writers of his ilk. Towards the end of his presidency, however, he made his views public, in the articles that were to give the nature faker controversy its name.

In "Roosevelt on the Nature Fakirs" the journalist Edward B. Clark quoted Roosevelt's attacks on the natural history contained in the animal stories of four men—Jack London, William J. Long, Ernest Thompson Seton, and Charles G. D. Roberts."[11] Roosevelt complained that erroneous or fantastical natural history was being retailed as fact by these men. His most scathing comments were reserved for Long's fantasies, but he quarreled at length with one of Roberts' stories, "On the Night Trail." His outrage was compounded by the fact that one of Long's books was being used as a school textbook, and all of these animal stories were often read by children. Misinformation about nature, he feared, would ultimately work against the efforts of the conservation movement, rather than support it.

A few months later, writing under his own name, Roosevelt continued the assault on Long in an article titled simply "Nature Fakers."[12] However, not everyone took seriously the spectacle of the President of the United States chiding a writer of children's stories. A cartoon by T.E. Powers in the *New York Evening Journal* satirized both sides of the quarrel. Long, Seton, London, and Roberts are pictured offering various bits of nonsensical nature lore, while arriving at a buliding pointedly named the Ananias Club. The Ananias Club appears intended to mock the exclusive Boone and Crockett Club, whose members combined wealth and social position with an interest in shooting big game. The club's members sometimes seemed to claim virtual ownership over the conservation movement—and over the wilderness this movement professed to protect for all Americans. In the cartoon several unhappy members look on in dismay from the porch of the Ananias Club as the upstart naturalist-writers draw near.

Powers' cartoon gives the nature faker controversy a comic-opera appearance, which it sometimes deserved. For example, Roosevelt complained that the lynx in Roberts' story "On the Night Trail" "would have stood no more chance with eight wolves than a house cat would stand in a fight with eight bull terriers."[13] In response, Roberts solemnly declared:

> I believe that the President undoubtedly had in mind a possible conflict between the Rocky Mountain lynx or Lynx rufus, with which he is familiar, and the big Western timber wolves. The story, in fact, concerned the real lynx, known as *Lynx Canadensis*, a vicious and powerful animal inhabiting the Northeastern parts of this country, and eight of our small Eastern wolves known as brush wolves, averaging less than half the size of the great timber wolf.

No wonder the dispute attracted the cartoonist's satirical eye at this point! This sort of pompous and self-serving hair-splitting deserves to be ridiculed.

Roberts, however, also went on to point out that behind Roosevelt's superficial quarrels with specific details in his story there was a long-standing and more fundamental disagreement:

> The statement made by the President and similar statements made by John Burroughs, the naturalist, mark the establishment of two separate and distinct schools of nature students in this country. The school headed by President Roosevelt and Mr. Burroughs maintains that the action of animals is governed purely by instinct. The school in which Jack London, Mr. Long and myself are classed believe that animals are actuated by something distinctly akin to reason.[14]

This is the nub of the controversy. Burroughs continued to doubt "that the lower animals ever show anything more than a faint gleam of what we call thought and reflectiveness."[15] Roberts, on the other hand, believed "that the actions of animals are governed, not only by instinct, but also, in varying degree, by processes essentially akin to those of human reason." Roberts admitted that some of his stories were pure entertainment. But he added: "in certain of the stories dealing with the results of my own observation and experience, I have dared to hope that I might be contributing something of value to the final disputed question of animal psychology."[16]

Roberts is referring here to the scientific quarrel over the sources of animal behaviour. This disagreement has a further significance that may not be apparent to modern observers. Darwin's theories not only challenged the natural theology that saw a divine harmony throughout nature, but also eliminated the gap between humanity and the animals. The traits of human beings, Darwin suggested in *The Descent of Man*, were elaborations of the traits visible in the higher animals. Nonetheless, despite the ascendancy of the evolutionary theory by the end of the century, many people—and some scientists among them—clung to the notion that humans were intrinsically superior to animals; above all, such people took comfort from the belief that humans alone had the ability to reason. Animals, they believed, were little better than automatons, governed solely by instincts present from birth. On the other hand, if Darwin's ideas were correct—if the higher animals evolved over time from lower forms of life, and if human attributes were different only in degree from animal attributes—then there was no need to invoke divine intervention to account for humanity's distinctive traits. Thus, the proponents of the theory that animals could reason were willy-nilly supporting the idea that humanity evolved from animal ancestors.

By the later years of the nineteenth century, most serious scientists accepted the Darwinian hypothesis of evolution as the origin of the earth's varied species of animals. Many animal stories present a ruthless struggle for survival between two or more animals, and such stories often culminate in the death of an animal character, a conclusion Margaret Atwood interprets as tragic. The authors, however, usually intend their stories to illustrate certain aspects of the Darwinian theory: specifically, competition for limited resources and the survival of the fittest—the Darwinian principles of natural selection. From a Darwinian perspective, both the loser and the winner in any competition for survival are part of a larger pattern of life and death. That is, there are no individual winners and losers in the Darwinian universe; there is only the continuance of species, and the continuance of life itself.

The animal story therefore drew fire from traditionalists on two counts: first, for portraying a Darwinian struggle for survival in a godless universe of chance events; and second, for supporting the idea that there was little distinction between humanity and the animals. By insisting that animal behaviour was governed almost entirely by instinct, Burroughs was keeping open the possibility of humanity's special status in relation to the animal world. The participants in the nature faker debate never posed the issues in quite these terms; nonetheless, it is apparent that the fundamental debate concerned more than the veracity of certain nature writers. The controversy was really a dispute between rival visions of humanity's place in the universe. Awareness of the deeper issues at stake helps to explain why an argument over the obscurer habits of certain wild animals could become so vehement and persistent.

Endnotes

1 Lionel Stevenson, *Appraisals of Canadian Literature* (Toronto: Macmillan, 1926), p. 163.

2 Alec Lucas, "Introduction," in Charles G. D. Roberts, *The Last Barrier and Other Stories*, New Canadian Library, No. 7 (Toronto:

McClelland and Stewart, 1958), pp. v-x; S. E. Read, "Flight to the Primitive: Ernest Thompson Seton," *Canadian Literature*, No. 13 (Summer 1962), pp. 45-57; William H. Magee, "The Animal Story: A Challenge in Technique," *Dalhousie Review*, No. 44 (1964-65), pp. 156-64; Alec Lucas, "Nature Writers and the Animal Story," in *Literary History of Canada: Canadian Literature in English*, gen. ed. Carl F. Klinck, 2nd ed., (Toronto: Univ. of Toronto Press, 1976), I, 380-404; Joseph Gold, "The Precious Speck of Life," *Canadian Literature*, No. 26 (Autumn 1965), pp. 22-32; Joseph Gold, "Introduction," in Charles G. D. Roberts, *King of Beasts and Other Stories*, ed. Joseph Gold (Toronto: Ryerson, 1967), pp. ix-xx; James Polk, "Lives of the Hunted," *Canadian Literature*, No. 53 (Summer 1972), pp. 51-59; James Polk, *Wilderness Writers* (Toronto: Clarke, Irwin, 1972); Margaret Atwood, "Animal Victims," in her *Survival: A Thematic Guide to Canadian Literature* (Toronto: House of Anansi, 1972), pp. 69-86; Patricia Morley, "Seton's Animals," *Journal of Canadian Fiction*, 2, No.3 (Summer 1973), 195-98; Tim Murray, "Charles Roberts' Animal Stories," *Canadian Children's Literature, 1,* No. 2 (Summer 1975), 23-37; Muriel Whitaker, "Tales of the Wilderness: The Canadian Animal Story," *Canadian Children's Literature, 1*, No. 2 (Summer 1975), 38-46; Patricia Morley, "Introduction," in Ernest Thompson Seton, *Selected Stories of Ernest Thompson Seton*, ed. Patricia Morley (Ottawa: Univ. of Ottawa Press, 1977), pp. 9-17; Alec Lucas, "Introduction," in Ernest Thompson Seton, *Wild Animals I Have Known*, New Canadian Library, No. 141 (Toronto: McClelland and Stewart, 1977), pp. vii-xii; Muriel Whitaker, "Afterword," in *Great Canadian Animal Stories*, ed. Muriel Whitaker (Edmonton: Hurtig, 1978), pp. 214-21; Alec Lucas, "Haig-Brown's Animal Biographies," *Canadian Children's Literature*, No. 11 (1978), pp. 21-38; John Coldwell Adams, "Introduction," in Charles G. D. Roberts, *The Lure of the Wild: The Last Three Animal Stories*, ed. John Coldwell Adams (Ottawa: Borealis, 1980), pp. 1-9; Robert H. MacDonald, "The Revolt against Instinct: The Animal Stories of Seton and Roberts," *Canadian Literature*, No. 84 (Spring 1980), pp. 18-29.

3 Atwood, pp. 79, 73.

4 The best account of the animal story's relationship with the development of ethology is found in John Henry Wadland, *Ernest Thompson Seton: Man in Nature and the Progressive Era, 1880-1915* (New York: Arno, 1978), pp. 165-297.

5 John Burroughs, "Real and Sham Natural History," *The Atlantic Monthly*, March 1903, p. 298. All further references to this work appear in the text.

6 William J. Long, "The Modern School of Nature-Study and Its Critics," *North American Review*, May 1903, pp. 692-93, 691.

7 Charles G. D. Roberts, *The Watchers of the Trails: A Book of Animal Life* (Boston: Page, 1904), p. vii. All further references to this work appear in the text.

8 Charles G. D. Roberts, *The House in the Water: A Book of Animal Stories* (Boston: Page, 1908), p. 27.

9 Ernest Thompson Seton, *Trail of an Artist-Naturalist* (New York: Scribner's, 1940), pp. 370-71.

10 John Burroughs, "The Literary Treatment of Nature," *The Atlantic Monthly*, July 1904, p. 42.

11 "Edward B. Clark, "Roosevelt on the Nature Fakirs," *Everybody's Magazine*, June 1907, pp. 770-74. Roosevelt's comments are reprinted in Theodore Roosevelt, "Men Who Misinterpret Nature," in *The Works of Theodore Roosevelt* (New York: Scribner's, 1926), v, 367-74.

12 Theodore Roosevelt, "Nature Fakers," *Everybody's Magazine*, September 1907, 423-27. The article is reprinted in Roosevelt, *Works*, v, 375-83.

13 Roosevelt, "Men Who Misinterpret Nature," p. 373.

14 E. M. Pomeroy, *Sir Charles G. D. Roberts: A Biography* (Toronto: Ryerson, 1943), p. 179.

15 John Burroughs, *Ways of Nature*, Vol. ii of *The Complete Writings of John Burroughs* (New York: Wise, 1924), p. vi.

16 Charles G. D. Roberts, *The Haunters of the Silences* (Boston: Page, 1907), pp. vii, vi.

Misao Dean
Political Science: Realism in Roberts's Animal Stories *

> In that country the animals
> have the faces of people
> ("The Animals in that Country,"
> Margaret Atwood)

Charles GD. Roberts's animal stories are usually discussed as an attempt to create a new kind of animal character, one which would not be an anthropomorphic copy of human psychology nor a one-dimensional allegory but a "real" animal based on the most up-to-date science and on accurate personal observation.[1] Critics read the stories as marking an important stage in the development of Canadian realism, citing the development of credible animal characters and the location of the stories in a meticulously accurate and recognisable New Brunswick landscape.[2] But these analyses of Roberts's animals stories as "realistic" have failed to take account of the ideology implicit in realist technique. Even in the most "realistic" text, "the thing represented does not appear in a moment of pure identity" (MacCabe 136). Far from "reflecting" reality, Roberts's stories create as reality a natural world which is inflected with assumptions about human personality and masculinity as norm which are endemic to his historical period.

Critical approaches to Roberts's stories are dominated by the assumption that in good writing language directly corresponds to material reality: "most critics have agreed . . . that an intimate, almost transparent connection between diction and object, between the word and the phenomenal world, is the hallmark of Roberts's best writing" (Whalen 172). Whalen sums up Roberts's "legacy to Canadian novelists" as his demonstration of how to represent in prose "the world as a tan-

* This article first appeared in *Studies in Canadian Literature*, 21.1 (1996), 1-16. It is reprinted here with the permission of the author.

gible reality, human beings as recognisable entities, and settings as actual locales" (168). Lennox praises Roberts's ability to depict, "in a realistic way, animals as animals in relation to their place in the actual, natural world" (121) and Joseph Gold locates "myth", which he argues structures all of Roberts's stories, "within the framework of an accurate survey of natural history" (Gold 23). While Gold, Atwood, MacDonald (1980) and Dunlap emphasise the way the stories result from a dialectical relationship between material reality and the "shaping consciousness" of the artist, ultimately their critical judgments are based on the tenet that the stories are "true" in some ultimate sense—"true" to an observable physical reality and (perhaps) "true" to an underlying and universally (or, in the case of Atwood, nationally) valid mythical structure.

The verisimilitude of the stories is often confirmed by contrasting them to contemporary animal stories such as the sentimental novels of Anna Sewell and Marshall Saunders, or the two *Jungle Books* of Rudyard Kipling.[3] Sewell's *Black Beauty* and Saunders's *Beautiful Joe* self-consciously create quasi-human "personalities" for their animal characters in order to foster reader identification, and so forward their animal-rights politics. Rudyard Kipling, whose *Jungle Book* is "in no sense realistic" (Ware xv), creates animal characters who are descendants equally of the proverbial animals of Aesop and of "Indian folk wisdom" (xv). All of these stories are infused with various kinds of Victorian ideological baggage: racist and colonialist attitudes in the case of Kipling, and the sentimental evocation of suffering innocence in order to arouse public concern in the case of Sewell and Saunders. In addition, their use of intrusive moralising and their romantic and implausible plots make them technically less "realistic." Placing Roberts's animal stories in the context of these (now) obviously unrealistic works has the effect of making them seem objective and materially "real" by contrast.

Roberts invites such judgments when he presents the creation of a "realistic" animal personality based on taxonomy and the new science of psychology as the major innovation of the animal story as genre. Roberts argues that previous generations of writers had imposed an anthropomorphic self upon their animal characters in order to create moral fables for their readers. In contrast, his stories grew out of the scientific observation evident in their immediate predecessors, the hunting "story of adventure and the anecdote of observation" (*Kindred* 21). The first, be states, generated a taxonomy of animals: "Precise and patient scientists made the animals their care, observing with microscope and measure, comparing bones, assorting families, subdividing subdivisions, till at length, all the animals of significance to man were ticketed neatly, and laid bare, as far as their material substance was concerned" (*Kindred* 22). The second generated an interest in animal psychology, which he considers to be an inductive science whose methodology led inevitably to the conclusion that "animals can and do reason" (*Kindred* 23). Observation confirmed Darwin's speculation that if humans evolved from "lesser" animals and shared many traits with them, then reason (in a rudimentary form) might also be a common attribute; from this Roberts developed his idea that animals must possess a "personality, individuality, mentality" (*Kindred* 28) which is distinctive, and which he contrasts positively to "mere instinct and automatism" (*Kindred* 24).[4]

But the language of Roberts's animal stories cannot transparently reproduce material reality, for no realism is transparent: "in so far as language is a way of articulating experience, it necessarily participates in ideology" (Belsey 42). All realistic works rely on the evocation of cultural codes which are ideological; they construct the real rather than reflect it. This is not to say that Roberts's stories are not technically accomplished, or that they are ideologically suspect: even less does it suggest that they are consciously deceptive or bad. Rather, despite their modernist technique of minimising the intrusion of the narrator, despite their evocative description and claims to scientific accuracy, we cannot judge naively that they reproduce reality. The stories demand analysis as "realist," that is, as attempts to create an illusion of reality. What they choose to signify as "real" is as important an area of analysis as how they signify it.

The ideology within which Roberts's stories speak is the masculinist discourse of the early twentieth century in which the "primal" experiences of hunting, scouting and woodcraft serve as an antidote for the feminised life of the industrial city dweller. "From 1890 to 1930 the 'Nature Movement' was at its height in the United States," providing a focus for "conventional western ambivalence about 'civilization"' (Haraway 54). North Americans in an increasingly urban society idealised the (American) frontiersman and the (Canadian) trapper or voyageur; the British created a popular image of "empire" which relied upon the enterprise of the "clean-limbed" and active irregular troops, offered as a model for the supposedly lazy and immoral members of the urban working class. The perceived "crisis of masculinity" in English, American and Canadian cultures consisted in the belief that men were becoming "soft," physically weak and morally corrupt through sedentary or industrial work. The construction of homosexuality in the discourse surrounding the trial of Oscar Wilde and the "decadence" of the 1890s produced a corresponding emphasis on "cleanliness," physical fitness and sexual autonomy in the first decades of the twentieth century. The popular literature of empire portrayed British colonies as appropriate fields for the exercise of British masculinity, preferably through a "cleansing" encounter with the natural world in adventures which emphasised "instinctive" reactions; the ability of the frontiersmen or backwoodsmen to adapt to and overcome any conditions was the stuff of popular novels set in the American West, along the Canadian Railway or in south central Africa.[5]

In order to provide the reader with a "return to nature" without requiring a "return to barbarism" (*Kindred* 29), Roberts's animal stories create animals as models of ideal autonomous self-hood, masculine and free from the taint of civilised life; by representing these animals in deep communion with human observers, they reproduce the selfhood of the reader as similarly autonomous, masculine and free. By encouraging identification with the animal subject, and with the position of the knowledgeable backwoodsman who lingers in the text as author and authoriser, the stories literally "naturalise" the position of reader as the result of this supposed primal return to the essence of being-in-nature.

But the human selfhood which is attributed to the animals is the ideological cover story for the subjectivity which the stories create. For while the animals as individuals are attributed freedom and agency, they are also "subjected" by a discourse which figures them as "the same as" humans, yet places them in a material and evolutionary hierarchy which is dominated by humans.[6] Similarly, the reader is "subjected" by the structural identification with animals, who are theorised as wholly material beings acting according to "natural laws," and with the predatory, male human observer for whose specular consumption the drama of animal life is offered. The "return to nature" promised by "The Animal Story" (*Kindred* 29) is promised to the male reader who by its means is offered a subject position of competence and mastery directly linked to his biological heritage as white male human being, crown and end product of evolution.

The theories of Charles Darwin were inevitably brought to aid this discourse. The struggle for existence, natural selection and evolution were widely thought to apply to the human species at the turn of the century, and their application formed the basis of the developing discipline of sociobiology. Despite Darwin's own careful disclaimers on this issue, responses to his work dominated the newly founded discipline of sociology, especially in the United States. One school of thought held that Darwin had merely projected onto the natural world the human society he saw around him; Marx, for example, wrote:

> It is remarkable how Darwin recognizes among beasts and plants his English society, with its division of labour, competition, opening up of new markets, inventions,' and the Malthusian 'struggle for existence'. . . . in Darwin, the animal kingdom figures as a civil society. (Quoted in Beer 58)

This contention was supported by Darwin's own admission that he had drawn his idea of the "struggle for existence" from Malthus's work on human population. Other thinkers, such as Herbert Spencer, argued that the "laws" of nature discovered by Darwin to govern the animal kingdom ought to be guides for social policy, and still others argued that Darwin's description of the struggle for existence, or "survival of the fittest," ought to motivate people to adapt and create co-operative, moral organisational structures which would similarly ensure survival.[7] In the United States, naturalists and museum collectors commented on the supposed nuclear structure of animal families and constructed a fantasy of the peaceable kingdom in order to naturalise a conservative solution to social unrest: "'naked eye science' could give direct vision of social peace and progress despite the appearances of class war and decadence" (Haraway 54). What all of these streams of thought held in common was the importance of biological science in determining appropriate ways to view human societies, and the salience of the "social analogy underlying Darwin's description of the natural order" (Beer 58).

In short, the animal "self" created by the stories, while naturalised by scientific theory and reported observation, is the very human self created by "classic realist fiction" (Belsey 73). The animals masquerade as "other," but like the bull, cat, fox and wolf of Atwood's poem, they are really (m)animals, reproductions of the ideological subject offered to turn-of-the-century readers of realist fiction. Like the sentimental and self-consciously human animals of Anna Sewell or Marshall Saunders these (m)animals cannot claim to convey "the non-human aspect of [their] existence" (Ware) except as absence. In a culture increasingly obsessed with the "biological" or "natural" basis of human action, in which responses to Darwinism were the dominant sociological theory, Roberts's (m)animals function as simulacra of social subjects, and their motivations, actions and fates are created by the conventions of realist narrative, turn-of-the-century gender politics, and the historical intersection of biological and sociological discourses.

The stories which fall into Roberts's category of "animal biography" offer examples of the way that conventional manipulation of realist "point of view" works to create subjectivity. Using conventional third-person narration, Roberts creates the physical perspective and psychological motivation to substantiate the subjectivity of his animal characters and to structure the identification of reader with character. In "The Little Homeless One" the title character encounters a goshawk in a rabbit run:

> The runway was narrow, and densely overarched by low branches, so it was impossible that the great bird

> could have seen him from the upper air. . . . The beautiful, fierce-eyed bird was not home upon the level earth. His deadly talons were not made for walking, but for perching and for slaying. His realm was the free spaces of the air, and here in the runway he could not spread his wings. His progress was so slow, laborious and clumsy that, but for the glare of his level, piercing eyes he could have seemed grotesque. (*Vagrants* 41)

The narrative here describes the scene from the physical point of view of the rabbit, which is the only perspective from which "the glare of [the goshawk's] level, piercing eyes" and his labourious clumsy movements would be visible. The rabbit's perspective is also represented in the focus on the talons, whose functions are described with the elevated diction (slaying) which gives them a mythic importance for the vulnerable rabbit. As the anecdote continues, the rabbit is attributed a psychology which includes not only fear, but "curiosity." "Gifted beyond his fellows with the power of learning from experience" the "Homeless One" learns to be "a little suspicious" (*Vagrants* 42) of rabbit runs, and retains this knowledge as a guide to future action.

The perspective of the rabbit in "The Little Homeless One" alternates with addresses to the reader which reproduce the discourse of romantic nature; the goshawk is described as "beautiful," an inhabitant of the "realm" of the "free air." Thus in addition to the positioning of the reader as identified with the subject animal, the narrative also invites the reader to participate in a discourse of "natural description" which positions him as knowledgeable observer, identified with the backwoodsman/author who directs his gaze. In "Mothers of the North" this identification is structured by the creation of a physical perspective on the action which writer and reader share. From the open water both the walrus herd and the attacking polar bear and her cub are visible. The narrative occasionally lodges a sweeping third person description of a scene in the consciousness of one animal, such as the old bull who is "on watch," or in the mind of the polar bear herself, who analyses the scene for the most effective angle of attack, but the dominant perspective is that of the human viewer, as in this description of the walrus herd:

> They were not, it must be confessed, a very attractive company, these uncouth sea-cattle. The adults were from ten to twelve feet in length, round and swollen looking as hogsheads, quite lacking the adornment of tails, and in colour of a dirty yellow-brown. Sparse bristles, scattered over their hides in rusty patches, gave them a disreputable, moth-eaten look. (*Vagrants* 2)

Specific dimensions, alternative vocabulary (sea-cattle) and colour references are "concrete details" that establish the referentiality of the description for the reader; the metaphors implied by "hogsheads" and "moth-eaten," in addition to the attributes of uncouthness, unattractiveness and disreputability provide the connotative aspects of the "authorial vision." This description, a demonstration of "reality" as "shaped" by the implied consciousness of the author, demonstrates the way that the text is constructed as a direct communication from one autonomous individual (author) to another (reader) and places both as observers of the scene.

In stories such as "King of the Mamozekel" and "The Little Homeless One" (in *Vagrants*) "King of the Flaming Hoops" and "The Monarch of Park Barren" (in *Kings in Exile*), Roberts uses the conventional biographical narrative pattern to reify both reader and character as subjects. In accordance with the conventions of the genre, the stories present a chronology of individuals from birth through maturity, offering the unified narrative of exposition, rising action, climax and denouement which reproduces "character" as the determinant of action in both life and art. Roberts's animal "personalities" are autonomous, and like the heroes of romance, create that autonomy by leaving home, undergoing adventures, and often returning to or re-establishing that home. Animals experience free choice through action which is "psychologically motivated"; they express their desire through action, and their desire is eventually contained in the achievement of full adult autonomy and the opportunity to mate. In " King of the Mamozekel" a moose is ejected from "home" by his mother's new mate; after winning his own mate, and sustaining challenges for her possession, he achieves full selfhood by confronting his unreasoning fear of bears (created by the memory of being mauled as a calf) in a duel with a bear who attacks his own son. In "The Odyssey of the Great White Owl" (*Lure of the Wild*) an arctic owl recently bereaved of his mate experiences a restless desire to travel which is only assuaged when he encounters a mateless female. In "The Little Homeless One" a snowshoe rabbit, abandoned when his mother nurses a new litter, learns through observation and experience how to preserve his life from cunning predators and pass on his superior physical traits to his young. In *Kings in Exile* animals removed from the wild soon after birth experience a relentless desire for freedom which creates a psychological kinship with man, and often results in their regaining freedom.

The values celebrated in these (m)animal "biographies" are predictable: independence, physical superiority, ability to learn and adapt, superior cunning, honesty, trust, ability to co-operate toward material ends. "The Little Homeless One" survives an attack on his abandoned siblings because he is independent enough to leave the nest; the "King of the Mamozekel" is admirable because of his physical size and ability to defeat rival males. Both survive because they learn from experience, the "King" from his encounter with bears, the "homeless one" from his observation of predators who stalk the rabbit runs. Blue Fox, the "Master of Supply" (*Vagrants*) prevails over his enemies because he shows prudence, "wise forethought," and "discretion," by burying the fruits of his summer hunting in "cold storage" next to the permafrost to be eaten in winter; this animal expression of the Protestant work ethic has also learned to organize, calling on the aid of his fellow foxes to drive away marauders.

The realist technique of closure formally resolves the issues of the protagonists' lives, whether structured to reinforce a positive teleology of progressive evolution or to shock the reader into recognising the impartiality of "science." The protagonists of Roberts' "anecdotes of observation" sometimes die meaningless deaths, dictated by random fate or undeserved bad luck: in these stories, such as "When Twilight Falls on the

Stump Lots" the strength of animal character, and the persistence of animal endurance, are irrelevant to the final disposition of things, and the reader's identification with the animal characters results in a sense of the irrelevance of spiritual values to the workings of "natural law." But the heroes of "animal biographies" often die the "good deaths" dictated by the genre. When the snowshoe rabbit makes himself a target for predators by thumping a warning to other rabbits, "The Homeless One, as truly as many a hero of history and song, die[s] for the safety of his tribe" (*Vagrants* 46). In both, "natural law" is triumphant, for despite the death of the individual, "The Homeless One" continues his line through his (numerous) offspring.

Following the conventions of biography, only outstanding *male* animals achieve the simple personality which characterises the animal biographies. In these stories the linguistic practice of referring to animals using generic male pronouns has the effect of producing a natural world in which the vast majority of animals are gendered male. A survey of the stories published throughout Roberts's career and posthumously reveals that the male is the norm; female animals appear only in the context of their reproductive functions, as "mate" or mother of the protagonist, actors in the struggle for existence only when procuring food for their (male) young. Animals who initially appear in the text as "it" (usually insects, such as the giant water-beetle in "In a Summer Pool") become "he" when credited with voluntary action, instinct or emotion (*Lure of the Wild* 33-4). Individual animals designated by a generic species name, such as "Red Fox," "Blue Fox," "The Little Homeless One," are always male; exemplars of the best of their breed, "King of the Mamozekel" or "Lord of the Air," or the captive animals in *Kings in Exile*, are always male. Realist technique in fiction depends upon the creation of such "typical" characters which, rather than representing the average or ordinary specimen, join together a myriad of qualities which were considered desirable: in scientific circles at the turn of the century, the concept of the "typical" animal specimen included not only extraordinary physique, physical perfection and virtuous character, but—definitively—maleness (Haraway 41). The effect whereby this "generic male" becomes simply male is well known: Miller and Swift, in *Words and Women*, recount the way that the generic "he" used to designate animals creates a presumption that "the male is the norm, and the assumption that all animals are male unless they are known to be female" (28).

Such (m)animals are not neutrally designated male as a matter of grammatical convenience; in Roberts's stories male animals display many of the characteristics typically associated with human masculinity at the turn of the century. Like the television programs on natural history, museum dioramas and Disney movies which they spawned, these stories reify gender difference as the primary category of human experience by projecting it onto the natural world: "Here in the animal kingdom, a natural world of male dominance and aggression is revealed. Here are males defending their property (territory or wives). Here are females selecting their mates as 'good' parents, either for their genetic endowments or their ability to provide" (Coward 212). Roberts's male animals achieve an independence marked by love of adventure, superior mental skills, competitiveness, instinctive love of hunting and virility.[8] In contrast, female animals are motivated primarily by mother-love;[9] the occasional unmated female characteristically displays simple cruelty and bloodlust (*Kindred* 233) and represents an uncontrollable, immoral wildness which demands human control.[10] Male animals are the agents of sexual desire in the stories: while cow moose sometimes feel "jealousy" at the idea of a female rival, male moose are driven into "an insurrection of madness, and suspense, and sweetness" (*Kindred* 185), owls into migrations, and ganders enticed to flee captivity by sexual desire. In an almost parodic representation of the rabbit's legendary potency, "The Little Homeless One" is offered numerous opportunities to mate, as female rabbits coyly lead him into the bushes, flashing their haunches enticingly:

> a sleek young doe met him in the runway, and waved long ears of admiration at his comely stature and length of limb. Tie stopped to touch noses and exchange compliments with her. Coyly she hopped away, leading him into a cool, green-shadowed covert of sumach scrub. (*Vagrants* 40)

He spends his days "hopping lazily after a pair of does who were merely pretending, by way of sport, to evade him" (41).[11]

Roberts's depiction of the female animal's role in reproduction is particularly inflected with contemporary debates about the nature of women. Progressive thinkers in the United States argued that species evolution demanded that women should actively choose their own husbands, offering as evidence numerous animals species in which the female is dominant. Charlotte Perkins Gilman believed that men, by valuing small, weak and frail "feminine" women as sexual partners, were unnaturally retarding the evolution of humankind, and with sociologist Lester Frank Ward argued that women, as guardians of the species, were more competent to choose the fathers of their children than men were to choose the mothers.[12] "King of the Mamozekel" depicts a cow moose who, while indifferently awaiting the outcome of a purely male battle in which she is the prize, yet has some concern in the affair beyond passive acquiescence:

> But as for the cow, she moved up from the waterside and looked on with a fine impartiality. What concerned her was chiefly that none but the bravest and the strongest should be her mate—a question which only fighting could determine. Her favour would go with victory. (*Kindred* 315)

Motivated by mother-love, she awaits the opportunity to become the mate of the most physically aggressive and strong male moose, a fit father for her children. The story intervenes in a debate about women by representing feminine animals who contradictorily exercise choice by remaining passive. "The Little Homeless One," in a popular distortion of Darwinian evolution, seems to assert that advantageous genetic traits can only be passed from male parent to offspring, and that the female has little role in the improvement of the species. The male rabbit is

> singled out, apparently, for the special favour of the Unseen Powers of the Wilderness . . . . to the end that

> he should grow up a peculiarly fine, vigorous, and prepotent specimen of his race, and reproduce himself abundantly, to the advantage, not only of the whole tribe of snowshoe rabbits, but all of the hunting beasts and birds of the wilderness, who chiefly depended upon that prolific and defenceless tribe for their prey. (*Vagrants* 39)

Mothers are represented as important in the nurture of their offspring, but random (in the case of the "Homeless One," exceedingly random) and biologically unimportant factors in their nature.

Roberts emphasises in "The Animal Story" the thematic and cultural importance of a mutual recognition of kinship between human and animal, ritualised as a look "deep into the eyes of certain of the four-footed kindred" (*Kindred* 23).[13] This encounter is the theme of "stories of adventure with beasts" (*Kindred* 21), another of Roberts's three categories of animal stories. In "The Moonlight Trails," the recurring character called simply "the boy" shares with predatory animals the excitement of hunting and the kill: "His heart leapt, his eyes flamed, and he sprang forward, with a little cry, as a young beast might in sighting its first quarry" (*Kindred* 51). Everywhere in Roberts's stories "man" is figured as a predator at the top of the food chain, sharing with animals the desire to hunt and needing meat to maintain physical health (see "Wild Motherhood" and "Savory Meats" in *Kindred*; also *The Heart ot the Ancient Wood*). Yet man also shares with animals more complex identifications: "the boy" also identifies with his victim, and in "Moonlight Trails" he vows never to snare rabbits again after he witnesses the desecration of his snare by foxes. The stories in *Kings in Exile* represent exchanges and partnerships between "man" and wild animal, in which an identification based on the temporary emasculation represented by civilised life is played out between captive zoo or circus animals and their "masters." In "Last Bull" a relic of the dying race of American Bison is named by "two grim old sachems of the Dacotahs" in symbolic recognition of their likeness; in "The Sun-Gazer" Horner feels such strong identification with a caged eagle that he purchases it in order to set it free: "Horner could almost have cried, from pity and home-sick sympathy" (168). Stories of loyalty and honesty in relationships between human and animal such as "Gray Master," "Lord of the Flaming Hoops" and "Lone Wolf" emphasise the homosocial culture in which these stories originate. The experience of identification, of seeing "a something, before unrecognised, that answered to our inner and intellectual, if not spiritual selves" (*Kindred* 23-4) in the lives and personalities of animals is represented as an exchange between male humans and male animals only.

Like the predators celebrated in Roberts's stories as intelligent and moral adversaries, "man is also a "king," "lord" and "master" of the natural world. In "Vagrants of the Barren," the woodsman hero becomes identified with his animal rivals in a struggle for existence.

> His anger rose as he realised he was at bay. The indomitable man-spirit awoke with the anger. Sitting up suddenly, over the edge of the trench his deep eyes looked out over the shadowy spaces of the night with challenge and defiance. Against whatever odds, he declared to himself, he was master."(*Vagrants* 150)

The language here associates the protagonist's animal defensiveness ("he was at bay") with his "indomitable man-spirit." The two become further identified as the story progresses, with the woodsman recognising that "No animal but man himself could hunt" in the blizzard he confronts, and later choosing to spare the lives of a helpless caribou herd, foundered in the snow:

> through contact there in the savage darkness, a sympathy passed between the man and the beast. He could not help it. The poor beasts and he were in the same predicament, together holding the battlements of life against the blind and brutal madness of storm. (*Vagrants* 157)

While the story is structured to ironically challenge the protagonist's "obstinate pride in his superiority to the other creatures of the wilderness" by requiring the protagonist to descend to animality, it in fact "strikes the chord of man's innate superiority" (Keefer 90), demonstrating it to consist in both the physical strength and cunning which ensures survival, and the moral ability to discern kinship and thus spare lives.

The moment of mutual recognition and identification in these stories reifies the subjectivity of reader and animal and situates that subjectivity within a network of ideological assumptions. The first of these is a mutual recognition of shared conditions of life: both human and animal are products of "natural laws," most especially the struggle for existence, and their lives are determined by material conditions. The second, and intertwined, assumption, is their mutual rebellion against these conditions of life and their expression of the will to triumph in the struggle for existence by killing, and in the achievement of a free, independent life. "Man" is here assumed to be a predator like others, participating in an implicit morality in which "good" predators learn to live peacefully among themselves through co-operation and kill only to survive (or to improve the breed through competition), and "bad" predators are loners, killing for sport and mad with "bloodlust." This morality is not guaranteed by supernatural powers, but implied by the "laws" of evolution and natural selection, which, as suggested in Roberts's sonnet, "In the Wide Awe and Wisdom of the Night," may be the utterances of God, but need not be.

"If representation is not to be conceive as a mirror held up to nature but as a signifying practice, then it and not nature is responsible for its statements, and political questions can be addressed to it" (Robbins 7). By masquerading as "*science*," Roberts's animal stories do the work of politics, creating and maintaining a hierarchical power structure which is dominated by humans, naturalising the masculine as norm and asserting unified autonomous human personality as a universal phenomenon. By effacing their status as ideological text and masquerading as "concrete reality," the stories "[do] the work of ideology' (Belsey 72) obscuring the arbitrary relationship between word and thing, discourse and subjectivity. The stories occupy a place in the critical narrative of the development of realism in Canadian fiction not by allowing "the thing represented" to "appear in a moment of pure identity" (MacCabe 136), but by constructing the reader as subject, "naturally" predatory, material and male.

Works Cited

Atwood, Margaret. "The Animals in That Country." *Fifteen Canadian Poets Times Two*. Ed. Gary Ceddes. Toronto: Oxford, 1989. 396

—. *Survival*. Toronto: Anansi, 1972.

Bannister, Robert C. *Social Darwinism: Science and Myth in Anglo-American Social Thought*. Philadelphia: Temple UP, 1979.

Beer, Gillian. *Darwin's Plots: Evolutionary Narrative in Darwin, George Eliot and Nineteenth Century Fiction*. London: ARK Paperbacks. 1985.

Belsey, Catherine. *Critical Practice*. London: Routledge, 1980.

Coward, Rosalind. "The Sex-life of Stick Insects." *Female Desire*. London: Granada, 1984. 209-15.

Dunlap, Thomas R. "'The old kinship of Earth': Science, Man and Nature in the Animal Stories of Charles G.D. Roberts." *Journal of Canadian Studies* 22:1 (Spring 1987): 104-20.

Gilman, Charlotte Perkins. *Herland*. Ed. Ann J. Lane. New York: Pantheon, 1979.

Gold, Joseph. "The Precious Speck of Life." *Canadian Literature* 26 (Autumn 1965): 22-32.

Haraway, Donna. *Primate Visions*. New York: Routledge, 1989.

Hutcheon, Linda. "Eruptions of Postmodernity: The Postcolonial and the Ecological." *ECW* 51-2 (Winter 1993-Spring 1994): 146-63.

Keefer, Janice Kulyk. *Under Eastern Eyes: A Critical Reading of Maritime Fiction*. Toronto: U of Toronto P, 1987.

Lennox, John. "Roberts, Realism and the Animal Story." *Journal of Canadian Fiction* II: 3 (Summer 1973): 121-23.

MacCabe, Colin. "Realism and the Cinema: Notes on some Brechtian Theses." *Modern Literary Theory: A Reader*. Eds. Philip Rice and Patricia Waugh. London: Edward Arnold, 1989. 134-42.

MacDonald, Robert H. *The Language of Empire: Myths and Metaphors of Popular Imperialism*. Manchester: Manchester UP, 1994.

—. *Sons of the Empire: The Frontier and the Boy Scout Movement 1890-1918*. Toronto: U of Toronto P. 1993.

—. "The Revolt Against Instinct: The Animal Stories of Seton and Roberts." *Canadian Literature* (Spring 1980): 18-29.

Miller, Casey and Kate Swift. *Words and Women: New Language in New Times*. New York: Anchor Press/Doubleday, 1977.

Robbins, Bruce. *The Servant's Hand: English Fiction from Below.* New York: Columbia UP, 1986.

Roberts, Charles G.D. *The Heart of the Ancient Wood.* 1900. Rpt. New Canadian Library. Toronto: McClelland and Stewart, 1974.

—. "In the Wide Awe and Wisdom of the Night." *Selected Poetry and Critical Prose.* Ed. W.J. Keith. Toronto: U of Toronto P, 1974. 107.

—. *The Kindred of the Wild.* Toronto: Copp Clark, 1902.

—. *Kings in Exile.* New York: Macmillan, 1910.

—. *The Lure of the Wild.* Ed. John Coldwell Adams. Ottawa: Borealis, 1980.

—. *The Vagrants of the Barrens and other Stories.* Ed. Martin Ware. Ottawa: Tecumseh, 1992.

Showalter, Elaine. *Sexual Anarchy: Gender and Culture at the Fin-de-Siecle.* New York: Viking, 1990.

Whalen, Terry, "Charles G.D. Roberts and his Works." *Canadian Writers and their Works* (Fiction Series) Eds. Robert Lecker, Jack David and Ellen Quigley. Toronto: ECW Press, 1989. 156-216.

Ware, Martin. "Introduction" *Vagrants of the Barren and other Stories.* Ottawa: Tecumseh, 1992.

Endnotes

1 See Atwood, *Survival*, pages 72-75 for a discussion of the ways these stories are considered to be a reply to the anthropomorphic stories of British writers.

2 See Lennox and Whalen, for example.

3 See, for example, Martin Ware's "Introduction" to *Vagrants of the Barren*, xv.

4 MacDonald (1980) and Dunlap disagree as to the relative weight Roberts placed on the two terms in the binary construction of reason and instinct; I'm not convinced that Roberts is consistent in this regard.

5 See Robert H. MacDonald, *Sons of the Empire* and *Language of Empire*; Donna Haraway, esp. chapter 3; also Elaine Showalter, *Sexual Anarchy*.

6 There is a direct analogy between this discourse and the more overtly political "colonialist discourse" discussed by Stephen Slemon, which works '"to *produce and naturalise* the hierarchical power structures of the imperial enterprise, and to mobilise those power structures in the management of both colonial and neo-colonial cross-cultural relationships" (qtd.. in Hutcheon 150).

7 See Bannister 14-33.

8 MacDonald, *Language of Empire* passim.

9 Primarily, but not exclusively. In "The Little Homeless One" the litter is abandoned by its mother in her struggle for survival: "She loved her young ones; but she loved her life better. She had but one life."

10 Both sexes of the weasel, wolverine and fisher are also represented as bloodthirsty animals who enjoy killing for its own sake ("Keepers in the Nest," in *Vagrants of the Barren*, and "The Den of the Otter," in *Lure of the Wild*), but in neither case is human intervention required.

11 Clearly, in the animal world of these stories, "no" means "chase me." This fantasy projection of sexual power is all the more offensive in the biographical context of Roberts's self-created image as a rogue and a successful ladies man.

12 See Gilman, *Herland.*

13 This moment became a conventional element of museum dioramas by the 1920s, which contained "at least one animal that catches the viewer's gaze and holds it in communion." Realistic technique creates the illusion that "There is no impediment to this vision, no mediation "between the animal and man," for "Only then could the hygiene of nature cure the sick vision of civilized man" (Haraway 30).

Bibliography

Primary Sources

Roberts, Charles G.D. *Orion and Other Poems*. Philadelphia: Lippincott, 1880.

____. *Later Poems*. Fredericton: privately printed, 1881.

____. *Later Poems*. Fredericton: privately printed, 1882.

____. *In Divers Tones*. Boston: Lothrop, 1886.

____. *Autochthon*. Windsor, N.S.: privately printed, 1889.

____. trans. *Canadians of Old*. By Phillipe Aubert de Gaspé 1890; rpt. New Canadian Library, No. 106. Toronto: McClelland and Stewart, 1974.

____. *The Canadian Guide-Book*. New York: Appleton, 1891.

____. *Ave: An Ode for the Centenary of the Birth of Percy Bysshe Shelley*, August 4, 1792. Toronto: Williamson, 1892.

____. *Songs of the Common Day, and Ave: An Ode for the Shelley Centenary*. London: Longman, 1893.

____. *The Raid from Beauséjour, and How the Carter Boys Lifted the Mortgage: Two Stories of Acadie*. New York: Hunt and Eaton, 1894.

____. *The Land of Evangeline and the Gateways Thither*. Kentville, N.S.: Dominion Atlantic Railway, 1895.

____. *Reube Dare's Shad Boat: A Tale of the Tide Country*. New York: Hunter and Eaton, 1895.

____. *Around the Campfire*. New York: Crowell, 1896.

____. *The Book of the Native*. Boston: Lamson, Wolffe, 1896.

____. *Earth's Enigmas*. Boston: Lamson, Wolffe, 1896.

____. *The Forge in the Forest*. Boston: Lamson, Wolffe, 1896.

____. *A History of Canada*. Boston: Lamson, Wolffe, 1897.

____. *New York Nocturnes and Other Poems*. Boston: Lamson, Wolffe, 1898.

____. *A Sister to Evangeline*. Boston: Lamson, Wolffe, 1898.

____. *By the Marshes of Minas*. Boston: Silver, Burdett, 1900.

____. *The Heart of the Ancient Wood*. 1900; rpt. New Canadian Library, No. 110. Introd. Joseph Gold. Toronto: McClelland and Stewart, 1974.

____. *Poems*. New York: Silver, Burdett, 1901.

____. *Barbara Ladd*. Boston: Page, 1902.

____. *Discoveries and Explorations in the Century*. Vol. XIV of *The Nineteenth Century Series: The Story of Human Progress and The Great Events of the Century*. London: Chambers, 1902.

____. *The Kindred of the Wild*. Boston: Page, 1902.

____. *The Book of the Rose*. Boston: Page, 1903.
____. *The Prisoner of Mademoiselle*. Boston: Page, 1904.
____. *The Watchers of the Trails*. Boston: Page, 1904.
____. *Red Fox*. 1905; rpt. Introd. David McCord. Boston: Houghton Mifflin, 1972.
____. *The Heart That Knows*. Boston: Page, 1906.
____. *The Haunters of the Silences*. Boston: Page, 1907.
____. *Poems (New Complete Edition)*. Boston: Page, 1907.
____. *The House in the Water*. Boston: Page, 1908.
____. *Red Oxen of Bonval*. New York: Dodd, Mead, 1908.
____. *The Backwoodsmen*. New York: Macmillan, 1909.
____. *Kings in Exile*. London: Ward, Lock, 1909.
____. *Neighbours Unknown*. London: Ward, Locke, 1910.
____. *More Kindred of the Wild*. London: Ward, Lock, 1911.
____. *Babes of the Wild*. London: Cassell, 1912.
____. *The Feet of the Furtive*. London: Ward, Lock, 1912.
____. *A Balkan Prince*. London: Everett, 1913.
____. *Hoof and Claw*. London: Ward, Lock, 1913.
____. *The Ledge on Bald Face*. London: Ward, Lock, 1916.
____. *The Secret Trails*. London: Ward, Lock, 1916.
____. *Canada in Flanders: The Story of the Canadian Expeditionary Force*. Vol. III. London: Hodder and Stoughton, 1918.
____. *In the Morning of Time*. London: Hutchison, 1919.
____. *New Poems*. London: Constable, 1919.
____. *Some Animal Stories*. London: Dent. 1921.
____. *More Animal Stories*. London: Dent, 1922.
____. *Wisdom of the Wilderness*. London: Dent, 1922.
____. *They That Walk in the Wild*. London: Dent, 1924.
____. *The Sweet O' the Year and Other Poems*. Toronto: Ryerson, 1925.
____. *The Vagrant of Time*. Toronto: Ryerson, 1927.
____. *Be Quiet Wind; Unsaid: Two Unpublished Poems*. N.p.: privately printed, 1929.
____. "Bliss Carman." *The Dalhousie Review*, 9 (Jan. 1930), 409-17.
____. *Eyes of the Wilderness*. London: Dent, 1933.
____. *The Iceberg and Other Poems*. Toronto: Ryerson, 1934.
____. *Further Animal Stories*. London: Dent, 1936.
____. *Selected Poems*. Toronto: Ryerson, 1936.
____. *Twilight over Shaugamauk and Three Other Poems*. Toronto: Ryerson, 1937.
____. *Canada Speaks of Britain, and Other Poems of the War*. Toronto: Ryerson, 1941.
____. *An Acadian "Buche de Noël."* N.p.: privately printed, 1945.

(Extract reprinted from the lecture "Echoes from Old Acadia," in G.M. Fairchild. ed., Canadian Leaves [New York: Thompson, 1887].)

____. *Thirteen Bears*. Ed. Ethel H. Bennett. Toronto: Ryerson, 1947.

____. *Forest Folk*. Ed. Ethel H. Bennett. Toronto: Ryerson, 1949.

____. *The Selected Poems of Sir Charles G.D. Roberts*. Ed. Desmond Pacey. Toronto: Ryerson, 1955.

____. *The Last Barrier and Other Stories*. Ed. Alec Lucas. New Canadian Library, No. 7. Toronto: McClelland and Stewart, 1958.

____. *King of Beasts and Other Stories*. Ed. and introd. Joseph Gold. Toronto: Ryerson, 1967.

____. *Selected Poetry and Critical Prose*. Ed. and introd. W.J. Keith. Toronto: Univ. of Toronto Press, 1974.

____. *The Lure of the Wild: The Last Three Animal Stories by Sir Charles G.D. Roberts*. Ed. and introd. John Coldwell Adams. Ottawa: Borealis, 1980.

____. *The Collected Poems of Sir Charles G.D. Roberts*. Ed. Desmond Pacey. Introd. Fred Cogswell. Wolfville, N.S.: Wombat, 1985.

____. *The Collected Letters of Sir Charles G.D. Roberts*. Ed. and introd. Laurel Boone. Fredericton: Goose Lane, 1989.

____. *Vagrants of the Barren and Other Stories of Charles G.D. Roberts*. Ed. and introd. Martin Ware. Ottawa: Tecumseh, 1992.

Secondary Sources

Adams, John Coldwell, introd. *The Lure of the Wild: The Last Three Animal Stories by Charles G.D. Roberts*. Ottawa: Borealis, 1980, pp. 1-10.

____. "A Preliminary Bibliography." In *The Sir Charles G.D. Roberts Symposium*. Ed. and introd. Glenn Clever. Reappraisals: Canadian Writers, No. 10. Ottawa: Univ. of Ottawa Press, 1984, pp. 221-49.

____. "Roberts, Lampman, and Edmund Collins." In *The Sir Charles G.D. Roberts Symposium*. Ed. and introd. Glenn Clever. Reappraisals: Canadian Writers, No. 10. Ottawa: Univ. of Ottawa Press, 1984, pp. 5-13.

____. *Sir Charles God Damn: The Life of Sir Charles G.D. Roberts*. Toronto: Univ. of Toronto Press, 1986.

____. "Sir Charles G.D. Roberts: Post Biography." *Canadian Poetry: Studies, Documents, Reviews*, No. 21 (Fall-Winter 1987), pp. 77-80.

"The Animal Story." *Edinburgh Review*, 214 (July 1911), 94-118.

Atwood, Margaret. *Survival: A Thematic Guide to Canadian Literature*. Toronto: Anansi, 1972.

Bailey, Alfred G. "Creative Moments in the Culture of the Maritime Provinces." *The Dalhousie Review*, 29 (Oct. 1949), 231-44.

Bellamy, Francis. "Evangeline and Her Sister." Rev. of *A Sister to Evangeline. The Bookman, 9* (June 1899), 352-53.

Boone, Laurel "Organizing Bohemia: The Letters of Charles G.D. Roberts."In *The Sir Charles G.D. Roberts Symposium*. Ed. and introd. Glenn Clever. Reappraisals: Canadian Writers, No. 10. Ottawa: Univ. of Ottawa Press, 1984, pp. 15-25.

Burroughs, John. "Real and Sham Natural History." *The Atlantic Monthly*, March 1903, pp. 298-309.

Cappon, James. *Roberts and the Influences of His Time*. Toronto: Briggs, 1905.

____. *Charles G.D. Roberts*. Toronto: Ryerson, 1925.

"Charles G.D. Roberts: His Interesting Collection of Short Stories." Rev. of *Earth's Enigmas. The New York Times Saturday Review of Books and Art*, 15 Aug. 1903, p. 558.

Clark, Edward B. "Roosevelt on the Nature Fakirs " [interview]. *Everybody's Magazine*, 16 (June 1907), 770-74.

Clever, Glenn, ed. and introd. *The Sir Charles G.D. Roberts Symposium*. Reappraisals: Canadian Writers, No. 10. Ottawa: Univ. of Ottawa Press, 1984.

Cogswell, Fred. "Charles G.D. Roberts (1860-1943)." in *Canadian Writers and Their Works*. Ed. Robert Lecker, Jack David, and Ellen Quigley. Poetry Series, Vol. II. Downsview, Ont.: ECW, 1983. 187-232.

____. "Charles G.D. Roberts: The Critical Years." In *The Proceedings of the Sir Charles G.D. Roberts Symposium*. Mount Allison Univ., 29-31 Oct. 1982. Ed. and introd. Carrie MacMillan. Sackville, N.B., and Halifax: Centre for Canadian Studies and Nimbus, 1984, pp. 117-29.

Dean, Misao. "Political Science: Realism in Roberts's Animal Stories." *Studies in Canadian Literature*, 21, 1 (1996), pp. 1-16.

Doyle, James. "The American Critical Reaction to Roberts." in *The Proceedings of the Sir Charles G.D. Roberts Symposium*. Mount Allison Univ., 29-31 Oct. 1982. Ed. and introd. Carrie MacMillan. Sackville, N.B., and Halifax: Centre for Canadian Studies and Nimbus, 1984, pp. 99-115.

Dunlap, Thomas R. "'The old kinship of Earth': Science, Man and Nature in the Animal Stories of Charles G.D. Roberts." *Journal of Canadian Studies*, 22:1 (Spring 1987), 104-20.

____. “The Realistic Animal Story: Ernest Thompson Seton, Charles Roberts, and Darwinism.” *Forest & Conservation History*, 36 (April 1992), pp. 56-62; rpt. in *The Wild Animal Story*, Ed. Ralph Lutts. Philadelphia: Temple Univ. Press, 1998, pp. 238-47.

Early, L.R. “Roberts as Critic.” In *The Sir Charles G.D. Roberts Symposium*. Ed. and introd. Glenn Clever. Reappraisals: Canadian Writers, No. 10. Ottawa: Univ. of Ottawa Press, 1984, pp. 173-89.

Edgar, Pelham. “Sir Charles G.D. Roberts and His Time.” Rev. of *Sir Charles G.D. Roberts: A Biography*, by Elsie M. Pomeroy. *University of Toronto Quarterly*, 13 (Oct. 1943), 117-26.

Eggleston, Wilfrid. “The Causerie.” *Winnipeg Free Press*, 10 Jan. 1948, p. 15.

____. *The Frontier and Canadian Letters*. Toronto: Ryerson, 1957.

Fisher, John. “The Bard of Tantramar.” *John Fisher Reports*. CBC, 12 Jan. 1947. TS. Hathaway Vertical File, Rufus Hathaway Collection. Harriet Irving Library, Univ. of New Brunswick, Fredericton.

Gold, Joseph. “The Precious Speck of Life.” *Canadian Literature*, No. 26 (Autumn 1965), pp. 22-32.

____. introd. *King of Beasts and Other Stories*. By Charles G.D. Roberts. Toronto: Ryerson, 1967, pp. [ix-xx].

____, introd. *The Heart of the Ancient Wood*. by Charles G.D. Roberts. New Canadian Library, No. 110. Toronto: McClelland and Stewart, 1974, pp. ix-xiv.

____, “The Ambivalent Beast,” in *The Proceedings of the Sir Charles G.D. Roberts Symposium, Mount Allison Univ., 29-31 Oct. 1982*. Ed and introd. Carrie MacMillan. Sackville, N.B. and Halifax: Centre for Canadian Studies and Nimbus, 1984, pp. 77-86.

Hornyansky, Michael. “Roberts for Children.” In *The Sir Charles G.D. Roberts Symposium*. Ed. and introd. Glenn Clever. Reappraisals: Canadian Writers, No. 10. Ottawa: Univ. of Ottawa Press, 1984, pp. 163-71.

Jewinski, Ed. “Michel Foucault, the AuthorS Charles G.D. Roberts, and Some Post-Structuralist Implications for Canadian Criticism.” In *The Sir Charles G.D. Roberts Symposium*. Ed. and introd. Glenn Clever. Reappraisals: Canadian Writers, No. 10. Ottawa: Univ. of Ottawa Press, 1984, pp. 191-206.

Jones, D.G. *Butterfly on Rock: A Study of Themes and Images in Canadian Literature*. Toronto: Univ. of Toronto Press, 1970.

Keith, W.J. *Charles G.D. Roberts*. Studies in Canadian Literature. Toronto: Copp Clark, 1969.

Kennedy, Roderick. “Dean of Canadian Authors.” *Family Herald and Weekly Star* [Montreal], 10 Feb. 1937, p. 36.

Kulyk Keefer, Janice. *Under Eastern Eyes: A Critical Reading of Maritime Fiction*. Toronto: Univ. of Toronto Press, 1987.

Lennox, John. "Roberts, Realism and the Animal Story." *Journal of Canadian Fiction*, II:3 (Summer 1973), pp. 121-23.

Lucas, Alec, Introd. *The Last Barrier and Other Stories*. by Charles G.D. Roberts. New Canadian Library, No. 7. 1958; rpt. Toronto: McClelland and Stewart, 1970, p. v-x.

____. "Nature Writers and the Animal Story." In *Literary History of Canada: Canadian Literature in English*. Gen. ed. and introd. Carl F. Klinck. Toronto: Univ. of Toronto Press, 1965, pp. 364-88.

Lutts, Ralph H. *The Nature Fakers: Wildlife, Science & Sentiment*. Golden, Colorado: Fulcrum, 1990.

____. Ed. *The Wild Animal Story*. Philadephia: Temple Univ. Press, 1998.

____. "The Wild Animal Story: Animals and Ideas." In *The Wild Animal Story*. Ed. Ralph Lutts. Philadelphia: Temple Univ. Press, 1998, pp. 1-21.

MacArthur, James. "A Gentleman in New France." Rev. of *The Forge in the Forest. The Bookman*, 5 (April 1897), 161-63.

MacDonald, Michael J., introd. *The Heart That Knows*. by Charles G.D. Roberts. Sackville, N.B.: Ralph Pickard Bell Library, Mount Allison Univ., 1984 pp. v-x.

MacDonald, Robert H. "The Revolt Against Instinct: The Animal Stories of Seton and Roberts." *Canadian Literature*, No. 84 (Spring 1980), pp. 18-29.

MacLulich, T.D. "The Animal Story and the 'Nature Faker' Controversy." *Essays on Canadian Writing*, No. 33 (Fall 1986), pp. 112-24.

MacMillan, Carrie, ed. and introd. *The Proceedings of the Sir Charles G.D. Roberts Symposium*. Mount Alison Univ., 29-31 Oct. 1982. Sackville, N.B., and Halifax: Centre for Canadian Studies and Nimbus, 1984.

Magee, William H. "The Animal Story: A Challenge in Technique." *The Dalhousie Review*, 44 (1964), 156-64.

Mallinson, Jean. "The Maiden Archetype in *The Heart of the Ancient Wood*." *Essays in Canadian Writing*, No. 3 (Fall 1975), pp. 47-51.

Massey, Irving. "Influence without Anxiety: Sir Charles G.D. Roberts – and Me." *The Kenyon Review*, NS 9, No. 1 (Winter 1987), 114-28.

Matthews, Robin. "*The Roman de la terre* and the Novel of the Land: Charles G.D. Roberts at Work in a Major Literary Genre." In *The Sir Charles G.D. Roberts Symposium*. Ed. and introd. Glenn Clever. Reappraisals: Canadian Writers, No. 10. Ottawa: Univ. of Ottawa Press, 1984, pp. 143-61.

McMullen, Lorraine. "Ernest Thompson Seton (1860-1946)." In *Canadian Writers and Their Works*. Ed Robert Lecker, Jack David, and Ellen Quigley. Fiction Series, Vol. II. Toronto: ECW, 1989.

Morell, A.C. "Symbolism and Spatial Patterning in Four Short Stories by Charles G.D. Roberts." *Studies in Canadian Literature*, 5 (Spring 1980), 138-51.

Morley, Patricia, "'We and the Beasts Are Kin': Attitudes towards Nature in Nineteenth and Early Twentieth-Century Canadian Literature." *World Literature Written in English*, 16 (Nov. 1977), 344-58.

Moss, John. "Writing to the Reader: The Novels of Sir Charles G.D. Roberts." In *The Proceedings of the Sir Charles G.D. Roberts Symposium*. Mount Allison Univ., 29-31 Oct. 1982. Ed. and introd. Carrie MacMillan. Sackville, N.B., and Halifax: Centre for Canadian Studies and Nimbus, 1984, pp. 87-98.

Muddiman, Bernard. "A Vignette in Canadian Literature." *The Canadian Magazine*, 40 (March 1913), 451-58.

Owen, William. "Vision and Revision in Roberts' Acadian Romances." In *The Sir Charles G.D. Roberts Symposium*. Ed. and introd. Glenn Clever. Reappraisals: Canadian Writers, No. 10. Ottawa: Univ. of Ottawa Press, 1984, pp. 117-25.

Pacey, Desmond. "Sir Charles G.D. Roberts." In *Ten Canadian Poets: A Group of Biographical and Critical Essays*. 1958; rpt. Toronto: Ryerson, 1969, pp. 34-58.

Pierce, Lorne. "Charles G.D. Roberts: An Estimate (The Qualities of His Thought: Part II)." *The New Outlook*, 20 Jan. 1926, p. 24.

____. "Lorne Pierce's 1927 Interview with Charles G.D. Roberts (as Reported by Margaret Lawrence)." Ed. and introd. Terry Whalen. *Canadian Poetry: Studies, Documents, Reviews*, No. 21 (Fall-Winter 1987), pp. 59-76.

Poirier, Michel. "The Animal Story in Canadian Literature: E. Thompson Seton and Charles G.D. Roberts." *Queen's Quarterly*, 34 (1927), 298-312, 398-419.

Polk, James. *Wilderness Writers: Ernest Thompson Seton, Charles G.D. Roberts, Grey Owl*. Toronto: Clarke, Irwin, 1972.

Pomeroy, Elsie M. *Sir Charles G.D. Roberts: A Biography*. Toronto: Ryerson, 1943.

____. "Sir Charles G.D. Roberts: Final Chapter." *The Canadian Author and Bookman*, 20, No. 20 (June 1944), 5-6.

____. "The Novels of Charles G.D. Roberts." *The Maritime Advocate*, April 1950. Rpt. privately in pamphlet form.

____. "A Poet's Dream World." *The Canadian Theosophist*, Sept.-Oct. 1959, pp. 89-93.

'The Relation of Man and Beast." Rev. of *The Kindred of the Wild. New York Times Saturday Review of Books and Art*, 12 July 1902, p. 467.

Rev. of *Earth's Enigmas. The Nation*, 21 May 1896, p. 399.

Rev. of *The Forge in the Forest. The Critic*, 10 April 1897, p. 247.

Rhodenizer, V.B. "Who's Who in Canadian Literature: Charles G.D. Roberts." *The Canadian Bookman*, 8 (Sept. 1926), 267-69.

Roberts, Lloyd. *The Book of Roberts*. Toronto: Ryerson, 1923.

Robertson, C.B. "Have Audiences Souls?" *The Toronto Star Weekly*, 3 July 1926, p. 34.

Rogers, A. Robert. "American Recognition of Bliss Carman and Sir Charles G.D. Roberts." *Humanities Association Bulletin*, 22, No. 2 (Spring 1971), 19-25.

Ross, Malcolm. "'A Strange Aesthetic Ferment.'" *Canadian Literature*, No. 68-69 (Spring-Summer 1976), pp.13-25.

Stringer, Arthur. "Eminent Canadians in New York, II: The Father of Canadian Poetry." *The National Monthly of Canada*, Feb. 1904, pp. 61-64.

Ware, Martin, introd. *The Vagrants of the Barren and Other Stories*. Ottawa: Tecumseh Press, 1992, pp. ix-xxviii.

Waterston, Elizabeth. "Roberts, Parker, and the Uses of History." In *The Sir Charles G.D. Roberts Symposium*. Ed. and introd. Glenn Clever. Reappraisals: Canadian Writers, No. 10. Ottawa: Univ. of Ottawa Press, 1984, pp. 107-16.

Whalen, Terry. "Roberts and the Tradition of American Naturalism." In *The Sir Charles G.D. Roberts Symposium*. Ed. and introd. Glenn Clever. Reappraisals: Canadian Writers, No. 10. Ottawa: Univ. of Ottawa Press, 1984, pp. 127-42.

____. "Charles G.D. Roberts (1860-1943)." In *Canadian Writers and Their Works*. Ed. Robert Lecker, Jack David, and Ellen Quigley. Fiction Series, Vol II. Toronto: ECW, 1989. 159-214.

Whitaker, Muriel, introd. *The Best Canadian Animal Stories: Classic Tales by Master Storytellers*. Toronto: McClelland & Stewart, 1997, pp. 1-9.

MARQUIS
MEMBER OF SCABRINI GROUP
Québec, Canada
2005